RUSSIA UNDER THE LAST TSAR

♠ ♠ ♠ RUSSIA UNDER THE LAST TSAR

THEOFANIS GEORGE STAVROU   EDITOR

University of Minnesota Press, Minneapolis

Library of Congress Catalog Card Number: 74-79047

Second printing, 1971

TO *Boris* AND *Irina,* MY LENINGRAD FRIENDS
in whose company I gained greater appreciation for Russian
history and culture of both the Tsarist and the Soviet period

Preface

∻ ∻ ∻

THE essays in this volume originally formed a series of lectures, "Russia's Golden Age? 1894–1917," at the University of Minnesota. The series was organized in connection with a seminar dealing with the reign of Nicholas II, and was an attempt to expose the students to the various interpretations of the two decades or so leading up to the revolutions of 1917. The series was rather unusual in that though the speakers well understood its purpose and general frame of reference, they did not consult with one another either in the preparation of their lectures or in the final writing of the essays. Needless to say, each was aware of the others' interpretations of the reign of Nicholas II, but the contributors all have refreshingly different approaches in assessing this most controversial period of Russia under the last tsar.

From the beginning, the purpose of the series and this volume was to present concisely and clearly in eight interpretative essays some of the most significant forces and issues in Imperial Russia during the two decades before the Revolution. As is readily noticeable, the essays represent the research and publication activities of the contributors during the last five or ten years. Our hope is that the volume will prove useful to students, undergraduate and graduate, to the intelligent general reader, and, to a certain extent, to scholars interested in this period of Russian history. In a volume of this kind, transliteration presents great problems, especially when the names of many literary and revolutionary figures have been spelled in a variety of ways and in some cases have been standardized despite violations of transliteration rules. Although no particular transliteration system was followed faithfully, the effort was made to be as consistent as possible while simultaneously striving to satisfy the transliteration idiosyncrasies of some of the contributors.

The editor wishes to thank the eight contributors, whose lectures in Minnesota not only made the symposium a success and the present volume possible but also served as a challenge and stimulus for students of Russian history. My thanks also go to Professor Robert H. Ferrell for his generous advice; to Miss Carol Leonard and especially to my teaching assistant, Mr. Janis Cers, for helping me with the compilation of the bibliography and the preparation of the index; to the staff of the University of Minnesota Press, especially the editor, for admirable cooperation and patience; to the World Affairs Center of the Extension Division at the University of Minnesota, which sponsored the series of lectures; and finally, to my wife Freda, who, besides being a gracious hostess, also helped with the final preparation of the manuscript.

THEOFANIS GEORGE STAVROU

University of Minnesota

Table of Contents

RUSSIA UNDER THE LAST TSAR

THEOFANIS GEORGE STAVROU

Introduction

✧ ✧ ✧

THE fiftieth anniversary of the Bolshevik Revolution occasioned several conferences and publications, scholarly and popular, attempting to evaluate the Soviet experiment by assessing its achievements and failures. This preoccupation with revolutionary and Soviet themes reveals, among other things, the undeniable impact of the Soviet Union on the Western and non-Western world as well as a profound interest in the course and ultimate fate of sweeping revolutions such as those which befell Russia in the twentieth century. This interest is even more significantly relevant because revolutions have occurred and are likely to continue to occur in various parts of the world, especially in the developing countries, whose social and economic base approximates that of Imperial Russia at the turn of the century. Russia and the Soviet Union have frequently been viewed as the prototype of countries which experience major political and social revolutions in the midst of vast experiments with modernization and industrialization.

The essays of this volume address themselves to the major issues that confronted Imperial Russia during the two decades leading up to the revolutions of 1917, one of the most exciting and controversial periods in modern Russian history. One should hasten to add that this excitement and controversy, in a modified form, of course, would have existed regardless of the revolutions of 1917 and their consequences. Judged on the merits of its own record, and despite the conservative philosophy and oppressive policy of Nicholas II, his reign witnessed a vivacious and in some cases, unprecedented bourgeoning of political, social, economic, and cultural activity whose diversity and richness are being uncovered by specialized studies of the period. It is a credit to the diverse achievements of the decades immediately before 1917 that so much of Nicholas II's Russia is still readily noticeable in the Soviet Union and that the Soviet achievement itself is, in a distorted sense, the realization of presentiments and dreams anxiously awaited by some and dreaded by others during the reign of the last tsar. Then there is the intense interest of Soviet intellectuals in the pre-1917 intellectual and cultural events — an interest which attests to the vitality, relevance, and permanence of some of the issues and aspirations of that time.

Against this background of considerable achievement, marking Russia's transition from agrarian backwardness and illiteracy to industrial progress and the paraphernalia of modernity, the person of the autocrat, Nicholas II, is almost forgotten or, rather, relegated to secondary importance. His tragic fate, far from spurring historians to write his biography, has instead encouraged detailed studies of the political, social, and economic forces which determined that Nicholas simply could not be allowed to continue as arbiter of Russia's fate. Thus, no satisfactory scholarly biography of the last Romanov has appeared. He is, of course, inevitably discussed in general histories and monographs dealing with the various aspects of Imperial Russia's decline and fall, and recently, popular accounts of Nicholas and Alexandra, his Germanic wife turned Orthodox, and their hemophiliac son have again dramatized the life of the tsar whose execution in 1918 was, among other things, an indication that the Bolsheviks were determined to push their revolution to the point where a return to the Romanov days would be as remote as such events as those of 1917–1918 would have seemed to Nicholas when he ascended the throne in 1894. The essays in this volume, too, make occasional references to Nicholas. Indeed, how could one discuss the various interpretations of the fate of Imperial Russia;

2

Russian conservative and radical thought; the problems of industrialization; constitutional developments; education and culture; or foreign policy without frequent references to the autocrat? For Nicholas viewed himself very much in the role of an unlimited autocrat both before and after the Revolution of 1905, despite the granting of the October Manifesto. And in Russian society, the autocrat remained the center of attraction to the end, even if by way of opposition to what he symbolized. Scholars' reluctance to engage in biographic studies of Nicholas perhaps stems partly from conviction that all has been said that needs to be said. Unless Soviet archives which may reveal new dimensions of Nicholas's personality and behavior become accessible, the reservation persists that the old story repeated may be charming as well as depressing but hardly original or instructive.

Nicholas was in reality a parachronism, a chronological mistake. He was possessed by the firm conviction that his and his family's fate, as well as that of Russia, were in the hands of God and that he, Nicholas, was, in turn, in God's hands. This conviction had both historical and personal explanations. His predecessors in the nineteenth century made similar claims. Alexander I's (1801–1825) life and death was clouded by religious mysticism. Nicholas I (1825–1855) personified Russian autocracy and had it expressed eloquently in the doctrine of "Official Nationality," consisting of the trinity of orthodoxy, autocracy, and nationality – a doctrine which, with a brief exception during the reign of Alexander II (1855–1881), dominated the thinking of nineteenth-century Russian rulers. Nicholas II inherited it from his father Alexander III, who had reactivated it intensely after the assassination of his father, the Tsar Liberator, Alexander II. But between the first and the last quarters of the nineteenth century, Russia had made significant strides in social evolution and political concepts. "Official Nationality" with Nicholas I at the helm could possibly be expected to work until the middle of the century. But only sheer madness or naïveté could expect it to function effectively at the end of the century under the direction of Nicholas II, especially since he lacked all the ruthlessness and the domineering characteristics of his

3

ancestor. The last Romanov was, as has repeatedly been told, of pleasant disposition and a model husband and father, but ill suited for the responsibilities which lay ahead in a dynamically changing society. Then there was the family tragedy concerning the health of the Tsar's only son, the Tsarevich Alexis, who was hopelessly afflicted with hemophilia. And in the midst of this family misfortune appears the notorious Rasputin, who mysteriously proved himself to be the only man able to prolong the life of the Tsarevich, the hope for the perpetuation of the dynasty. To be sure, the role of Rasputin, who was at worst a symptom, not the cause for the fall of the monarchy, has been overstated. But this familiar story of the relation among the Tsar, the Tsarina, and Rasputin over the health of the heir to the Russian throne still has to be considered seriously along with the most readily recognizable disruptive forces at work during the reign of Nicholas II. It can be a study of how, after all, in some cases the failure of the human body may affect the course of history.

The decades under consideration have traditionally been treated by Soviet and Western historians as a prelude to the Soviet period. In the West, such treatment usually takes place in the context of the old but ever present controversy between the "optimists" on the one hand, the "pessimists" on the other. The optimists understandably emphasize the advances of Imperial Russia in industry, agriculture, education, labor, and the creation of responsible, educated citizens who were gradually becoming constructive contributors to the government's political activity. All these elements were moving consciously or unconsciously toward full parliamentary government — all that was needed was time. But alas, the war, with its accompanying strains and tensions, frustrated these efforts and put an end to constitutional hopes. The pessimists, as could be expected, describe all this activity as a "superficial glow," brought about partly by the government's half solutions but offering no justification for the outcome expected by the optimists.

It is in the context of this debate that Professor Arthur Mendel, himself uncertain about his position but strongly favoring the optimists, sets out to comment on the various interpretations of

Nicholas II

Alexandra Feodorovna

Sergei von Witte. Photograph courtesy of
Theodore Von Laue

Konstantin P. Pobedonostsev

Paul N. Miliukov

Left: Alexander Blok. Photograph courtesy of Nicolas Zernov. *Right*: Dmitrii Merezhkovskii

Left: Dmitrii Mendeleev. *Right*: Ivan Petrovich Pavlov

V. I. Lenin in Red Square during the celebration of the second anniversary of the October Revolution. Photograph courtesy of Novosti Press Agency

the fate of Imperial Russia by surveying the vast literature on the subject by participants in the events and by émigré and Western scholars. Basically, however, Professor Mendel's essay renews his debate with the two most outspoken exponents of the "pessimistic school," Professors Theodore Von Laue and Leopold Haimson. Von Laue boldly and dogmatically states that Russia's political, social, and economic experience, especially in the decades leading to the revolutions of 1917, was not conducive to the establishment of Parliamentary government or any other type of government but the one forcefully provided by the Bolsheviks, an unavoidable fate which would have occurred with or without World War I. Haimson's pessimism is based on the divisions or polarizations within Russian society, polarizations which led both to the overthrow of tsarism and the defeat of liberalism. Mendel finds it difficult to accept either of these views and instead agrees with Lenin's pessimism, which seems to suggest that the Bolsheviks stood no chance without the confusion and strains resulting from the war.

Since the writing of Professor Mendel's essay, there has appeared another worthy of note by a recognized authority on Russia and the Soviet Union, George F. Kennan.* The essay is remarkable not only because of the cogency with which Mr. Kennan presents the main weaknesses and failures of the regime which led to the breakdown of the tsarist autocracy, but also because of Mr. Kennan's change of opinion while reviewing the events of these two decades. Mr. Kennan readily acknowledges the efforts of the tsarist government and the actual results of these efforts at modernization, especially in such fields as industry and education, but he lists four major causes of tsarism's downfall in 1917. By far the most important was "the failure of the autocracy to supplement the political system in good time with some sort of parliamentary institution" which would have enabled the landowning nobility and the intelligentsia emerging from all classes to participate in the governmental process. Obviously, autocracy had this opportu-

*"The Breakdown of the Tsarist Autocracy" was originally presented at a conference on the Russian Revolution held at Harvard University in the spring of 1967, and appears in Richard Pipes, ed., *Revolutionary Russia* (Cambridge, Mass.: Harvard University Press, 1967), pp. 1–15.

5

nity in 1862 when the gentry of Tver under the leadership of Unkovskii presented Alexander II with the idea of a central zemstvo organ and again in 1895 when zemstvoists tried to impress on Nicholas II the crucial importance of a more representative system of government. The failure of the Russian tsars to respond responsibly and realistically to these overtures robbed them of their chance to employ talents of good will and turned the opposition hostile. Had the regime acted in the 1860's — and one may be expecting too much farsightedness from Romanov autocrats, even Alexander II, who were pressed down by a heritage of unfettered absolutism — there was the possibility of preserving and perpetuating a limited monarchy, but the united support of the conservative and liberal intelligentsia was essential to the survival of the dynasty. By 1905, when revolution gave a forced birth to the Duma, it was already too late. The political experience of nearly half a century had not only split the conservative and liberal intelligentsia, it unified the radical ones and above all it colored their attitude toward the dynasty and their outlook toward the solution of political and social problems.

The second major cause was the irresponsible policy of extreme Great Russian nationalism, which was intensified in the last thirty years of the monarchy and which proved crucially detrimental to the unity of the Empire. In such a multinational empire, one has to look hard to find justification for a policy which offended national minorities, alienating them from the government and forcing them to make substantial contributions to the "revolutionary groups" bent on destroying the monarchy. Anti-Semitism, manifested in a series of pogroms, was of course the most outstanding example of extreme Great Russian nationalism. The temporary unity that the government could achieve by this kind of policy (which, incidentally, did not fail to find support among both the upper class and lower classes of Russian society) was more than offset by the real disunity gradually setting in and contributing significantly to the fall of the monarchy. Equally disastrous was the role of this extreme nationalism in foreign affairs; it was largely responsible for Russia's involvement in the Russo-Japanese War and World War I, with their well-known ensuing catastrophes.

The last two causes discussed by Mr. Kennan are the personality of Nicholas II and the revolutionary movement. The heart of Russian autocracy's deficiency was the imperial family — the autocrat himself was inadequately qualified to meet the demands of his position in his time. As Mr. Kennan epigrammatically and incisively points out, "It is ironic that this man who fought so tenaciously against the granting of a constitution, had many of the qualities that would have fitted him excellently for the position of a constitutional monarch and practically none of those that were needed for the exercise of that absolute power to which he stubbornly clung." But one must not ignore the fact that one main reason for Nicholas's and his government's political behavior was the existence of the revolutionary movement, which, besides depriving the bureaucracy of badly needed talents, also sought to frustrate the government's efforts at successful modernization.

This, then was the general picture when war broke out to contribute to the collapse of tsarism. But Mr. Kennan's review of these developments forced him to change camps — or more accurately, question his initial optimism, for none of the failures mentioned above originated with the war. Rather, there was the fact that no steps had been taken to correct "the consequences of these deficiencies" by the eve of World War I. Thus, in panoramic perspective, "the spectacle of the final years of tsardom prior to 1914 is that of an impressive program of social, economic, and cultural modernization of a great country being conducted, somewhat incongruously, under the general authority of a governmental system that was itself in the advanced stages of political disintegration."

Nicholas's Russia required the conscientious cooperation of all sections and classes of society and government if it were to weather without violent revolution the gigantic transformation it was undergoing. Perhaps the tragedy of Russia lay precisely in the conspicuous absence of such cooperation. Both before and after the Revolution of 1905, dialogue between official and unofficial Russia — or more specifically, between conservative and radical Russia — was minimal, an eloquent expression, perhaps, of their determination to resist each other's way of life and plans for Russia's future. The atmosphere was one of hostility and bitter criticism. The conservative philosophy of the Tsar underlay all his actions, public or private; he continued to be unreceptive to any suggestion of changes that might limit his authority. Russian conservatism sought to maintain the existing political and social institutions, by force if need be, and thus to maintain the unity and strength of the autocratic state.

Until recently, Russian conservatism was a much neglected subject both in the West and in the Soviet Union, chiefly because of its ultimate failure to conserve the old order intact or in part. Yet the study of this conservatism can yield useful insights into the continuities of Russian history and culture. Many of the conservatives had strong roots in the land and could provide direction and discipline for succeeding generations; hence, they helped preserve institutions and transmit values. The government's policy of industrialization and its accompanying forces, however, undermined Russian conservatism. Thus, ironically, when the government needed their services desperately, the conservatives could no longer perform their functions.

Russian conservative thought before the revolution is discussed by Professor Robert F. Byrnes who, after an introduction on the nature of nineteenth-century Russian conservatism, concentrates on the ideas of Konstantin Pobedonostsev, the Overseer of the Russian Holy Synod from 1880 to 1905. Konstantin Pobedonostsev was, of course, the epitome of Russian conservatism; even though Nicholas was forced to dismiss him during the revolutionary upheaval of 1905, Pobedonostsev's conservative ideas continued to influence Nicholas's thinking and the thinking of the conservative order in general until 1917. Now, it is quite clear that Pobedonostsev's conservative philosophy was by its very nature anachronistic. It was, as Professor Byrnes points out, not "an acceptable conservative philosophy," for it refused to acknowledge the complexity of the problems facing Russian society — problems that required imaginative, not simplistic, solutions. The deficiency of this philos-

THEOFANIS GEORGE STAVROU

ophy is, of course, basic also to conservatism in general, which is at its best in a tranquil environment and at its worst when caught in the tumult of revolution. Their writings attest that the Russian conservatives realized the magnitude of the revolution threatening their society; they understood the threat as well as the threateners understood the nature of the conservative opposition. It is, however, in the nature of conservatism not to rise to the occasion and provide solutions which a revolutionary situation demands.

In a revolutionary situation radical solutions have greater appeal, and the failure of Russian conservatism is often juxtaposed to the relative triumph of radicalism. But as Professor Donald W. Treadgold points out in his essay, Russian radicalism enjoyed only "superficial success" during the reign of Nicholas II — in fact, having reached its peak of popularity and influence, it "went into a period of decline." A historical explanation for this phenomenon is that since the eighteenth century, certain sections of Russian society began to grow at the expense of the hitherto all-encompassing state, and by the turn of the twentieth century could express their discontent. This partly explains why radical slogans and programs did not attract the majority of Russian society, frustrating the radicals after 1905, and also why radicalism played so small a role in the fall of tsarism as compared with anarchy, which held sway in 1917 and was simply exploited by the radicals. Furthermore, it is instructive to keep in mind that radicalism was only part of the nonconservative thought during Nicholas's reign. Professor Treadgold includes in his discussion other nonconservative groups, such as the Liberals and the Socialist Revolutionaries, as well as those intellectuals who abandoned radicalism and concentrated on the arts and sciences. He also summarizes the Russian political, social, and cultural thought of the time.

Understandably, constitutional developments in Russia during the reign of Nicholas II have been the subject of special interest and speculation ever since the issuing of the October Manifesto in 1905. Professor Thomas Riha carefully portrays the political temper of the Russian government and society as he discusses the various opportunities (and their limitations) available to Russians for

9

participation in the governmental process. In many respects, this is a depressing period: even though the Duma, however imperfect, could serve to bridge the gap between official and unofficial Russia, ironically enough, it alienated the monarch from the nation — on the eve of his dethronement, Nicholas was less a constitutionalist than in earlier years, and his disregard for individual liberties remained offensive to the end. Equally depressing was the fact that the Russian masses did not develop sufficiently (perhaps justifiably) the attitude of looking to a parliament for real solutions to their problems. In the context of Russia's rapid changes between the revolutions of 1905 and 1917 and the added strains of World War I, the record seems to suggest that liberal constitutionalism stood no reasonable chance, despite its successes in the passage of essentially nonpolitical bills. Professor Riha may concede to the pessimists (who, after all, can cite history to support their thesis), but he asks the question which is imperative if one is to appreciate Nicholas's Russia for its own sake instead of judging it by its collapse in 1917: Was the constitutional experiment entirely unsuccessful? The record of accomplishments is impressive enough to convince one easily that the answer is no. One of the most important overall gains was educated Russians' learning during this period to understand the significance of democratic concepts and institutions; they obtained an understanding far superior to that possessed by their counterparts in the Soviet period — during Stalin's reign, at any rate.

All major developments contributing in any way to the gradual transformation of Russia at the turn of the century hinged on industrialization, the heart of the Russian government's efforts at modernization. Professor Von Laue, who has contributed much to the study of Russian industrialization, has also systematically been one of the most devastating pessimists about pre-1917 Russia. Permeated by a pessimistic theory of rapid industrialization mercilessly engulfing society and destroying institutions and values faster than it can create replacements, his essay emphasizes the political, social, and economic problems besetting Russia before the Revolution. All these problems increase in magnitude when viewed in the context of Russia's urge for global competition, an urge that made

10

"modernization imperative." But modernization through industrialization, it gradually became acknowledged, could not be achieved without adopting revolutionary measures not initially anticipated by the Russian autocracy. Thus, Witte, the driving force behind Russian industrialization and a believer in autocracy, challenged the educational philosophy of conservative Russia, which he discovered to be inadequate to meet the needs of an industrializing society. Similarly, in his view, the traditional conservative institution of the peasant commune failed to produce enough or to serve efficiently in the industrialization process; therefore, Witte advocated the abolition of the commune, anticipating the famous Stolypin reforms. But the source of pessimism permeating Von Laue's argument (the same pessimism discussed by Professor Mendel in the first essay of this volume) is his thesis that some of the basic motives underlying Russian industrialization, such as the urge for global competition, made rapid industrialization imperative, and the experience of World War I showed that Russia had not industrialized fast enough. Furthermore, and this seems to be a basic problem, Professor Von Laue views rapid industrialization as incompatible with liberal constitutionalism, which explains why a government like that of the Bolsheviks was inevitably needed to complete the industrialization begun under tsarism.

Although no essay in this volume deals in detail with the agricultural situation and policy during the period 1894–1917, there are references to the Stolypin reforms in several essays. The cultural scene is treated by the essays of Professors Alexander Vucinich and Gleb Struve, each approaching the subject from a different point of view. Professor Vucinich is concerned primarily with the growth of Russian scientific thought, and he discusses a galaxy of scientists who made significant contributions to twentieth-century science, some of whom also became winners of the Nobel Prize. He discusses this in the context of the growth of Russian universities, other educational institutions, and professional societies, governmental or private, all of which contributed to the promotion of Russian culture. Here again one notices the dilemma in which the government consistently found itself throughout this period: the government

11

needed the universities in its modernization drive, yet the universities became centers of political and social unrest and criticism, a phenomenon which became more noticeable as university enrollment multiplied and its social basis broadened. Nicholas I's description of Moscow University as "the wolf's den" could apply to numerous other educational institutions at the turn of the century.

The growth of Russian universities was part of the great cultural renaissance which swept Russia during the reign of Nicholas II. Indeed, if there is an area where disagreement about definite and positive achievements is hardly justifiable it is this field. As Professor Struve points out, this cultural renaissance was all encompassing including the arts, letters, philosophy, and religious, social, and political thought. Critics or the pessimists may describe it as the last flower of a doomed society, but nevertheless there it was. Its contributions were felt outside Russia, and in some cases this cultural renaissance persisted into the Soviet period, exercising great influence on Soviet intellectuals. Western scholars visiting the Soviet Union frequently meet Russian intellectuals manifesting deep interest even in those aspects of pre-1917 Russian culture which are proscribed by the Soviet authorities.

There will always be a debate about the relation between war and revolution in Russia — that is, there will be those who will argue that a change of order was unavoidable regardless of the war and others who will argue that revolution, and definitely the Bolshevik victory, would have been unthinkable without the war. Nobody can reasonably argue, however, that the war did not heighten the various crises which existed and even created new ones, with the result that the unbearable strain made gradual solutions to pressing problems impossible. The essay by Professor Roderick McGrew deals with the imperatives of Russian foreign policy that ultimately brought Russia into World War I, with its momentous repercussions for Russian, European and indeed world history.

ARTHUR MENDEL

On Interpreting the Fate of
Imperial Russia

⚕ ⚕ ⚕

WHAT accounts for the resurgence of interest in the Russia
of Nicholas II and the revolutions it spawned? One of the chief
reasons lies in our understandable concern today with the fate of
the economically "backward" societies, with the economic, social,
psychological, and political transformations that are tearing these
communities out of their preindustrial rituals and routines, and
forcing them into the "modern" mold. The center of our interest
is obviously political — Does this great transformation favor authoritarian government, or does it promote, indeed, is it even compatible
with, some variety of popular, representative, parliamentary government?[1] Ours being an age of historicism, scholars and politicians

[1] For Soviet historians the lessons are as clear as day. The history of
Russia at the turn of the century demonstrated, as one Soviet historian recently wrote, "the inability of capitalism under twentieth-century conditions
to direct a backward agrarian country along the path of economic progress . . . that neither Tsarism nor the Provisional Government could solve
the problems facing the country, move it along the path of industrial progress
and assure its economic independence" (I. N. Olegina, "Sovremennaia
Amerikanskaia i Angliiskaia istoriografiia ob industrializatsii v SSSR" (Contemporary American and English Historiography on Industrialization in the
USSR), *Voprosy Istorii*, No. 3 (1966), pp. 53, 55). We in the West, in
turn, often hope through such lessons to learn how better to frustrate precisely this outcome. Since, as Hugh Seton-Watson writes, conditions similar

ARTHUR MENDEL

turn to the lessons of history, sometimes for help in understanding and responding wisely to this current revolution, sometimes in search of evidence for preconceptions about its character and direction. Among other early examples of supposedly backward societies, we study the history of Russia, focus particularly on the half century or so following the Crimean War, and ask repeatedly, Why in the middle of Russia's modernization did power pass to the Bolsheviks? Why did the liberal, constitutional, Western form of government that seemed to be emerging fail dismally to take root and flourish? Is there a lesson here for our thinking about the politics of industrialization in general? Or was this particular history just that, a particular evolution of a particular country under a particular set of conditions?

And what about the particular case itself? Was the victory of the Bolsheviks inevitable or, more moderately, probable? Were the predominant conditions — the anachronistic, medieval structure of state and society; the prerequisites and consequences of rapid industrialization; the pattern and impact of international relations; the bizarre character of the Russian intelligentsia with their quixotic passions and fantasies — all together simply too antagonistic to parliamentary government and "open" society? Or are some of the essential reasons for the victory of Bolshevism and the failure of liberal government and society in Russia to be found in such purely accidental factors as a weak-willed tsar, a hysterical wife, a hemophiliac son, a personality like Lenin, and a weighty batch of comparable bits and pieces of history that were necessary, irreplaceable links in the actual chain of events. If this is the case, then the whole experience, and others like it, offer little for the generalizer and policy maker, however enthralling they might be for the narrative historian and

to those prevailing in Russia at the turn of the century are today "giving birth to various types of national and social revolutionary movements in many parts of the world, from Peru to Nigeria and from the Lebanon to the Philippines, the history of the last decades of Imperial Russia is of more than academic interest. It throws light on some of the problems that most urgently beset the statesmen of our own day, and provides an impressive array of mistakes which they would do well to avoid." (Hugh Seton-Watson, *The Decline of Imperial Russia 1855–1914* (London, New York: Praeger, 1952), p. 381.)

14

potent with meaning and "lessons" of another kind, the kind that humanists talked about in the days before models, methods, and memory machines.

As in all cases of retrospective prophecy, historians of the period are divided into pessimists and optimists. For the sanguine, these last decades of Imperial Russia display a potential, if trying, evolution toward something like a Western parliamentary government and open society, an evolution cut short by a convergence of many factors and events that was by no means ineluctable. On the other hand, the somber deplore the optimists' view as naively superficial, blind to the deeper forces determining the fate of Russia, driving it along, agonizingly and precipitously, toward its Bolshevik denouement. The optimists have stated their case in the following ways:

For, as a result of the events of 1905 and the social processes then set in motion, Russia on the eve of the war was well advanced on the path of evolution toward a modern democratic state. Had the war not intervened, she could have advanced much further, peacefully, through the pressures of the growing labor movement, the liberal middle classes, and the socially-conscious intelligentsia.

Russia before the First World War was still a relatively backward country by any quantitative criterion. . . . Nevertheless, as far as the general pattern of its industrialization in the second period was concerned, Russia seemed to duplicate what had happened in Germany in the last decades of the nineteenth century. One might surmise that in the absence of war Russia would have continued on the road of progressive westernization. . . . Modest as the improvements in the situation of the peasants were, they were undeniable and widely diffused. . . . There is little doubt that the Russian labor movement of those years [the years before 1914] was slowly turning toward revisionism and trade-unionist lines. As was true in the West, the struggles for general and equal franchise to the Duma and for a cabinet responsible to the Duma, which probably would have occurred sooner or later, may well have further accentuated this development.

The most rapid and substantial progress in all fields of Russian life was made during the Duma Monarchy (1906–1914), which was the closest Russia ever came to constitutional government.

15

In Russia and its borderlands, the years of Nicholas II's reign witnessed a speedy industrial growth; a sweeping transformation of the peasantry into small proprietors; the rapid spread of education; new, diverse, and original cultural developments; the schooling of a generation in political experience through the zemstvos, municipalities, the Duma and the courts. . . .

Russia still had to solve many complicated and difficult problems, but the possibility of their peaceful solution was by no means excluded. To the extent that the country was growing economically more prosperous and culturally more advanced, this possibility was constantly gaining strength and the danger of a violent upheaval was becoming more remote.

Constitutional government, the liberties enjoyed that were non-existent before 1905, the enormous vitality shown by Russian society, the growth of self-activity on all fronts, the unusual economic prosperity, all these suggest that a revolutionary situation was remote in 1914. Finally, the Stolypin reforms, the rapid transfer of the land of the nobility into the hands of the peasantry, and the growth of heavy industry at the same time that the rural standard of living was rising were removing the chief cause of the social upheaval of 1917 — the peasant revolt. This, as we have seen, was Lenin's opinion, and on this subject he had no peer.

The changes of the last half-century had been so rapid, however, that contemporary reforming statesmen could look forward with confidence to the day when the empire would attain the level of achievement of Western societies.

There has grown up on the wide basis of theories, economic and otherwise, a tendency to regard everything that has happened as inevitable, and those who have not lived through this period or have not made a really detailed study of it sometimes rest content with such an assumption. The opposite is the view of those who saw the issues at the time and realized how easily things might have moved and nearly did move in quite a different direction. . . . Sergius Shidlovsky, a Liberal in Russia who might have been an intelligent Conservative in this country [England], and later Chairman of the Progressive Bloc, had said before the war: "Give us ten more years and we are safe." Ivan Petrunkevich, the veteran Liberal leader, had pointed out in 1905 the path which led to a "new order of things, without convulsions, without bloodshed, without thousands of unnecessary victims." Shidlovsky meant that

16

those essential changes which were required in Russia could come without convulsions, and they very nearly did.[2]

Had the bourgeois revolutions of 1905 and 1917 succeeded in establishing something like the familiar Western European state and society, it would have seemed, through the optimists' perspective, the most natural consequence of everything that had gone before: a beginning phase of technological borrowing from the West in, say, the mid-sixteenth century; a period of superficial custom-costume mimicry beginning in about the mid-seventeenth century, including the reigns of Peter the Great and his daughter Elizabeth; then, predictably, the century of ideological reflection, coinciding happily in its first phase with the Western Enlightenment; and, finally, the climax of the long evolution, the crucial decades, beginning with the Crimean debacle, of remodeling Russian institutions on the Western pattern — how neatly it all seemed to be unfolding![3]

It is in the last of these waves of Westernization that the optimists find, of course, their most forceful arguments. Not only can one see everywhere in this period evidence of dramatic social, economic, intellectual, and even political change in the direction of a Western society; but there is also an impressive general theory argu-

[2] These "optimistic" quotations are from, respectively, Raphael R. Abramovitch, *The Soviet Revolution 1917–1939* (New York: International Universities Press, 1962), p. 1; Alexander Gerschenkron, "Patterns of Economic Development," in Cyril Black, ed., *The Transformation of Russian Society* (Cambridge, Mass.: Harvard University Press, 1960), pp. 57–58, 60; Sergei Pushkarev, *The Emergence of Modern Russia, 1801–1917* (New York: Holt, 1963), p. 413; Donald W. Treadgold, *Twentieth Century Russia* (Chicago: Rand McNally, 1959), p. 121; Michael Karpovich, *Imperial Russia 1801–1917* (New York: Holt, 1932), p. 94; Jacob Walkin, *The Rise of Democracy in Pre-Revolutionary Russia: Political and Social Institutions under the Last Three Czars* (New York: Praeger, 1962), p. 233; Cyril E. Black, "The Nature of Imperial Russian Society," in Donald W. Treadgold, ed., *The Development of the U.S.S.R.: An Exchange of Views* (Seattle: University of Washington Press, 1964), p. 187 (see also pp. 185–186); Bernard Pares, *The Fall of the Russian Monarchy* (New York: Knopf, 1939; Vintage, 1961), pp. 238–239. See also the optimistic prognosis for the Russian state and society in the decades preceding World War I in Henry L. Roberts, "Russia and the West: A Comparison and Contrast," in Treadgold, ed., *The Development of the U.S.S.R.*, pp. 364, 369–370, and in response to Roberts's article, Marc Szeftel, "The Historical Limits of the Question of Russia and the West," in *ibid.*, pp. 383–384.

[3] Szeftel, "Historical Limits," p. 383.

ing that things could hardly be otherwise. To appreciate this general approach, we must recall briefly the character of the old system. Autocracy was a political instrument required to mobilize the severely sparse resources of a medieval rural economy to meet major external challenges, whether real or, more often, imagined through the prism of nationalistic, dynastic, religious, or ideological fantasies. Now, a glance at the familiar — and extraordinary — map of Russian expansion from the sixteenth through the nineteenth century demonstrates the remarkable success of that system. But besides being grandly successful, the system was also finely and stably balanced. What class or institution would oppose Autocracy? Once the independent aristocracy had been crushed and supplanted by the "service" gentry, the landed class was totally dependent on the State for income, land, and, above all, the preservation of the serf system. A few skirmishes with the Church only enhanced the dominance of the State. The peasants, of course, rose, and rose again, but the only political result was to strengthen the bond between the State and the gentry, the only class that might have restricted the autocrat's power, as it did elsewhere. As for the middle class, their number and attitudes made them politically irrelevant.

But this well-ordered and successful system had operated, for the most part (the Swedes are the exception), against peoples and nations no more developed than Russia — Mongols, Poles, Turks, and the diverse defenseless tribes that dotted the routes to the Pacific. The Crimean War brought this heretofore gloriously successful system to grips with nations that had a four-century lead in the gargantuan transformation from the medieval to the modern world. It is incredible that the lesson of Crimea was not learned by Russia a half century earlier during the Napoleonic invasion, but Russia mistook Napoleon's retreat and the exhilarating parade down the Champs Élysées as evidence of Russia's victory over France — that is, as evidence that the archaic system was as good against advanced foes as it had been against primitive.

Nicholas I carried this delusion of power to the absurd limits of thinking Russia a major or even *the* major European power. Had it been conscious bluff, it would have been splendid. But still floating in the illusive aura of 1815, he seems to have believed that something substantial stood behind his wildly speculative gambits in the international power market. The bubble burst at Sevastopol. The response seemed obvious — the old system of mobilizing resources for international conflict had to be replaced by one comparable with the system of the new, advanced enemy. And from the point of view of the autocracy, that is all that was involved in Alexander's emancipation of the serfs, the beginnings of railway development, the improvements in fiscal practice, the leap forward in education and backward in censorship, and, less directly, even the marvelously liberal innovations in local self-government and judicial procedure. Through all these daring alterations in the structure of society, its directing apparatus, the autocracy, was to be untouched or, if influenced at all by the reforms, strengthened.

But the optimist insists that fundamental changes in the economy, in social and cultural forms, and even in the area of local government could not be carried through without corresponding changes in the Autocracy, and any hopes along these lines by traditionalists were utopian delusions. In the best Hegelian-Marxist sense, the autocracy, by the very means it used to bolster itself, was, in effect, sowing the seeds of its own destruction. To see this, one need only compare the comic opera of December 1825 with the remarkably successful revolution of October 1905, the revolution that established an elective, legislative body alongside the bureaucracy and, thereby, went far beyond even the "senseless dreams" of the liberal Westerners of only a decade before. In 1825 soldiers milled about, as aimless as they were powerless, until dispatched by a few blasts of grapeshot. In 1905 there existed a powerful urban working class, able by its general strike to cripple the urban society (and implicitly thereby, the administrative system); a large, audacious, and embittered student body; a well-organized, united, and effective stratum of urban professionals — businessmen, engineers, accountants, university professors, and the like; and a generation of liberal-minded, practical men of affairs trained in the judicial and self-government institutions established by the great reforms.

19

What were all these new and effective opposition forces but the inevitable offspring of the innovations that the autocracy had considered, and rightly so, prerequisites for conflict with Western enemies? The new positions leading to and opened by the manifold Westernization could not be filled without throwing open the doors of the university and gymnasium to all those sons of cooks and butchers that Dmitrii Tolstoi tried to keep out. These upstarts could not be expected to stay out of politics, to stick to the narrow careers charted for them in the service of the State. It is the same story with the new working class and urban bourgeoisie: unavoidable, and unavoidably oppositional. As for the zemstva, the local self-government bodies, they may well have been designed as simply an inexpensive means of local administration after the dissolution of manorial management under serfdom. It can hardly be doubted that the zemstva were largely manned and directed by the traditional rural elite, most of whom showed little interest in the job. But it is no less true that even the most moderate zemstvoists came constantly into conflict with the bureaucracy on a variety of issues, and that the zemstva not only educated thousands in de facto self-government but, as a result of these continued conflicts, inspired a common ground of opposition. As Witte correctly realized, the conflict between zemstvo and autocracy was as probable as was that between the autocracy and the new urban forces, the professional and commercial middle class and the proletariat.

But this only begins the list of ways that modernization begun by the autocracy as a means toward greater strength had precisely and decisively the reverse effect. Besides dangerously concentrating a proletariat, a professional class, and a rebellious student body in the centers of political power, industrialization infuriated both these new forces and the traditional rural classes. It radically displaced the intensely status-conscious gentry and oppressed the peasantry through forced exports, monopoly prices, and regressive taxation that ultimately paid the bill of modernization. It furthered in all segments of society the painful collapse of old roles, values, motivations, and expectations — with the politically explosive consequences now familiar. It left no money to ameliorate the deplorable urban conditions into which the already distressed and disoriented peasantry flocked in quickly disillusioned hope of something better. It tied the entire economy by foreign loans and investments to a highly erratic international money and power market, thus paving the way for the economic crisis that aggravated the discontent throughout society in the five years or so preceding the Revolution of 1905.

In short, whereas there had been a well-balanced, symbiotic, mutual dependency among the participants in the traditional mobilization system of State, Church, and service-gentry, this was decidedly not the case in the new, post-Crimean system. The reforms required for defending the integrity of the *Nation* undermined the traditional power of the *State*. This is most dramatically clear in times of greatest national trial, international war: first in the East against Japan, then in the West, war impelled Russians toward the common conclusion that the autocracy could not meet the first duty of all governments, defense of the integrity and honor of the nation.

When we consider the varieties and the force of discontent amassing at the turn of the century, we can easily understand von Plehve's attraction to a little war with Japan — as, he thought, an outlet for this pent-up resentment, a stimulant for the predictable patriotic fervor that would supplant it, and perhaps, a booster for the sagging economy. After all, precisely such conflict had always been the ultimate goal of the great transformation, the reason for undertaking the political gamble (would modernization strengthen or weaken the regime?) that the autocracy was obviously loosing. Moreover, what could be more cautious than to test out the new resources in the East, the direction of traditional Russian success, against a country that, notwithstanding the Meiji reforms, could hardly be compared with the potential Western opponents. And then: the sinking of the flagship *Petropavlovsk* almost immediately after the war began; the defeat at Turechen; Kuropatkin's constant retreats through 1904; the unbelievable fall of Port Arthur in December; the defeat near Mukden, which Kuropatkin had vowed would be the final point of retreat; the further retreat toward Kharbin; and, as though Russia's cup of humiliation and despair had not long since flowed over, the tragicomedy of Rozhdestvenskii's

21

Baltic voyage to the East and the final outrage at Tsushima. After this, the State had no choice but to concede to the demands of the parties that had emerged in the preceding decade, parties that incorporated the very groups that had been created by modernization and that gave political voice to the distress suffered by all segments of society, traditional and new, that had resulted from it.

But if the opposition had grown vastly more powerful than it had been in 1825, had not the instruments of the State's defense grown proportionately? The answer is obvious: the humiliation of defeat that sparked the already highly inflammable popular discontent into open rebellion emasculated the army. This was admittedly the reason for granting a constitution and the elected Duma rather than enforcing a military dictatorship, the alternative that Witte frankly offered, along with the constitution proposal.[4]

So it continued, one step after another, from the reforms of the 'sixties, through the establishment of the Duma, into the decade of "Constitutional," "Duma" Russia. The rapid dissolutions of the first two Dumas, the illegal change in the franchise, and Stolypin's martial-law violence against the "extremists" are easily managed in the optimists' presentation, for together these merely indicate that the favorable opportunity provided by military disaster gave the opposition more power than it could hang on to under more normal conditions. But it was clearly a case of two steps forward, one step back. The third and fourth Dumas not only continued through their lawful spans, but made significant strides toward firmly rooting the system of election and parliamentary procedure. Through its participation in the affairs of state, particularly those concerned with national defense, the Duma was establishing itself in the mind of the public as a far more responsible, effective manager than the archaic bureaucracy. Moreover, the regularized consultations between the ministers and the Duma committees proved to the more reasonable bureaucrats, those who had the interests of the nation in mind, that the Duma, not the Court, was their true ally. In other words, the foundations of ministerial responsibility were being laid.

[4] *The Memoirs of Count Witte*, trans. and ed. by Abraham Yarmolinsky (New York: Doubleday, 1921), pp. 240–241, 244.

The limitations on the franchise were hardly an unusual feature in the early stages of parliamentary history — this shortcoming, the absence of ministerial responsibility, the lack of influence over certain reserved sections of the budget, and the frustrating veto power of a troglodyte upper house were all matters for later political struggle, to be won in later crises.

From about 1912 rumblings could be felt again. A new revolutionary wave began its ascent. As in the years preceding the 1905 crisis, there was an increase in strikes, an intensification of strain between the opposition and the State, this time partly manifested through the Duma, and trends toward the kind of united front political activity that had been so successful a decade before. History may never repeat itself, but it made a grand try at this juncture. For once again, as in 1904–1905, it was the desperate experience of war that raised discontent accumulating in the years immediately preceding the war to revolutionary pitch, this time giving the opposition an opportunity to move ahead from where it had left off in 1905, to regain what had been taken away by the Fundamental Laws and franchise revision. Everything seemed to favor complete success. Once again, the Court and the bureaucracy appeared unable to mobilize effectively the resources that they had created to fight the modern war. Once again, urban discontent, radically intensified by the wartime shortages, strains, and dislocations, was led by a well-organized, united front opposition.

But it was more than a repetition of 1905. Everything was heightened. In place of a year and a half of distant fighting, which had, in fact, ended before the revolution reached its peak, Russia was suffering a third winter of war on its very threshold, a war to which none could see an end. To add to its prodigious bungling, which everyone had come to expect, there was now the bizarre Rasputin affair, so radically exaggerated by fevered rumor, that cost tsarism what legitimacy it still had. Correspondingly, the opposition was now far stronger than it had been during and after the Russo-Japanese War. We must keep in mind that the intervening years had provided a well-established alternative government in the Duma. In addition, the educated urban and provincial public

23

was now able to form, with surprising rapidity and effectiveness, a variety of organizations that proved incomparably more skilled than the disdained Court camarilla in directing the war effort. And so patently was this clear that by 1916 the united front of opposition included virtually everyone except a handful of intimates and sycophants rotating around the Tsarina and "Our Friend" Rasputin. No wonder the chorus shouting for a ministry having the confidence of the people — that is, the Duma — now included the ministers themselves. The evolution begun at Crimea seemed nearing its end. The essential question — could the social and economic transformation take place without altering accordingly the political system? — was in the process of finding its unequivocal no. It was not only the resources, most widely defined, that had to change through modernization. The traditional political regime must go as well, to be replaced, naturally enough, by the very forces, the urban classes led by the commercial and professional bourgeoisie, that were the offspring and principal benefactors of the transformation. One could say with Marx that a new economic substructure, the urban, industrial complex, was in the process of creating its corresponding superstructure, a parliamentary government. Or one could argue, in Weberian terminology, that the several "orders" of society — economic, social, and political — must be in phase, and that tension persists until they are.[5] There are any number of such plots, forms and models, to embrace the process, which, from the optimists' point of view, was not merely aiming toward a bourgeois, "open," parliamentary government, but which had already taken by 1914 the most crucial steps toward its achievement.

If this encouraging political evolution was occurring in isolation from relevant developments elsewhere in the society, the force of the optimists' argument would be seriously weakened. But this is not the case, for the direction of changes throughout Russian culture and society paralleled and bolstered the political trend. First of all, there was the steady and rapid spread of general education, perhaps the most powerful of all motivating forces in moderniza-

[5] Alex Inkeles, "Social Stratification in the Modernization of Russia," in Black, ed., *The Transformation of Russian Society*, pp. 338–350.

24

tion and the most reliable assurance of its continuation.[6] In the economic sphere, industrialization had already begun in this crucial decade before the war to shift from its unhealthy dependency on foreign investment and government control to domestic capital and more self-sufficient entrepreneurial direction.[7] By tearing away the pillars of the primitive rural commune and promoting the establishment of individual farms, the Stolypin policies were on their way to surpassing in magnitude of change even the Great Reforms, and, along the way, establishing a firm popular foundation for those familiar Western attitudes that have proved so congenial to bourgeois representative government. Similarly, one should note the dramatic spread of rural cooperatives, the increase in rural savings and consumer purchasing power, the diverse and extensive rural development programs sponsored by a variety of public and official bodies, the elimination of one after another of the discriminatory fiscal and juridical procedures that had for centuries set the peasant off as, at best, a third-class citizen.[8] Even the labor movement was entering its moderate phase, and its leaders, including many of the Marxist faction, were abandoning their romantic extremism and their cherished underground. Finally, and perhaps most promising of all, even the intelligentsia showed signs of abandoning its puerile

[6] "The institutions of higher education were the chief training ground for this new class, and their enrollment in proportion to the population increased more than nine times between 1885 and 1914. The increase in secondary-school enrollment was even greater, and by the time of the First World War Russia had made substantial progress toward a system of universal elementary education. The social mobility accompanying the growth in higher education is reflected in the fact that the proportion of children of peasants, craftsmen, and workers enrolled in the universities grew from 15.7 per cent in 1880 to 38.8 per cent in 1914, and in the higher technical institutes was 54 per cent in the latter year. The officer corps was no doubt the most conservative branch of the bureaucracy, but it appears that by the end of the empire a majority of the new officers came from non-noble families as did some of the leading generals in the First World War." (Cyril E. Black, "Nature of Imperial Russian Society," in Treadgold, ed., *The Development of the U.S.S.R.*, pp. 186–187.)

[7] Alexander Gerschenkron, *Economic Backwardness in Historical Perspective* (Cambridge, Mass.: Harvard University Press, 1962), Chs. I–II.

[8] Aleksei N. Antsiferov et al., *Russian Agriculture during the War* (New Haven: Yale University Press, 1930).

omnipotence fantasies and fin de siècle postures and maturing into responsible contributors to society.[9]

Had all this been topped with a full parliamentary government and bourgeois culture and society, it would have seemed so natural, so obvious a climax of what had gone before that any prophetic history that put some Pestel, Nechaev, Bakunin, or Lenin in power would have appeared the rankest nonsense, the ravings of some Dostoevskyian underground man.

The rankest nonsense became the fact. Most optimists blame the overwhelming burdens and tensions of the war, which, they argue, tore to shreds the social and political fabric, fostering, after the revolution in February, a cataclysmic anarchy which favored the unprincipled opportunism of the Bolsheviks and which, in turn, could be crushed only by unlimited Bolshevik violence. But other optimists believe that the burdens of war were not by themselves sufficient causes for this disastrous sequence.[10] Had the tsar made the least effort to cooperate (as he did for a time after the Galician retreat) with the public forces that were beginning to mobilize effectively the war effort, had he taken the lead of the patriotic fervor that swept the nation in the first months of the war, had he allowed the competent ministers installed in 1915 to remain in power and had he sanctioned their desire to work with the progressive groups in the Duma, Zemgor, defense councils, and so forth, then the revolutions of 1917 would have been avoided. That final year of war would not only have passed without the fateful breakdown and anarchy, but the military showing would have continued to improve, as it had been doing and as the Germans feared it would continue to do. To determine why the Tsar did not follow this policy and why his actions and those of his Court appeared, insanely, to undermine the war effort rather than to lead it as one might normally have expected, we must turn to the character of the Tsar,

[9] Wladimir Weidlé, *Russia: Absent and Present*, trans. by A. Gordon Smith (New York: Hollis & Carter, 1952, 1961), pp. 91–108; Boris Elkin, "The Russian Intelligentsia on the Eve of the Revolution," in Richard Pipes, ed., *The Russian Intelligentsia* (New York: Columbia University Press, 1961), pp. 32–46.

[10] Black, "The Nature of Imperial Russian Society," p. 190; Karpovich, *Imperial Russia*, p. 25.

the tragic Tsarina, and the nightmare of madness and mediocrity that dominated the inner Court and stifled the national effort to such an extent that it appeared in the public mind as out and out treason. The optimist sees no inevitability here — of course the tsarist system was more congenial to such conditions than, say, a fully parliamentary system, but the conditions themselves were no more ineluctable, nor even probable, than was the hemophilia of the Tsarevich. Certainly, one could not imagine any of the three Alexanders charged with treason in a national war.

Such, in general, is the case for the optimists. It is a case that has been under persistent attack both before and after the Bolshevik victory. The most vigorous and resourceful of the recent assaults is, I think, that of Professor Theodore Von Laue, who has probably gone further than anyone else, Soviet scholars included, in allowing "no chance for a liberal constitutional Russia whatsoever." [11] He is quite willing to acknowledge many of the progressive developments listed by the optimists — the remarkable economic expansion, the rapid advance in education, the improvement in peasant status and conditions, the increase in political security and spontaneity, the broadening and deepening of civil rights, the establishment of an elected Duma, and so forth.[12] But he easily discounts them all, arguing that, notwithstanding such progress, "next to nothing was accomplished in regard to the basic necessities confronting the country"; that the optimists see only the "superficial glow"; that the Revolution of 1905, leading to most of the gains that encourage the optimists, "was more like a passing squall of bad weather," a "disintegrating half-way stage rather than a hopeful beginning"; that peasant educational opportunities remained "but a drop in the bucket"; that "Stolypin's agrarian measures merely offered a half-solution"; and that even the momentous achievement of Witte, which Von Laue has himself done so much to publicize, must be judged "foredoomed to failure," an unenduring "gloss of success." [13] But

[11] Theodore H. Von Laue, "The Chances for Liberal Constitutionalism," *Slavic Review*, XXIV (March 1965), 46.

[12] See also his *Why Lenin? Why Stalin?* (Philadelphia, New York: Lippincott, 1964), pp. 72–73.

[13] *Ibid.*, pp. 68, 73; "The Chances for Liberal Constitutionalism," pp. 41, 43; "Of the Crises in the Russian Polity," in John S. Curtiss, ed., *Essays in*

why was all that seemed so promising, that provides the optimists with some of their weightiest evidence, all so fundamentally hopeless? Von Laue's answer, and by no means his alone, is that Russia was fatally trapped in an agonizing contradiction which precluded the establishment of a parliamentary government or, in fact, any government but the one hammered out by the Bolsheviks. This is tragic, Von Laue admits, and "only a villain will gloat over the unspeakable misfortune,"[14] but it was nonetheless the essential fact of Russian life.

Von Laue's major proof of this rests on an alignment of factors remarkably similar to that used by the optimists to support their case. At one pole stands global conflict; at the other, backward society. It is the desperate and tragic struggle to bridge the gap implied in this that, according to Von Laue, creates the conditions so hostile to Russian liberalism. The real culprit seems to be rapid industrialization: global conflict makes gradual economic development impossible, and rapid industrialization is incompatible with liberal constitutionalism.

Since it is the bedrock of his argument, Von Laue repeatedly emphasizes the inevitability of this global conflict, if not for one reason, then for another. There is, first of all, Imperial Germany, with its "appetite for eastward expansion which needed only military and political opportunity to grow to unlimited proportions." But should one argue that Wilhelm's Germany, unlike Adolf's, held out no such threat to Russia's survival, no such "profound challenge to its existence," to Russia's being ruled by her own "native masters";[15] that it was quite possible for Russia to act in 1914 as she had in 1908 and 1913, swallow for a time her Balkan pride and put off fighting until prepared; then Von Laue can argue a second cause of inevitable international conflict: Russia's own messianic complex. Russia's own craving for unrestrained expansion,

---

Russian and Soviet History (Leiden: E. J. Brill, 1963), p. 310; *Sergei Witte and the Industrialization of Russia* (New York: Columbia University Press, 1963), pp. 276, 305.

[14] "Of the Crises in the Russian Polity," p. 322.

[15] "The Chances for Liberal Constitutionalism," pp. 38–39; "Of the Crises in the Russian Polity," pp. 303–305; *Sergei Witte*, p. 307; *Why Lenin?*, p. 76.

for "global pre-eminence," or for "the subtler satisfactions of global prestige"[16] is the ineluctable force driving Russia into the war and preparation for it, both radically unfavorable to liberalism. But one might then draw from a vast literature, including Von Laue's own biography of Sergei Witte, to show the large number highly placed in Russian government and society who were against war. In reply to this, Von Laue has the argument that the Russian people themselves would drive the nation to war. In an early statement of this theme Von Laue noted that "there is no evidence that the bulk of the population did not favor the basic political ambitions of the government." Later, he argued more forthrightly that "the government and its subjects were of one mind" on the issue of Russian "global pre-eminence," that on this question, the force driving Russia to Armageddon, "the individual ego and the state ego became ever more closely fused." In another exposition of this thesis, Von Laue depicts the people as even more belligerent than the State: "But suppose that Nicholas II, under the pressure of the conservatives, had decided to stay out of the war over Serbia. What effects would this surrender have had on the state of Russian opinion? Might it not have escalated the agitation into open rebellion, pushing the liberals into the streets on the side of the workers? . . . Unhesitant participation in the war kept the liberals on the side of the autocracy; it prevented a major domestic crisis."[17] For those who still remain skeptical of Von Laue's views on this essential point, he offers the general truths that "world wars were the order of the age," and that "as Thucydides had observed, societies like individuals are engaged in a constant wrangle for ascendancy."[18]

Thus, whether one explains it by Germany's boundless "appetite for eastward expansion," or a comparable messianic drive by Russia toward "global pre-eminence," or a humbler concern for "global prestige" by the State and/or the people, somehow Russia's entrance into the conflict of war must be made inevitable. I happen to be

[16] "Of the Crises in the Russian Polity," p. 304; "The State and the Economy," in Black, ed., *The Transformation of Russian Society*, p. 210.
[17] "The State and the Economy," p. 221; "Of the Crises in the Russian Polity," p. 304; "The Chances for Liberal Constitutionalism," pp. 39–40.
[18] "The Chances for Liberal Constitutionalism," p. 39; *Sergei Witte*, p. 307.

reading now the correspondence of Lawrence Durrell and Henry Miller. How well it recalls the "inevitable war" between Russia and the United States: "this coming month of August [1947] will see some sort of diabolical conjunction, very similar to the set-up in August 1914 and September 1939. . . . By the time we get back to Europe it will be about as interesting as the deserts of Texas. I think a very short war — say six months — could account for all the major cities of Europe [March 1948]. . . . I've resigned my post here and propose to reach London by Christmas — probably an atomic Christmas [September–October 1948]. . . . If World War III doesn't break out in a few weeks (as I firmly expect) [August 1953] . . ." [19] Had war actually occurred at any one of these times or, say, at the time the Hungarian Revolution of 1956 or the Cuban Missile crisis, the evidence of all that came before would have provided an overwhelming case for the inevitablists.

But assuming that Von Laue is correct in his portrait of an ineluctable collision course together with the rapid industrialization it implies, there remains the question of why they were so incompatible with the parliamentary government that was also apparently emerging in the prewar Russia. We already know from Von Laue that the people were militant nationalists who were, if anything, more belligerently messianic than the Court. Why not assume their support, through the Duma, of the economic program required by such attitudes? Why is Russian rapid industrialization incompatible with Russian liberalism? Von Laue offers several answers. First, rapid industrialization "would never have found majority support under a parliamentary regime" because "Russian liberalism was largely agrarian in orientation and opposed to foisting economic sacrifices upon the population." Second, there is the vital connection between political liberalism and private economic initiative. Lacking prior accumulation of bourgeois capital, talent, and drive, the State must take the lead in rapid industrialization, and "the freedoms of the Western model were incompatible with government initiative in the Russian tradition": rapid industrialization from the

[19] *Lawrence Durrell and Henry Miller: A Private Correspondence*, ed. by George Wickes (New York: Dutton, 1963), pp. 246, 250, 252, 296.

top "crippled the sense of independence and dynamic initiative which is such an essential ingredient of Western urban-industrial society." Third, parliamentary government, "under Russian conditions," simply could not solve Russia's problems: "Parliamentary government, it would seem safe to speculate, would have considerably slowed down the decision-making process. The administration would have been decentralized, more power devolved upon the zemstva. And at the center one could have expected, in view of the variety of political programs and the deep-seated penchant for maximalist solutions, a protracted wrangling of antagonistic groups, which in themselves lacked cohesion, leadership, or a mass following. A period of costly, and possibly quite fruitless experiments would have followed." [20]

This brings us to a major point in Von Laue's argument, the leitmotiv of much of his writings: The only way that Russia might advance fast enough to avoid the disasters waiting for her from the inevitable global conflict was through a total transformation forced from the top and involving all segments of Russian culture and society. In other words, only a Soviet revolutionary transformation, a totalitarian planned economy and controlled society, might hope to save the integrity and independence of the nation. Not only was liberal parliamentarianism out of the question, but even the tsarist system lacked the necessary power for this; thus, Witte's program failed to be carried through to its logical (that is, Soviet) conclusions. [21]

This is Von Laue's principal argument against the optimists, who reach opposite conclusions from the great transformation Russia was then undertaking to meet the requirements of modern war — they see emerging as a consequence of this transformation, first, a successful advance toward Western economic, social, and cultural patterns and, second, the establishment of solid foundations for a Western parliamentary government. But Von Laue has a second approach in his general position which, in contrast with his main

[20] *Sergei Witte*, pp. 304–306; "Of the Crises in the Russian Polity," pp. 308–309.
[21] "The State and the Economy," pp. 222–225; *Sergei Witte*, p. 306; "Of the Crises in the Russian Polity," pp. 314–322; *Why Lenin?*, pp. 58–65.

interpretation, argues that defeat in global conflict was not necessary for the failure of Russian liberalism and the Bolshevik victory, that this denouement was, in fact, well on its way in 1914. At the center of this line of thought are the well-publicized fissures that cracked Russian society, separating the educated society from the "dark" masses, the villages from the towns, the sectarians from the Orthodox, the officials from the intelligentsia, the intelligentsia from everyone else including themselves, minority people from minority people and Great Russian majority from them all, and so on. To all this must then be added the fact that "the inevitable advance of industrialization even at the current rates would have intensified the existing social tensions, as in fact it did." [22] Under such strife and confusion, "what guarantee was there that once the external compulsion [of autocracy] was removed and spontaneity of thought and action encouraged, the multitude of tongues, levels of civilization, social groupings, and ranks would not result in anarchy? Under any circumstances, *in war or peace*, the political awakening of the peoples of Russia in an era of freedom would have, most likely, accented the proverbial disunity of the empire to the breaking point, as it did in the fall of 1917." [23]

Thus, "in war or peace," liberalism was doomed. In fact, not only can Von Laue dispense with the war and still arrive at his pessimistic view of the prospects of Russian liberalism, but he can also dispense with the contribution of rapid industrialization, so torn was Russia by these gaping splits: "*What ever* the tempo of industrial development, the surrounding framework of political institutions and social custom in autocracy as well as in liberal society was obviously unprepared to withstand the shocks" of this economic development.[24]

The shocks that were too much for both the autocracy and liberal society were all too successfully managed by the Bolsheviks. Only this highly disciplined party, with its techniques of mass organization could replace the autocratic system that had heretofore held the compoundly fractured empire together, and, more important,

---

[22] "Of the Crises in the Russian Polity," pp. 307–308, 311; *Why Lenin?*, Ch. II.
[23] "The Chances for Liberal Constitutionalism," p. 41. Italics added.
[24] *Ibid.*, p. 45. Italics added.

32

only a complete state socialism of the Bolshevik variety — not the halfhearted Witte program — could solve the problem of industrialization and thereby catch up with the West militarily. In short, "the Soviets have provided what seem to be highly effective solutions to the crises that confronted the Russian state under the Tsars. The global position now occupied by the Soviet Union testifies to their validity." [25]

Through such theories Von Laue seeks the "deeper historical necessity," "the connecting necessity not seen on the surface of events," the "pattern of coordinates into which the development of modern Russia *has to be set* and into which, furthermore, *have to be charted all* the barely explored ingredients of power politics, socio-political cohesion, and industrialization that have determined the course of modernization in Europe and the world." [26] One may wonder at the process by which such necessities and "coordinates" are gleaned from "barely explored" areas: although one can only applaud Von Laue's pleas for "patient, humble, and self-effacing search," it seems to me that things more fundamental than "the elusive telling detail" still remain undisclosed.[27]

Whereas Professor Von Laue has two roads to inevitable Bolshevik power — one with war, another without it — Professor Leopold Haimson seems to risk all on the even-without-war approach. In place of Von Laue's "coordinates," Haimson has two "polarizations," which, added together, give Bolshevik power. The first polarization is between the educated society and the official bureaucracy, and leads to the overthrow of tsarism. The second is between the educated society and the masses, mainly urban. It either frustrates all efforts at constitutional, parliamentary government or quickly demolishes such a government if, by chance, one should get a foothold in power. Everything that the optimists call upon to defend the possible survival of parliamentary government, Haimson dismisses in much the same manner as does Von Laue. The Revolution of 1905 and establishment of an elected, legislative Duma is no

[25] "Of the Crises in the Russian Polity," pp. 320–321.
[26] *Ibid.*, pp. 303, 314 n. 1; "The Chances for Liberal Constitutionalism," p. 46. Italics added.
[27] "The Chances for Liberal Constitutionalism," p. 46.

more than "a brief historical interval," the remarkable united front that brought about this achievement is a "grab-bag" of political tendencies, the moderating tendencies in the labor movement associated in part with the Mensheviks are "deceptive," and so on.

Above all, and this is the crux of his argument, there could be no further merger of interests between the liberals and the masses of the sort that produced the successes of 1905, since Haimson has learned somehow that "by 1912–14 the vast majority of the liberal intelligentsia no longer entertained so glowing an image of the working class"[28] as they had, presumably, in 1905, and that the workers, in turn, felt the same toward the liberals. Thus, the rise in opposition evident to all in the years before the war — opposition that the optimists see as the beginning of another advance along the road charted in 1905 — according to Haimson necessarily led not to liberalism but to Bolshevism.[29]

At one point Haimson urges the historians to turn aside from ifs and address themselves "to *what in fact was happening.*"[30] Yet, from the optimists' point of view, if one recalls what *happened*, not what according to Haimson was *happening*, it is difficult to imagine a Bolshevik victory apart from the cataclysmic impact of the war experience. I have elsewhere expressed at length my doubts about Professor Haimson's interpretation[31] and want here only to raise several of the questions that I think important for its evaluation. Did mass disaffection in the prewar period compare with what it became as a result of three years of wartime suffering? Can the presence of a battered, weary, untrained peasant army, at the front

[28] Leopold Haimson, "Reply," *Slavic Review*, XXIV (March 1965), 54. Italics added.

[29] For an exposition of Professor Haimson's argument, see his two-part article, "The Problem of Social Stability in Urban Russia, 1905–1917," *Slavic Review*, XXIII (December 1964) and XXIV (March 1965). For a more elaborate statement of my own evaluation of Haimson's theories, see Arthur Mendel, "Peasant and Worker on the Eve of the First World War," *Slavic Review*, XXIV (March 1965), 23–33.

[30] "Reply," pp. 55–56. Very much like Professor Von Laue, Professor Haimson somehow manages to reconcile a firmly welded, grand synthesis with his belief that the study of this phase of Russian history is "at a stage where even the most basic data have not yet been sifted and individually understood, let alone properly correlated" (p. 56).

[31] See n. 29 above.

34

and, more crucially, barracked in the rear, be left out? Apart from the three-year war experience, would a professional army have responded as the soldiers did in 1917 to the strikes and demonstrations? Is it mere coincidence that both revolutions, 1905 and 1917, emerged out of war crisis? Similarly, is there anything comparable in the prewar years with the degree and extent of hostility toward the Court felt by educated society, from socialist to monarchist, that emerged during the war? It seems to me, in fact, that Professor Haimson's attempt to derive a victorious Bolshevik revolution from prewar conditions is more unreasonably speculative than the arguments of the optimists who see the years 1912–1914 as the beginning of another phase in the long process of establishing a constitutional government, a period of struggle led by the already established alternative government, the Duma, but involving groups from all segments of society, liberal and labor included.

After all — and this relates to both Von Laue's and Haimson's positions — from the mid-1800's through the Revolution of 1905 into and including the prewar Duma period, the advance toward a liberal, open, Western society is steady and, in comparison with early similar processes in the West, remarkably rapid. One should keep in mind that men and women born as serfs in the reign of Nicholas I were participating in elections for a central representative government under Nicholas II. Considering the years before the war, who is more the speculator, one who extrapolates a future of comparable evolution from what had already happened, or one who predicts the radically contrary conquest of power by the Tkachevs and the Bakunins? It is my own view, therefore, that neither Professor Von Laue nor Professor Haimson has demonstrated the inevitability, probability, or even likelihood of a Bolshevik government emerging apart from the specific experiences of World War I. I should agree, rather, with Lenin's ultra-pessimistic views of the Bolshevik prospects in these years.

This brings us to the most fascinating question of all, Did the war, then, make this outcome inevitable or even probable? I do not believe that the Bolsheviks would have had much chance of coming to power were it not for the war. I also do not consider

35

ineluctable a war with Germany when Russia was knowingly vastly unprepared for it, but I am ambivalent about the probability of outcomes once Russia was in the war. As was suggested at the outset, there are two principal interpretations: According to one, essential structural features of the Russian state and society, under the impact of prolonged war, caused the overthrow of tsarism, the ensuing anarchy, and the ultimate Bolshevik victory. From this viewpoint, little could have been done to divert this evolution toward other outcomes. The other interpretation argues that notwithstanding all structural defects, the existing system could have remained intact through the war had it not been for the extraordinary circumstances associated with the bizarre behavior and policies of Nicholas II and his intimate Court circle.

The inadequacy of railroads — which both directly and indirectly contributed significantly to the desperate food shortage, an essential factor in the revolution in February — and the comparable deficiency in industry, which undermined provision of military supplies and of urban facilities, were both symptoms of economic backwardness. These crucial inadequacies, together with the consequent military failures, promoted discontent in the cities, where political power was centered, and among the troops. The strikes and bread marches in the third winter of war that precipitated the February Revolution may indeed follow predictably from such structural weaknesses, although even this is debatable. But such demonstrations were hardly novel either in Russia or elsewhere: it took the defection of the defense forces, the police, and the army to turn them into open revolution, a defection not necessarily traceable to structural weaknesses. Notwithstanding ghastly losses, the morale of the troops on the front was hardly worse than it was among the other armed forces in the war — that is, miserable, but not critically revolutionary. Also, after the debacle of 1915 and the consequent public participation in the war effort, the supply of military and auxiliary facilities improved.

There is a theory of revolution which argues that no amount of distress at the lower levels of society is lethal to the Establishment as long as the elite hold together. I think the war experience in Russia provides an example. By the end of 1916 the Court was virtually isolated from all educated society, from all the power elites in military, commercial, political, and even governmental circles. The highest officials, members of the Cabinet, sided with a united Duma front, which included even dedicated monarchists, in opposition to the camarilla that seemed to hold final authority. It seems to me that were it not for this complete isolation of the Tsar, his wife, and their most intimate circle, the Putilov strike, bread march, and Women's Day demonstration would not have been followed by defection of the troops and, in a single week, the overthrow of tsarism and the subsequent anarchy that gave Lenin his chance to take over.

But assuming that this disaffection of the elite was in fact a necessary link in the chain leading from military and civilian shortages to the overthrow of tsarism, the problem of evaluating the disaffection remains. I see several possible approaches. One can argue that such isolation of the Tsar from the rest of society, including his erstwhile dedicated supporters, was a highly *improbable* situation resulting from the particular attitudes of this particular Tsar and the weird role of his wife, her sycophants, and her Friend Rasputin. Had the Tsar kept the position he took after the retreat of 1915, remained behind the capable ministers he installed at that time, and led the patriotic Duma and public efforts to bolster the sagging war effort — had he done, in other words, what practically any other tsar in Russia's past would have done, what others even in the royal family were endlessly haranguing him to do — would the defection of the elite have occurred? Far from "necessary," the actions of the Tsar and his Court responsible for this total disaffection, for the extraordinary public accusation of treason, are unprecedented. To say, as Lenin and his followers do, that such behavior together with the influence of personalities like Rasputin are characteristic of such medieval courts or that they are the expected result of the equally characteristic break in communications linking the State and society is not a convincing reply. Other tsars broke through such barriers to support vital reforms. And what could be more vital than the survival of Russia itself during the war, a survival that for some fantastic, incomprehensible reason the Tsar himself was jeopardizing?

This is one approach. But there is another, more determinist view of this essential divorce of the elite from the State, involving a dramatic conflict of illusions. Were Nicholas's actions really so irresponsible? Could he not have been very well aware of the likely outcome of the patriotic, public war effort, the Progressive Bloc activities, and the sympathy for both overtly manifested by his own leading ministers — the outcome that the optimists cherish? The war with Japan had made the first disastrous crack in the system of autocracy by introducing the Duma to share power with the Court and bureaucracy. Everything happening during World War I seemed all too clearly to be moving toward still another, perhaps final, blow at what remained of autocracy. Peter the Great and Alexander II did break out of medieval isolation and wave the standard of progress, but they did so to strengthen not only the nation but the State, the autocracy. Progress for Nicholas, however, would mean collaborating in its destruction. The Tsarina and Rasputin were hardly needed to urge Nicholas's opposition to these tendencies. He had already demonstrated throughout the Duma period his resistance to any further such decline in his prerogative as seemed latent in Stolypin's rapport with Guchkov, for example. His illusion was to think that this defense of the medieval prerogatives, a theme that occurs throughout Pares's intimate study of the Court mentality, was consistent with, indeed indistinguishable from, the welfare of Russia.

But this illusion might not have had such disastrous consequences had it not encountered comparable illusions in the opposition, who seemed convinced that the Tsar and the Court were responsible for the poor showing in the war. Behind this illusion the opposition had another — that Russia was already an advanced society and that if she suffered grotesque defeats, vast shortages, and administrative chaos, they were the result of conspiracy and even treason at the top, not of the relative backwardness of the economy and society or of the disorders suffered by all participants in World War I. Faced with the opposition's self-deception, what could the Tsar have done, even had he been willing to risk further loss of power by leading the war effort? Could his lead have improved supplies of fuel, food, and housing to the deprived towns; won more battles; trained more effectively the mass of raw peasant recruits; provided more track and rolling stock? Probably not. And if such improvements were not forthcoming in these critical areas, the opposition would have continued to cry out against what remained of tsarist prerogative, going from ministry of confidence to full ministerial responsibility, then to the ouster of all the private advisers of the Tsar — along a continuum, that is, such that the Tsar would have been forced at some point to stop and defend the remnants. Once the public took on a major share in the war effort, through the Duma and the various public bodies, the only alternative to attacking the Court was responsibly facing the fact of Russia's backwardness — an alternative which, judging from memoirs of the period, the opposition was loathe to adopt.[32]

The case of Rasputin seems to illustrate this: it was far easier to blame such "dark forces" than to accept the backwardness of Russia, far easier to believe that this or that person was to blame and should be removed than to alter the more fundamental weaknesses that were truly responsible for the deprivations and defeats. The remarkable progress that the liberal opposition had achieved in the prewar decade, the further strengthening of its influence and position during the war, and a host of other specifically wartime conditions enabled the opposition to achieve the goal of its illusory dream: driving out the Tsar and putting in his stead a government, albeit provisional, of its own. But the opposition had a final and still more fateful illusion, that the Russian "people" were as committed to the war as was the educated society and no less antagonistic to the Court for undermining the war effort.[33] Just the opposite was true. The people hated everything about the war; rather than the Tsar's impeding the war effort, he was the keystone, as Miliukov

[32] See, for example, Mikhail V. Rodzianko, *The Reign of Rasputin: An Empire's Collapse*, trans. by Catherine Zvegintzoff (New York: A. K. Philpot, 1927).

[33] This remains Kerensky's view, as we see from his book *Russia and History's Turning Point* (New York: Duell, Sloan, & Pearce, 1965), Ch. IX.

39

realized too late, that kept the system, particularly its soldiers, workers, and peasants, functioning at all.[34]

As I have said, I am undecided which of these interpretations of the war years is correct. For that matter, I am uncertain about the "objective" validity of either the optimists' or the pessimists' general position, although I strongly incline toward the former. There can be no certainty where such complex historical subjects are involved. The "unseen necessities" that Von Laue is after remain and, fortunately, will continue to remain, unseen.

I therefore return to the theme with which this essay opened: the relation between historical studies of such "backward" countries as Russia, and present and future development in Asia, Africa, and Latin America. There is all too often a close association between the historian's portrait of the past and his predilections about the present and future. A retrospective pessimist whose account of underdeveloped tsarist Russia excludes liberal constitutionalism as an alternative to autocracy is not likely to find hopeful prospects for liberalism in present-day societies that he considers comparably backward, and there is always the temptation to carry over the "unseen necessities" from one to the other. But more serious is the danger that those engaged in politics might honor the historian's claim to having disclosed the "unseen necessities," the "pattern of coordinates into which . . . have to be charted all the barely explored ingredients of power politics, socio-political cohesion, and industrialization that have determined the course of modernization in Europe and the world."

In one sense, harm is done whether the "patterns of coordinates" are pessimistic or optimistic, since their acceptance in either case

[34] Summarizing this interpretation, which meshes nicely with Haimson's approach, one might say that Russian liberalism failed because it had been succeeding too fast, that it had gained enough power to dislodge tsarism, given the war crisis, before society had provided the necessary conditions for erecting a constitutional, parliamentary government in its place. Too much remained of the traditional, "medieval" world both at the top and at the bottom. At the top, anachronistic illusion of autocratic prerogative prevented a bonafide cooperation between the Court and the Duma leaders of a sort that might have prevented the disastrous split in the elite. Too much remained at the bottom, among the peasants, workers, and soldiers, to allow sufficient support for the ideals and programs of the liberals.

40

unnecessarily narrows the range of endeavor, discouraging approaches that are inconsistent with the historian's predictions. But when the patterns are pessimistic, there is the added detriment of promoting a self-fulfilling prediction, establishing policies on pessimistic expectations that in fact foster precisely such outcomes, if only by discounting alternative programs. When we consider the fact that in Asia, Africa, and Latin America there prevail today many of those conditions that, according to the pessimists of Russian history, made liberal constitutionalism impossible in pre-Bolshevik Russia, we can readily appreciate the potential harm of such spurious "objectivity."

And it is, to repeat, always spurious. No historian can avoid projecting his own being as he selects and orders his data, outlines his plot, portrays character, shifts his moods and stress, ranks influences and attributes, distributes punishments and rewards, and implicitly passes judgment in every line he writes. Some personalities, moreover, are attracted to highly structured, deterministic, abstract patterns; others feel more at home in a richly textured, intensely personal, even phantasmagorically chaotic milieu. Some seem to find a remarkable amount of conflict, tension, and pain; others glide leisurely along happier contours. Some range far and wide for comparisons and analogies, for echoes and correspondences; others want only to deepen their intimacies with the unique something or other. When to this unavoidable subjectivity we add the fact that each situation has a wealth of unique features distinguishing it from its apparent analogue and recall as well the striking role of accident in history, we should realize that what the historian has to say to those who are involved in working out concrete policies must be cautiously limited, immersed in layer after layer of reservations and qualifications. Above all else, the policy maker should beware of those who claim to have found the *really real*.

ROBERT F. BYRNES

Russian Conservative Thought before the Revolution

♟ ♟ ♟

CONSERVATISM and the history of conservative thought
have been neglected by historians, Americans as well as those in
other countries. Noisy, lively, and successful radicals and revolutionaries have naturally attracted the attention of scholars, most
of whom write in societies which are, or consider themselves, revolutionary or which were the products of successful revolutions. Moreover, the study of conservatism involves analysis not only of highly
complicated and complex forms of thought but also of institutions,
customs, and values, all of which are more irksome to analyze and
define than are radical and revolutionary movements. Consequently,
the level of our knowledge concerning conservative thought and
conservative traditions is low, in Russia as well as in other countries.

The word *conservative* is extremely difficult to define, particularly
because it is so frequently misused and because its character and
meaning change from one society to another and from one time
to another. Thus, the conservatism of an American in the last
third of the twentieth century differs considerably from the conservatism of a Russian at the same time, because the two seek
to preserve different national values and institutions. [Moreover,
conservatism is a matter of taste more than of doctrine. It is,

as John Buchan wrote, "above all, a spirit, and the fruits of that spirit are continuity and unity." It reflects an appreciation of the complexities of social systems and a respect for the wisdom inherent in established institutions and ideas. It has at its core a strong sense of continuity and of the impotence of words and ideas. It reflects a certain moral satisfaction concerning status and rank. Above all, it assumes that means and methods are as important as goals. In American slang, a conservative believes that "it ain't what you do, it's the way that you do it." [1]

Generally, a conservative is one who seeks to keep in safety, from harm, decay, or loss, "those institutions and values which he considers at the core of his society." Conservatism is "characterized by a tendency to preserve or keep intact unchanged." Scholars have identified a number of kinds of conservatism, all of which come together in what one might call philosophical conservatism. For example, temperamental conservatism reflects the natural disposition of some men to oppose change and to love authority, tradition, and habit. Lord Hugh Cecil defined this kind of conservatism as "a natural disposition of the human mind. It is a disposition adverse from change, and it springs partly from a distrust of the unknown and a corresponding reliance on experience rather than on theoretic reasoning; partly from the faculty in men to adapt themselves to their surroundings so that what is familiar merely because of its familiarity becomes more acceptable and tolerable than what is unfamiliar." [2] Temperamental conservatism, in short, is based on habit, fear, and inertia.

A second kind of conservatism, which is probably of especial significance in the twentieth century, has been defined as possessive conservatism. Generally, this reflects the values and views of the middle class, and it seeks to defend status, power, property, and the past. It is self-centered, and emphasizes property or possessions.

A third kind is practical or pragmatic. This was more common in the nineteenth century than it is in the twentieth century. It is the

[1] Arthur Bryant, *The Spirit of Conservatism* (London: Methuen, 1929), pp. 7–23, 61–64.
[2] Lord Hugh R. H. Cecil, *Conservatism* (London: Williams, 1911), p. 9.

view of a member of a society clearly on the defensive, and it is at the core of conservative parties, such as the Tory Party in England in the nineteenth century.

The most important form of conservatism — one which combines these three and adds a reflective quality — might be defined as philosophical conservatism. This is pessimistic, organic, and ethical. It is not substantially different from philosophical liberalism. Indeed, Clinton L. Rossiter noted that "the essential difference between liberal and conservative is one of mood and bias. No line separates one camp from the other. Out somewhere between them stands a man who is at once the most liberal of the conservatives and the most conservative of the liberals. In genuine liberalism, there is a strain of conservatism, and in genuine conservatism there is a strain of liberalism." [3]

At the heart of all conservative thought and of conservative political and social systems, one finds a series of essentially common characteristics. Perhaps the most important of these is the view of the nature of man, who is considered by all conservatives a weak instrument who must be bolstered or supported and maintained by institutions and ideas, such as those of the Russian Communist Party or of the Catholic Church or of an aristocratic political system. Thus, a true conservative believes that man is not able to stand independently on his own feet, that he reflects the past and its values and its traditions, and that he must remain a part of this complex arrangement if he and his society are to survive and prosper.

The true conservative also views society, any society, as a complicated, complex, and truly remarkable series of institutions and ideas, which reflect a folk wisdom developed over a long period of time. The society is always of such a character that the conservative believes change must be introduced slowly and carefully, lest the very foundations of the system be destroyed. In short, the conservative believes that the means or methods of change are just as important as the goals of a society. Thus, change is not opposed, but must come carefully and slowly because violent or radical change will inevitably be destructive and disruptive.

[3] *Conservatism in America* (New York: Knopf, 1955), pp. 5–9.

44

In the nineteenth century, as in earlier periods, Russia was essentially a conservative society. [The great majority of Russians, which Avvakum in the seventeenth century called "the ignorant, self-sufficient majority," were men and women with such limited knowledge and such a restricted view of the world that they were almost inevitably conservative. The political and intellectual leaders of the state at the same time were also essentially conservative, in part because of their isolation and ignorance and in part because of the Russian traditionally reverent view of society and of the established ways of doing things. Russia in the nineteenth century was and had been a service state, with weak estates or classes, a powerful controlled church, and a firmly established and respected autocracy, so that conservatism was part of the atmosphere or climate. The principal threats to conservative views and institutions were Western ideas and Western ways, the introduction of which had begun with Peter the Great and Catherine the Great in the eighteenth century. However, Russian isolation and Russian satisfaction with the established system as such were so great that Western ideas had little influence, except on the very highest levels of society, where some members of the aristocracy were more foreign than Russian.]

The struggle between conservative thought and institutions on one hand and radical or liberal ones on the other in the nineteenth century began basically with the publication by Chaadaev in 1836 of his "Philosophical Letters," in which he wrote that "not one useful thought has germinated on the barren soil of our country; not one great truth has sprung up in our midst." Chaadaev and those who accepted his views, who came to be called Westerners, believed that Russia was not and could not be an independent state or society, that Russia must borrow extensively from Western Europe, and that Russia must become in fact an essentially European state. The view of Chaadaev and his supporters was opposed in what one might call the Great Debate of the 1840's by the Slavophils, who created the first clearly conservative position for Russian intellectuals. The Slavophils were much influenced by Western thought and values, particularly those of England and Prussia. They came from leisured manorial families, generally from the Moscow area, they were often closely related or represented a closely knit Moscovite society, and they were convinced that Russia was a truly unique civilization which had been and must remain separate and distinct from other societies. The values which they found unique and of particular value in Russia were those of a peaceful, harmonious, and patriarchal society, tied basically to the land and to agriculture and shaped in essence by the Russian Orthodox Church, which had created in Russia a free community of believers united with the state in a peaceful manner. They thought that this unique society should remain isolated from the West and other societies, because the introduction of foreign ideas would create distortions and would be poisonous and destructive. In particular, they feared ideas from the West, some of which at the time emphasized that man was a perfectible creature; that individualism, freedom, and diversity were essential characteristics of any healthy society; and that the rule of law would and should lead ultimately to constitutional, and then to democratic, government.[4]

Russian conservative thought throughout the nineteenth century has a number of characteristics that distinguish it from conservative thought as it developed then in Western Europe and in the United States. Perhaps the most important distinction was the conviction of most Russian conservatives that man is not simply weak, but is in fact evil and therefore requires restraints and controls significantly greater than those which Western conservatives thought essential.

[In addition, Russian conservatives placed greater faith in ancient institutions and beliefs than did their Western counterparts. In particular, Russian conservatives had a deep respect for the autocratic form of government, for the absolutely essential role of the Russian Orthodox Church, and, generally, for the position and role of the landowning aristocracy.]

The Russian conservatives also tended to be extremely nationalistic. They believed strongly in the rule of Russia by Russians and

[4] Albert Gratieux, *A. S. Khomiakov et le mouvement slavophile* (Paris: Les Editions du Cerf, 1939), Vol. I, pp. 115–126; Vol. II, pp. 33–34; William J. Birkbeck, *Russia and the English Church in the Last Fifty Years* (London: Rivington & Percival, 1895); Nicholas Riasanovsky, *Russia and the West in the Teaching of the Slavophiles* (Cambridge, Mass.: Harvard University Press, 1952), p. 108.

in severe control of minorities, non-Russian ethnically and non-Orthodox religiously, by Russian members of the Russian Orthodox Church. On occasion, this conservative Russian nationalism became quite aggressive, as in the Panslav movement in the 1860's and 1870's and in the growth of a Pan-Russian movement in the years before World War I.

Finally, perhaps the most important characteristic of Russian conservatism was its spirit or style, particularly its emphasis upon force and violence. This characteristic was an essential violation of established conservative creeds, because it reflected an attitude toward change as disruptive and destructive as were the attitudes of Russian radicals and revolutionaries. In short, the style and character of Russian conservative thought in the nineteenth century did not reflect what Walter Bagehot called the "calm rational mind" which should constitute the essence of any established or conservative society. The vicious attacks on foreign influence, the assault by many conservatives against Jews, Catholics, and socialists, the emphasis on fear and force, and the aggressive spirit which dominated conservative thought and policy are all violations of the essential conservative creed.

There were many significant statements concerning conservative thought in Russia late in the nineteenth century — by poets such as Fedor Tiutchev, historians such as Michael Pogodin, lawyers such as Boris Chicherin, propagandists and columnists such as Michael Katkov, educators such as Sergei Rachinskii and Nicholas Ilminskii, and philosophers such as Vladimir Soloviev and Konstantin Leontiev. However, probably the most important Russian conservative political thinker in the quarter of a century before World War I was Konstantin P. Pobedonostsev, who was not an original philosopher (as no conservative philosopher should be), but whose views reflect and are typical of Russian conservative thought of that time.[5]

Pobedonostsev was a native of Moscow and a Moscovite throughout his life, although he lived his last fifty years in St. Petersburg. He began his career as a bureaucrat and scholar, publishing, particu-

[5] A full description and analysis of Pobedonostsev's philosophy may be found in Robert F. Byrnes, *Pobedonostsev: His Life and Thought* (Bloomington: Indiana University Press, 1968).

larly between 1858 and 1865, significant essays and books concerning the history of serfdom and of Russian civil law. During those years, he was an informal member of the Slavophil movement. He was later associated with the Panslav movement. By 1880 or 1890, he was the spokesman for conservatism in Russia, reflecting the government and the bureaucracy on one hand and the views of the conservative intellectual establishment on the other.

Pobedonostsev's personal qualities and temperament help explain both the fundamentals and the style of his political philosophy, which was in the Karamzin tradition of Russian thought in its attitude toward the state. He thought first of the State as naturally as an American thinks first of the individual. The individual, indeed humanity itself, was relegated to fourth place behind the State, the Church, and the family. The State, and the Church in union with the State, were the foundations upon which his political philosophy was erected, with the family a cooperating instrument of these senior agencies, to all of which the individual was subject. Even so, and perhaps because of this, his philosophy can best be explained by beginning with his view of the nature of man, of Russian man in particular, and of the evils of his age.

Pobedonostsev was an eternal foe of abstractions or general theories and of those who used them. At the same time, his own views inevitably hardened into abstract theories which became sharply defined as he grew older and more conservative. For him, man by nature is "weak, vicious, worthless, and rebellious." Like Hobbes, who has been called "the Baroque forerunner of the modern police state" and like the philosophers and practitioners of authoritarianism, he "vilified the human nature." His writings are saturated with descriptions of the frailties and follies of man and of the particular evils of the age which nourished these inherent weaknesses. In fact, he viewed man with a combination of pity and horror and was mildly surprised that humanity had survived.[6]

Russians constituted a particular case, and he was convinced that Russians by nature had peculiar flaws. Thus, he believed that

---

[6] Konstantin P. Pobedonostsev, *Prazdniki Gospodni* (St. Petersburg, 1894), p. 14; Thomas a Kempis, trans., Pobedonostsev, *Fomy Kempiiskago o podrazhenii Khristu* (5th ed.; St. Petersburg, 1893), pp. 276, 282, 287–289.

48

"inertness and laziness are generally characteristic of the Slavonic nature" and that Russians for these reasons required more relentlessly firm and vigorous leadership than most people. He thought Russians were particularly obsessed with money, power, and drink and marked by "decomposition and weakness and untruth."

A corollary to his assumption that man is by nature evil and weak was his condemnation of those who assumed that man can reason or that reason can be an effective tool for any but a tiny minority, whom he called "the aristocracy of intellect." Except for the minority, he saw man as a vessel, an object of soft wax molded and formed by three forces utterly beyond his control: the unconscious, land, and history. Noting that "the healthy do not think about health," he urged that society be allowed by men to operate as an organ of the body does, "simply and unconsciously." He declared that "true, sound intelligence is not logical, but intuitive, because the aim of intelligence consists not in finding or showing reasons but in believing and trusting."

Under this philosophy, of course, knowledge itself is evil, except for knowledge of one's national history. He would have accepted the apothegm of Barrès that the necessary foundation of a state is a cemetery, for he saw the "congenial need" of a nationality in "the unconscious sphere of feeling, accumulated from our ancestors." Since the capabilities of all but the minority are so limited, man must realize simply that his roots are in the past and that he derives from his ancestors. More he cannot understand. The man who is not satisfied with instinctive feeling and who by himself seeks truth and his own equilibrium automatically idolizes reason and becomes a dangerous fanatic, threatening the unity and the very existence of society. The great, essential, and living truths are above the mind, and the great mass of men can receive ideas only through feeling. The only supports of man's will can be faith and religious feeling, and the Christian faith alone can perforate the principles of egotism and pride, reach the core of man, and give him true freedom in his recognition of necessity.[7]

[7] Pobedonostsev, *Pis'ma Pobedonostseva k Aleksandru III* (Moscow, 1925–1926), Vol. II, pp. 38–41, 223–225; Pobedonostsev, "Le-Plè," *Russkoe*

There were exceptions, of course, and his view was not always that bleak. He had a special affection for childhood and believed either that children did not possess the faults and frailties he noted among their elders or that corrupt society was responsible for the flourishing of these hidden qualities after childhood. Pobedonostsev's "good society," if he could envision one, was like Carlyle's, with freedom in discipline, no sense of time, rest and sleep, and a mother's love.

[Like most dour and pessimistic philosophers and statesmen, Pobedonostsev was convinced that his own age was subject to particularly corrosive evils, all thriving because of the basic weakness of Russian character and of Russian society. The principal danger he fought was the presumption that man was perfectible, which led to doubt, discontent, irritation, and fantasies on one hand and explained laziness, the vogue of credit, and other modern and artificial approaches to life on the other. In his view, at the heart of this basic misconception and in part responsible for it is the belief that man is a rational creature and that "the fanaticism of formal logic" could resolve the problems the State faced. He urged that knowledge is the root of evil, and that doubt provides access to it. He considered speculative thought "destructive, suicidal, and sinful." Proud, sophisticated intellectuals in particular do not recognize that rationalism is an art, not a science. They are instead seduced by arguments, abstractions, and swollen self-interest into attitudes which are irrelevant, subject to vast and rapid fluctuations, and highly dangerous. The belief that man and society can be improved by individual or group action and that reason, not faith, should guide Russia is responsible for most of Russia's problems, particularly for the subversive doctrines concerning parliamentary and democratic government and concerning unbelief.[8]

obozrenie, XXIII (1893), 14–15; Pobedonostsev, "Otvet russkago cheloveka Kropotkinu," *Moskovskiia Vedomosti*, October 15, 16, 1901.

[8] Pobedonostsev, *Moskovskii sbornik* (3rd ed.; Moscow, 1896), pp. 57–76, 92–99, 116–119, 126–130, 238, 275–276, 286–288; (4th ed.; 1897), pp. 259–260, 282–283, 296–298; (5th ed.; 1901), pp. 151–158, 327–329; Pobedonostsev, "Kritika i bibliografiia. Svoboda, ravenstvo i bratstvo," *Grazhdanin*, No. 35 (August 27, 1873), pp. 958–960; Iurii F. Samarin and O. Dmitriev, *Revoliutsionnyi konservatizm* (Berlin, 1875), p. 10.

50

In this grim picture, he identified three institutions which might save Russia and even enable her to provide guidance for other threatened peoples. These institutions, which were at the heart of his philosophy, are the State, the Russian Orthodox Church, and the family, with their functions and authority overlapping and inter-mingled, but with the State central. As a highly educated, widely read intellectual from an academic family, he was also much interested in the educational system as a contributor to the establishment of a stable society. However, he was convinced that an educational system reflects a society, its character, its history, and its climate, and that it neither can nor should be used to transform it. He did agree that "learning is light," but he ridiculed the proposal that Russia should consider the establishment of compulsory and free primary education. He thought laws restricting child labor unreasonable and senseless. He was certain that the educational system in its every aspect should remain under the direct control of the State and the Church.[9]

His views with regard to the character and role of education were consistent throughout his life, except for his recognition after 1880 that elementary education of a primitive kind was a necessity and for the lively interest he developed in his last decade in secondary school education for the elite. He paid remarkably little attention to higher education until the 1890's, apparently because he did not believe that some of the ills of which he complained within the government could be eliminated by improved training for bureaucrats. When he did begin to direct his attention to the secondary and higher education of Russia's future ruling group, he borrowed heavily from studies of England's public schools, which impressed him in every way. For the future statesmen and the "enlightened minority," a detailed knowledge of their family, nation, and church, and of the climatic and geographic conditions of Russian society were vital. Since they were to be educated for important state duties, they were to know foreign languages, literatures, and societies, though not so well as their own. They were to acquire

[9] Pobedonostsev, *Uchenie i uchitel'* (2nd ed.; Moscow, 1905), Vol. II, pp. 49–50.

knowledge of the antagonistic states and racial groups surrounding their nation. They were not only to be learned, but they were also to be experienced "social authorities," sagacious, intelligent, and respected. They should, moreover, possess wives who would read with them evenings and who would cooperate in charitable work in the neighborhood. The ideal professor is one who devotes his entire life to his students, with great patience, enthusiasm, and love for them and for his service. He is specifically not to be an intellectual, because this frequently leads to irreligion, liberalism, and poisoning of the entire educational system.[19]

So far as the mass of the Russian people were concerned, he declared too that "schools must fit the people." Since most children in the community must earn their living, most of their education must be conducted at home, where they should master their father's work. Sons of miners should become miners, sons of sailors sailors, and sons of peasants peasants. The only formal education of these millions should be provided by the Church in a brief period of primary school, which should not be a step to higher education. Knowledge should not be the goal: indeed, no well-ordered schools should have examinations. The main purpose of primary education was to instruct the youngsters to know, love, and fear God, to love their native land, and to honor and obey their parents. The emphasis was therefore moral, rather than intellectual, and the brief period of primary school should therefore concentrate on the four R's, reading, writing, arithmetic, and religion. He would have agreed with Wellington that "instruction without religion produces only clever devils," and he was convinced that "educated and unemployed fools," marred by vanity and conceit, constituted a tremendous danger for Russia.

Thus, for Pobedonostsev, the primary school should provide Russian children with "the basic elements of intellectual and moral culture" and should also "leave them in that place and in the milieu in which they belong." He emphasized that everyone should remain

[19] Pobedonostsev, trans., *Novaia shkola* (Moscow, 1898), Preface and pp. 3–4, 25–30, 69–72, 95–102; Pobedonostsev, "Ob universitetskom prepodavanii," *Moskovskiia Vedomosti*, June 26, 1899; Pobedonostsev, *Uchenie i uchitel'* (5th ed.), Vol. I, pp. 31–38; (1st ed.; 1904), Vol. II, pp. 38–54.

"in that place, in that area, in that corner where fate has placed him." The place of women was therefore in the home. He feared lest primary education excite a love of learning or create "discontent and ambition."[11]

Just as the curriculum of the primary school should emphasize virtue and native Russian skills, so should the teacher exemplify the best qualities of his country. He should naturally be an Orthodox Christian from the same strata of society as his pupils. He should be concise, clear, patient, lively, attentive, well mannered, highly disciplined and well prepared. Finally, he should be completely absorbed by and dedicated to his work, not a hireling who considered his position a "temporary stage towards a better arrangement of his own life." Like Socrates, or an unsung hero, he should love his work and should be prepared to give his life to his calling.[12]

The family for Pobedonostsev is clearly a more central institution than was the primary school. Indeed, he saw the family as the primary instrument for educating and controlling man — "the ultimate social institution." He referred to it as "the spiritual and cultural nursery of citizens," "the foundation of the state," and "the eternal element of prosperous societies." It reflects the character of the society of which it is a part and therefore illustrates it.

Pobedonostsev was convinced that the family is "the foundation of all social life and order," that moral development and all human welfare are based upon it, that it is "the foundation of all enduring happiness," and that it even resembles and anticipates the Kingdom of God. In Russia and among Russians, "for all those familiar with our history and conditions of life," it has its origins both in Christian doctrine and in history. It is based upon religious faith and upon

[11] Pobedonostsev, *Moskovskii sbornik* (3rd ed.; 1896), p. 69; Pobedonostsev and Ivan K. Bapst, *Pis'ma o puteshestvii gosudaria naslednika tsesarevicha po Rossii ot Peterburga do Kryma* (Moscow, 1864), pp. 88–89; Pobedonostsev, *Vechnaia pamiat'. Vospominaniia o pochivshikh* (Moscow, 1896), pp. 9–20; Pobedonostsev, *Uchenie i uchitel'* (5th ed.), Vol. I, pp. 27–44; (1st ed.; 1904), Vol. II, pp. 48–49, 54; Leonid Grossman, "Dostoevskii i pravitel'stvennye krugi 1870-kh godov," *Literaturnoe nasledstvo*, No. 15 (1934), p. 138; Heinrich W. Thiersch, *On the Christian Commonwealth* (Edinburgh: T. & T. Clark, 1877), p. 141.

[12] Pobedonostsev, *Uchenie i uchitel'* (5th ed.), Vol. I, pp. 3–61; (2nd ed.; 1905), Vol. II, pp. 38–39.

a religious ceremony. Marriage therefore is an indissoluble contract of a sacred character, broken at peril to society when that society allows "personal egotism" to triumph over higher values. Pobedonostsev opposed civil marriage, separation, and divorce. He considered divorce a blow against the highest interests of the State, as well as a violation of a solemn contract sanctified by the Church, recognized by the State, and approved by society. He agreed that women might suffer because of such views, but he reasoned that this religious definition of marriage defended their "high moral position" and dignity better than did or could any other marriage system.[13]

For Pobedonostsev, the family is assigned the function of repressing the nature of the child, harnessing and controlling one of man's most fundamental instincts, providing for the orderly perpetuation of the human race, ensuring social stability, and maintaining history and tradition. He believed that the child from birth is weak and that God in entrusting it to the parents gives them the choice of raising either a dutiful or a parasitic and destructive child. The parental power, "the only power established by God in the Decalogue, is the highest power," and "willing obedience . . . is the only virtue of the child." The function of the parents, particularly the father, is therefore to repress the child's instincts firmly and surely, through force, love, and fear. "Faithfulness, love, sacrifice, and obedience" should be learned by the child in the home. The father should also instill into the child knowledge of and respect for the Decalogue and provide him the physical and moral education to enable him to assume his allotted place in society.[14]

The Church was incomparably more important for Pobedonostsev than even the family, the institutions related to the family, or the

[13] Pobedonostsev, *Kurs grazhdanskago prava* (2nd ed.; St. Petersburg, 1880), Vol. II, pp. 23–24, 45–54, 75–112, 146–168, 210, 644–666; Pobedonostsev, trans., *Osnovnaia konstitutsiia chelovecheskago roda* (Moscow, 1897), pp. 66–69, 180–182; Pobedonostsev, trans., *Khristianskiia nachala semeinoi zhizni* (Moscow, 1861), *passim*, especially pp. 7–20, 28–30, 122–145, 193–206; Pobedonostsev, "Le-Plè," pp. 9–25.

[14] Pobedonostsev, *Pis'ma k Aleksandru III*, Vol. II, pp. 147–148; Pobedonostsev, *Kurs grazhdanskago prava* (2nd ed.; 1880), Vol. II, pp. 5–9, 99–101, 103–112, 149–155; Pobedonostsev, *Uchenie i uchitel'* (1st ed.; 1904), Vol. II, pp. 11–12.

organization of economic life in the countryside. In fact, the Church and religion were central to his life and saturated his beliefs and policies. When he wrote in general terms about Russia or about the State, Orthodoxy meant the membership of the Russian Orthodox Church or the ethnic Great Russians. Although he did recognize that Russia contained other religious groups and many national minorities, he saw the Russians in the Russian Orthodox Church, with those White Russians and Little Russians who were also Orthodox, at the center of his world. The Old Believers and the sects resided in an outer circle, and the non-Russians — Finns, Germans, Poles, Jews, Uzbeks, and others — lived on the empire's borders in a shadowy, distant circle, given serious thought only when he had to consider issues or policies involving them. Doctrine was simply not a subject of discussion for him, in part because he was not interested in doctrine and in part because he thought it such a rooted matter for any religious group that it was beyond discussion.

He was convinced that Russia was more than a country, that Orthodoxy was more than a religion, and that they together constituted a world. He considered Russia not necessarily superior to other societies and cultures, but different — so different that perhaps only a Russian could understand his religion and country, just as perhaps only an Englishman could understand his religion and country. He believed that churches, like races or ethnic groups, have distinct virtues and defects, reflecting their history and tradition. The Russian Orthodox Church, for example, was weakened by ignorance, superstition, and inactivity, but these were temporary and reflected the country's backwardness. Similarly, Roman Catholicism, Anglicanism, and other forms of Protestantism had particular weaknesses which reflected their histories. Whatever its shortcomings, he saw the Russian Orthodox Church as "the church of all of the people," one which answered a deep-seated popular need, and "a living organism held together by sentiment and conscience."

The Church became "identical with and inseparable from the history of the Russian *narod*" in the ninth century and has since then been the "life, truth, and full foundation of our existence." He

ROBERT F. BYRNES

believed that "the power of the state is based solely on the unity of consciousness between the people and the state, on the national faith." Because the history of the Church and the State have been so entwined for almost a thousand years, the Church is and should always be the state or national church, with no other religious groups allowed or tolerated. In fact, he sought to reduce and ultimately to destroy the power of all other religious groups within the empire. He thought that the Russian state should ignore and refuse to provide official recognition of beliefs other than Orthodoxy, because recognition gives legal status, which strengthens the rival religions and helps delay the day when everyone in Russia would share the same faith. However, although he was vigorous in advocacy of forceful policies with regard to the religious minorities, at the same time he recognized that elimination of these groups would inevitably require time, because "even lies should be removed slowly." [15]

Pobedonostsev believed so strongly that the character and fate of each state are determined by religion and that sooner or later one religious group would acquire absolute dominance that he could not understand the policy of the American government regarding religious toleration. Indeed, he predicted that the Catholic Church would take advantage of the freedom the American Protestant rulers granted and would one day seize power, establish Catholicism as the state religion, and seek to root out all other faiths.

Just as he believed that the nature of society and religion makes coexistence of two or more religions in one state inconceivable, so also he was convinced that the union or even the close cooperation of two creeds is impossible. He declared that each racial group possesses distinctive customs and traditions, that these shape their religious beliefs and their political institutions as well, and that it is

[15] Pobedonostsev, *Moskovskii sbornik* (3rd ed.; 1896), pp. 17–19, 23, 173, 219–222; Pobedonostsev, *Istoriia pravoslavnoi tserkvi do nachala razdeleniia tserkvei* (2nd ed.; St. Petersburg, 1892), pp. 11, 122–130, 161–162; Fedor M. Dostoevsky, *Polnoe sobranie sochinenii* (16 vols.; Paris: YMCA Press, 1945–1946), Vol. IV, pp. 384–385; Claude G. Bowers, *Beveridge and the Progressive Era* (Boston: Houghton Mifflin, 1932), pp. 147–148; Emile J. Dillon, *The Eclipse of Russia* (New York: Doran, 1918), p. 83; Eduard Winter, *Russland und die slawischen Völker in der Diplomatie des Vatikans, 1878–1903* (Berlin: Akademie, 1950), p. 75; Riasanovsky, *Russia and the West*, pp. 130–131.

both impossible and dangerous for one society to attempt to borrow ideas and beliefs from another or to impose its values upon another. Faith is "parcelled out according to nationalities," and is "intolerant and uncompromising." Moreover, the most important elements of a faith cannot be defined, expressed, or separated even by an articulate believer.[16]

⌈The role of the Russian Orthodox Church is to maintain the unity in faith and belief essential for the maintenance of stability — in other words, religion is to act as a cement for society. The strong and stable society should therefore have only one religion, regardless of the number of races it contains. He believed that "the Church and the Church alone has allowed us to remain Russians and to unite our scattered strength." In fact, the greatest quality of the Church is its unity with the *narod*. He was persuaded that Orthodoxy alone can provide the unity without which no one would have confidence in the government or in the State. He considered that one of the greatest advantages deriving from this system is the equality provided by the unity. "Our Church is the house of the Russian man, the most hospitable house, the house where all are equal." The Church in thus satisfying one of man's elemental desires helps at the same time to strengthen the stability of society.[17]⌉

The nature of Pobedonostsev's ideas concerning religion and society ensured that he not be a supporter of Russian expansion or of an aggressive, or even active, foreign policy. He was as conservative in his approach to foreign policy as he was to political or social change. He saw Russia as a member of a European state system and as one of a number of states in the world with some, but only

---

[16] Pobedonostsev, *Moskovskii sbornik* (3rd ed.; 1896), pp. 179, 192–193, 201–204; Pobedonostsev, *Pis'ma k Aleksandru III*, Vol. I, p. 404; Pobedonostsev, "K voprosu o vozsoedinenei tserkvei," *Grazhdanin*, No. 33 (August 13, 1873), pp. 893–896; Pobedonostsev, "Bor'ba gosudarstva s tserkoviu v Germanii," *Grazhdanin*, No. 34 (August 20, 1873), pp. 915–917; Pobedonostsev, "Novaia vera i novye braki," *Grazhdanin*, No. 39 (September 24, 1873), pp. 1047–1048.

[17] John S. Curtiss, *Church and State in Russia: The Last Years of the Empire, 1900–1917* (New York: Columbia University Press, 1940), pp. 169–170; General Hans Lothar von Schweinitz, *Denkwürdigkeiten des Botschafters General v. Schweinitz* (Berlin: R. Hobbing, 1927), Vol. II, p. 384; Louise Creighton, *Life and Letters of Mandell Creighton* (London: Longmans, 1904), Vol. II, pp. 160–161.

some, of the others of which, it had to maintain formal relations, and then "only at the top." However, he did not believe that Russia should participate actively in world affairs. Indeed, there is some evidence that he resented and opposed all foreign alliances.

In other words, he was an isolationist. The only exception to this stand helped solidify the rule, for in 1876 and through much of 1877 he was an ardent advocate and later a supporter of war with Turkey to free the Balkan Slavs and to unite them with Russia in a Slavic federation. However, as the war progressed, Pobedonostsev reversed his opinion. From that time forward, he turned Russian state power inside, not outside. He considered the Russian empire a jerry-built system plagued by so many fundamental problems that it could not expend energy on areas beyond its frontiers. He continued to believe that it was impossible and dangerous for one society to attempt to borrow ideas and institutions from another or to impose its customs and political system upon another. Each society to him was an independent organism. After 1878, he therefore remained generally aloof from participation in the formal discussion or definition of Russian foreign policy, even in time of great tension. He was opposed to alliances, rejected Pan-Slavism after his one escapade had ended, and resisted any policy actively or forcefully promoting Russian interests abroad.

Since Pobedonostsev did not develop his thought into a consistent philosophic system, he did not describe with any systematic clarity his view of the nature and purpose of society and of government. There was, of course, a very clear distinction in his mind between the best procedure to adopt under given circumstances and the ideal practice under ideal circumstances. There was, too, a clear recognition of the distinction between the present community and the best attainable human community. This distinction for him was not so great as it has been for most people interested in politics. First of all, as a conservative he believed that the society which he surveyed contained many highly satisfactory institutions and that the changes which should be made were by no means drastic or revolutionary. In addition, and this is certainly even more significant, his view of human capabilities was not high. He ridiculed any idea of an "ideal society," and he would certainly have used the word "utopian" as a term of ridicule. He sought the best attainable society, not the unattainable perfect community.

It is important also to recognize that his Russia was not a secure or unchanging society. He believed that stability was the supreme virtue of a social organism, and his entire system was one which glorified static relations. However, he did not believe that the struggle between good and evil, right and wrong, darkness and light, would cease, even in the best attainable society. Actually, even the best attainable society would not be reached. Even this finite community would always be "becoming," would never "be."

It should be clear now what his view of the principal function or purpose of the autocratic state is: simply to provide balance, stability, or equilibrium, and to supply "the daily interests and needs of society." These are its ultimate goals. To reach these goals, the absolute government is to provide "rational direction" by means of a "calm, humane, indulgent, and arbitrary administration." It is to distinguish between light and dark, good and evil. It is, above all, to prevent the rise of nationalisms in the multinational Russian empire, through providing both force and equality. It is to override established laws and institutions whenever those laws and institutions interfere with the maintenance of equilibrium.

From this peace and quiet, he believed that splendid fruits would develop. These fruits, of course, compared to those envisioned by Aristotle or Sir Thomas More or Edward Bellamy — or even the makers of the Constitution of the United States — are quite meager. Pobedonostsev declared that the first great consequence of the "establishment" of a well-organized and stable state would be reliance upon inertia, which he considered a vastly underrated force. Once stability had been obtained, inertia would work its slow magic, the "good side" of man would flower, and there would be a "slow moral improvement and uplift of the soul in society." [18]

If one compares Pobedonostsev's aims with those expressed in

[18] Pobedonostsev, *Moskovskii sbornik* (3rd ed.; 1896), pp. 242–252; (4th ed.; 1897), pp. 253–259; Pobedonostsev, *Pis'ma k Aleksandru III*, Vol. I, pp. 116–120; Vol. II, pp. 38–40, 46–47, 144–145, 223–226; Pobedonostsev, *Kurs grazhdanskago prava* (2nd ed.; 1880), Vol. III, pp. 78–82.

the Preamble of the Constitution, it becomes apparent that two of the goals sought by the American leaders, unity and tranquility, were also sought by Pobedonostsev. For the founders of the United States, however, unity and tranquility were not to the same degree *ends*, as they were for him — they were also to a considerable degree *means* to the acquisition of three of the other expressed aims, justice, the general welfare, and the blessings of liberty. Of these Pobedonostsev says nothing.

It is not surprising, given his view of the nature of man and his philosophy of government, that he viewed the Russian State in some ways as a family, with absolute parental authority and paternal care on one hand and unquestioning obedience and love on the other. He was certain that the ideal time for each individual was his childhood, and his state was designed to make that era permanent. As a child, with no responsibilities or sense of time, with firm but gentle parental care and direction, surrounded by love and certain truth, and above all, with instinct and feeling ruling over the illusions of reason and freedom, man is truly happy.[19]

He hoped to organize a Christian society such as the one which for a thousand years had made religion more important than race, except that the Christendom he sought was simply a national Christendom. He would have agreed with Ammianus Marcellinus that "life is never sweeter than under a pious king." His ideal monarch was Louis IX, king of France in the thirteenth century, when everyone in each of the estates knew his place, social peace prevailed, the Church and the State ruled in harmony, and the king, a saint, sat under a tree and decided those few disagreements which arose within the society. In the 1880's, he thought the reign of Nicholas I one of the "most clear and brilliant periods" of Russian history, with few and simple problems, clear policies, gifted advisors for the Tsar, and a government strong enough to persuade the lion to lie down with the lamb. The reign of Alexander III, during which

[19] Pobedonostsev, *Moskovskii sbornik* (3rd ed.; 1896), pp. 268–274; Pobedonostsev, *Pis'ma k Aleksandru III*, Vol. II, p. 271; Pobedonostsev, *Prazdniki Gospodni*, pp. 10–11, 16–20, 26–27, 31–32, 48–51, 55–58, 64; Catherine A. Pobedonostsev, trans., *Istoriia detskoi dushi* (Moscow, 1897); Marie Corelli (pseud. of Minnie Mackay), *The Mighty Atom* (Philadelphia, London: Hutchinson, 1896).

Pobedonostsev played a very important role, was a highly satisfactory one, though far from perfect, because it at least had preserved the principle of divine right and "the rule of the fittest."[20]

[The State, and the Church in union with the State, were the foundations upon which his political philosophy was erected. Although he wrote a great deal about the vital question of the sanctions of authority, his ideas are not completely clear. He wrote on occasion that the Russian ruler derives his power from divine right, but more frequently and insistently he spoke of the power of the tsar as "based solely on the unity of consciousness between the people and the state, on the national faith." In his most important statement of this philosophy, the impassioned attack upon the proposals of Loris-Melikov which he gave at the Council of Ministers meeting on March 8, 1881, he asserted that "Russia was strong, thanks to the autocracy, thanks to the unlimited mutual confidence and intimate relationship between the *narod* and the tsar." The most important justification for autocracy, of course, was historical, but he so clearly assumed this that he wrote little about it. The family played an important connecting role between the *narod* and the state, especially in the essays he wrote in the last decade of his life. However, the idea of *sobornost'*, or community, so dear to the Slavophils, he never mentioned. Moreover, he did not seek to provide a legal rationale for the autocracy and would have scorned the very idea that this was necessary or even useful. Thus, the State for him was an expression of truth. "Power is founded on truth, and truth on power." The State, power, good, and the *narod* were, thus, all connected in one indissoluble and blurred unity.[21]]

[20] Pobedonostsev, *Pis'ma k Aleksandru III*, Vol. II, pp. 4–5; Pobedonostsev, trans., *Pobeda, pobedivshaia mir* (10th ed., Moscow, 1905), pp. 16–49, 57–92, 133–184; *The Confessions of St. Augustine* (New York: Boni & Liveright, 1927), pp. 1–40; William S. Lilly, *Chapters in European History* (London: Chapman & Hall, 1886), Vol. I, pp. 48–87; Pobedonostsev, trans., *Osnovnaia konstitutsiia chelovecheskago roda*, pp. 117–120.

[21] Pobedonostsev, *Moskovskii sbornik* (5th ed.; 1901), pp. 54–57; Pobedonostsev, *Pis'ma k Aleksandru III*, Vol. I, pp. 170–171; Vol. II, pp. 3–4, 46–47, 145; Pobedonostsev, *K. P. Pobedonostsev i ego korrespondenty. Pis'ma i zapiski, Novum Regnum* (Moscow, 1923), pp. 832–835, 1004–1006; Pobedonostsev, "Gosudar Imperator Aleksandr Aleksandrovich," *Russkii*

Pobedonostsev recognized that autocracy is not a perfect form of government, but it is built on Russian history and tradition and "the evils of autocracy are the evils of society itself." He vigorously opposed a *zemskii sobor* or territorial assembly or other arrangements to provide some kind of representation for the most important and most highly educated groups in Russia. During the last ten or fifteen years of his life, the best defense of autocracy he could devise was a series of blistering attacks upon other forms of government, especially parliamentarianism, in which the "personal ambition, vanity, and self-interest" of the members prevail, eloquence and ambition are the most important qualities required, and "manipulators" acquire rule. They combine bribery and dogma in maintaining control, and the national interest is not even considered. Constitutions for him are "the instruments of the unrighteous, the weapon of intrigue." Popular sovereignty is "the great falsehood of our time," and democratic government is the most complex and difficult form of government known to man. It cannot survive in a state which contains a number of nationalities, and it leads inevitably to a Napoleonic dictatorship by way of materialism, infidelity, disorder, violence, and anarchy.[22]

In short, autocracy is the best form of government and the only conceivable one for Russia. It operates most effectively when the monarch is a dutiful father or shepherd for his country, distinguished by high moral standards. The autocrat is to represent the *narod*'s interests. By his travels and his presence at ceremonies, he is to strengthen the love of the *narod* for the state. In addition, he is to select able and energetic executive aides and to accept their advice in directing the state. These executive agents for Pobedonostsev are the principal instruments of rule, and efficient operation of the system depends upon them. Essentially, he sought to modernize

arkhiv, I (1906), 619–624; Egor A. Peretts, *Dnevnik E. A. Perettsa, 1880–1883* (Moscow-Leningrad, 1927), p. 38.

[22] Pobedonostsev, *Moskovskii sbornik* (3rd ed.; 1896), pp. 25–52; Pobedonostsev, "Kritika i bibliografiia. Svoboda, ravenstvo i bratstvo," pp. 958–962; Pobedonostsev, "Ispaniia," *Grazhdanin*, No. 37 (September 10, 1873), pp. 1807–1810; Pobedonostsev, "Zopisnaia knizhka. Velikaia lozh' nashego vremeni," *Grazhdanin*, No. 10 (June 10, 1884), pp. 1–4; Pobedonostsev, trans., *Osnovnaia konstitutsiia chelovecheskago roda*, Appendix, p. 222.

the autocracy. His advice to Alexander III was, "Cherchez des capables."

These executives are first of all to be men of courage, willing to accept responsibility and to speak frankly to the tsar. They are to be hardworking, practical, sagacious, efficient; they are to have organizing ability; they are to operate with clear lines of authority and responsibility. In their advice to the Russian ruler, they are to consider "history, tradition, the actual position of the state, and the needs of national life." Thoroughly schooled in the history and tradition of their nation, they are also to ignore and smash its binding laws and institutions when they believe this is required in the State's interest. He justified violent and arbitrary governmental action and angrily denounced the moralistic interpretation of history and of political action for ignoring or giving insufficient weight to the national interest, which should always be the main concern of the State and its rulers. He defended "the conscious lie" of the statesman in a world which inevitably contains a considerable amount of evil, and he believed that superior men should be beyond criticism in life as well as in recorded history.[23]

In short, although he was a supporter of autocracy, he really believed in the forms of absolutism and in rule by an "aristocracy of intellect" or "social authorities." This group was quite different from those whom Burke called a "true natural aristocracy" and "an essential integral part of any large body rightly constituted," because Pobedonostsev neglected the cultural framework or social institutions within which they would work. Authority by men such

[23] Pobedonostsev, *Moskovskii sbornik* (3rd ed.; 1896), pp. 228–234, 259; Pobedonostsev, *Pis'ma k Aleksandru III*, Vol. I, pp. 49–53, 73–78, 111, 170–171, 193–196, 208–209, 215, 248–252, 259–260, 270, 338–339, 346–347; Vol. II, pp. 3–5, 32–34, 46–47, 53, 144–145, 197–202, 215–219, 319–321; Pobedonostsev, *Novum Regnum*, pp. 1004–1005; Pobedonostsev, *Istoricheskiia izsledovaniia i stat'i* (St. Petersburg, 1876), pp. 14–15, 47–55, 116–185; Pobedonostsev, "Graf V. N. Panin," *Golosa iz Rossii*, VII (1859), 3–10, 15–31, 37–39, 76–92; Pobedonostsev, "Ispaniia," pp. 991–994; Pobedonostsev, *Vsepoddanneishii otchet ober-prokurora Sviateishago sinoda K. Pobedonostseva po vedomstvu Pravoslavnago Ispovedaniia za 1883* (St. Petersburg, 1885), pp. 1–3; Pobedonostsev, "Privetstvie starago vospitatelia Velikomu Kniaziu v den ego sovershennoletia," *Starina i novizma*, XII (1907), 1–9; Pobedonostsev and Bapst, *Pis'ma*, pp. 85–86; Pobedonostsev, trans., *Osnovnaia konstitutsiia chelovecheskago roda*, p. 221.

ROBERT F. BYRNES

as these in a strong and respected centralized government would ensure stability, just as the absence of such men and confusion in policy had led to a series of disasters and destroyed popular faith in the system.

Throughout his years of service in the Russian State system, he poured scorn on the bureaucrats. He wrote that "all the evil from which we suffer came up from the bureaucracy, not down." He noted that "paper will tolerate all things." He declared that one of the great curses of Russia is the spineless government official who is smooth and polished, solves small and unimportant problems, eliminates personality and efficiency from government, and skillfully evades major issues. One of them he noted "resembled an inadequate meal." He did not identify any relation between the size and quality of the Russian bureaucracy and the autocracy, although he did wonder why the English were successful in identifying immensely able men and in giving them authority. In fact, of course, his proposal for a kind of dictatorship of the few within the autocracy was a proposal to resolve the problems the government itself created.[24]

He wrote remarkably little about the landowning nobility. In fact, industrialists and merchants were much more often the subject of his comment than were landowners, and he clearly preferred representatives of the middle class (but not intellectuals!) for executive positions. However, he did believe that the nobility had acquired a special place of honor by their labors throughout Russian history, and he was convinced that they are more loyal to the State than were the bureaucrats, intelligentsia, merchants, or peasants.

Moreover, he was certain that "it is important in the highest degree that the landowning nobility remain on their estates within Russia and not crowd into the capitals." He resisted those who sought to arrange congresses of the nobility, but he urged that their

[24] Pobedonostsev, *Moskovskii sbornik* (3rd ed.; 1896), pp. 250–266; Pobedonostsev, *Pis'ma k Aleksandru III*, Vol. I, pp. 259–260, 267–269; Vol. II, p. 153; Pobedonostsev, *Novum Regnum*, pp. 856–867; Pobedonostsev, *Kurs grazhdanskago prava* (2nd ed.; 1880), Vol. I, pp. 287–289; Pobedonostsev and Bapst, *Pis'ma*, pp. 249–251, 338–340, 346; Pobedonostsev, trans., *Osnovnaia konstitutsiia chelovecheskago roda*, p. 222; M. N. Knorring, *General Mikhail Dmitrievich Skobelev* (Paris, 1939–1940), pp. 192–196, 226–227.

economic and political position be strengthened in every way possible and that they retain their preponderant position in the administration of justice, in the army, and in the creation of national
ideals. It is significant that he urged that the landed nobility live
in the country and did not propose that their role in the central
administration or even at the highest levels of provincial administration be increased or even maintained. In short, the "aristocracy of
intellect" and the "social authorities" could include members of
the aristocracy, but that class should not dominate the government
and should instead be one of the pools of talent from which the
State should select its leaders. Pobedonostsev explicitly opposed on
grounds of efficiency a system restricting the possibility of positions
of authority to only one class, and he did believe that merit should
ideally be the determining factor.[25]

The base of the triangle of the Russian State system was the *narod*,
a word he used frequently but failed to define clearly. The virtues
he considered desirable and necessary for this group are duty and
sacrifice, obedience, love of work and love of order, Christian love
for one's fellowman, and submission to one's inner, unconscious
balance. He recognized that a man with these virtues would be considered uncreative by many, but he reiterated that a stable society,
composed of placid and obedient citizens "who knew their place,"
would develop a force more productive of enduring achievement
than any other kind of society. In summary, then, his ideal citizen
is the unsung hero, working constantly, quietly, and peacefully in
his own sphere, seeking no reward but life itself, uncomplaining,
and devoted to service to his community. The examples he offered
most frequently were the rural teacher and the rural priest, poorly
paid, unrewarded by the authorities for their contributions, but
blindly devoted to their work and to service.[26]

In summary, a brief analysis of Pobedonostsev's political philosophy and a quick survey of his State's armory of instruments reveal

[25] Pobedonostsev, *Pis'ma k Aleksandru III*, Vol. II, pp. 46–47; Pobedonostsev, *Novum Regnum*, pp. 452–453, 521–522; George L. Yaney, "The
Concept of the Stolypin Land Reform," *Slavic Review*, XXIII (1964), 280.
[26] Pobedonostsev, *Uchenie i uchitel'* (5th ed.), Vol. I, p. 35; (1st ed.;
1904), Vol. II, pp. 15–19, 42–48; Pobedonostsev, *Novum Regnum*, pp. 865–
866.

several striking characteristics. To begin with, his ideas concerning the nature of man are fundamental to his entire philosophy and "justify" the arbitrary and authoritarian government he advocated. In addition, his belief that the character of the State is shaped by its national religious faith and by its traditional political and social institutions provided a base from which he could oppose "alien" ideas and institutions.

Nevertheless, Pobedonostsev's system is not so well organized or traditional as it appears. Perhaps this can be shown most clearly by neglecting for the moment the obvious weapons in the State's hands and by identifying some of the principal instruments or elements he ignored or slighted. Neither justice nor the general welfare are of great significance to him. He did not appreciate the significance of a political facade, and there is a striking absence of color and trappings, except for the song and ceremony of the Church. Neither the army nor the police play an important role. However, it is in his treatment of the established nineteenth-century political trinity, the throne, the altar, and the aristocracy, that the most serious lacunae appear. For Pobedonostsev, of course, the main bulwark of the State is the Orthodox Church. The other two members of the trinity, though, are very shaky indeed. He fervently supports autocracy, but his advocacy is based neither on functional nor on religious grounds, and his arguments are generally vague. His autocrat is in effect a figurehead, and Pobedonostsev sought to replace the landed nobility with a group of middle-class executive managers and efficiency experts, the technocrats of the twentieth century.

As a reflection of Russian conservative thought in the years before World War I, Pobedonostsev's philosophy also reflects the weaknesses of Russian conservatism. Perhaps the most serious flaw, one which marks much of modern conservative thought, is its vengeful, nihilistic character and its ultimate reliance upon and encouragement of violent, destructive action. In fact, Pobedonostsev's ideas are in some ways as radical and revolutionary as those of Lenin. A second serious weakness is the extreme pessimism and lack of faith of many Russian conservatives, which is represented in the

66

scholasticism and trivialities of the ideas of Pobedonostsev and many of his conservative contemporaries.

A third weakness is the remarkable absence of religious thought, or thought by important religious philosophers, in the Russian intellectual scene. The Orthodox Church exerted remarkably little influence on Russian intellectual life in the nineteenth century, in part because the Church itself paid so little attention to ideas, in part because the Church did not attract outstanding men into its leadership, as the French and English churches did, and in part because the position and views of the Orthodox Church seemed irrelevant for most of those interested in the problems Russia faced at that time.

The rapid decline of the aristocracy, particularly in the last third of the nineteenth century, also contributed to the weakness of Russian conservative thought. The ruling class in a sense simply disintegrated as the nineteenth century passed.

Russian conservatism suffered also from the absence of civil liberties. It is now paralyzingly clear that both conservative and liberal thought in an unfree society tends to lack quality and substance. Russia was not only an unfree society in the nineteenth century, but it was also an underdeveloped or backward country. Both of these qualities restricted the development of a positive and clear conservative philosophy. Thus, the policies of the Russian government and of the ruling class, particularly in the last half of the nineteenth century, were themselves radical and revolutionary. The revolution in Russia, in terms of the modernization or rapid transformation of the society, was begun from the top by the government itself, beginning with the fundamental transformation of society by Alexander II. The industrialization of Russia was, after all, immensely hastened by the Russian government itself in the 1890's, under Count Witte, whose impact on Russian political and economic development may in the long run have been as significant as that of the revolutionary Lenin. The policies of Stolypin in the first decade of the twentieth century were also radical and revolutionary. Moreover, a review of Russian foreign policy in the last half of the nineteenth century reveals that the government, which called itself and was considered conservative, contributed substantially to the reorganization of the map of Central and Eastern Europe, because Russia assisted in the reunification of Italy and in the formation of a united German state, both revolutionary measures carried out with Russian assistance and support. In short, the relative weakness of Russian conservative thought during these years is connected with the radical domestic and foreign policies which the Russian government itself adopted.]

However, the weaknesses of Russian conservative thought and policy must be considered in the larger framework of the weaknesses of conservatism in modern times in general. The very nature of conservatism leads to an aversion to political philosophy, and the nature of conservative thought inevitably creates a vagueness and inarticulation concerning goals and ideas. This is a general or permanent characteristic of conservatism, and inevitably weakens it in its competition with liberal and radical views.

One should also remember that political and intellectual leaders in modern times have faced an astonishing number of large and complicated problems, which have often baffled even the most intelligent and well-informed leaders. The size and nature of the issues which modern states face are such that they support the likelihood and the attractiveness of radical and revolutionary approaches. This is, in short, an era of enormous change in both free and unfree societies. Conservatism in general requires well-established societies and tranquility, neither of which have been common factors in our era.

[In summary, the failure of Pobedonostsev and his contemporaries to create an effective and acceptable conservative philosophy reflects, on the one hand, the weaknesses of the society in which they were writing and, on the other, the nature of the challenges which that society and the modern world in general face.]

*break b/n Conservative thought
and role adopted by government.*

68

DONALD W. TREADGOLD

Russian Radical Thought, 1894-1917

☥ ☥ ☥

THE nineteenth century was, in the eyes of many Westerners, a time when Russia had an oppressively autocratic regime but
when its thought was predominantly radical — that is, devoted to
the aim of overthrowing the regime and violently replacing the
existing political and social order with one something like that of
Western Europe or North America. It is possible to make a case
for this view; almost the entire apparatus of Soviet publishing does
so every month, every year, but many Westerners not at all in sympathy with the Soviet regime have also contributed to such a case.
It is understandable that the Soviets tend to depict a tsarist Russia
polarized between good and evil, with themselves as heirs of the
good emerging triumphant, as it is natural that Westerners in looking at Russia should lay stress on those elements of political struggle
that seem most closely to approximate their own experience, at least
such aspects of it as are connected with the American and French
Revolutions. Such a polarized picture of prerevolutionary Russia,
however, requires considerable qualification.

It is quite true that Russian radical thinkers played a significant
role in the history of nineteenth-century Russia and that they had
a powerful impact on the world of literature, journalism, and even

scholarship, as well as publishing and higher education generally. This world was, of course, a restricted one with respect to the numbers of people, magazines, and institutions concerned — but nevertheless, this world was influential out of all proportion to its numbers. The highest officials of tsardom read Alexander Herzen's newspaper in exile, *The Bell*, and took it seriously; the secret police assiduously tracked and recorded the movements of a few zealous young men and women in Russia who never had the slightest chance of putting their revolutionary principles into practice, though from time to time they did turn to a job they could hope to do — that of murdering high officials. They thought, talked, and wrote furiously, not concealing their enmity to the kind of Russia they had to live in. That was enough to attract the attention of the vast and apparently limitless power of the Russian imperial government. When Nicholas I was once passing Moscow University, he remarked, "There is the wolf's den."

The reign of Nicholas II, beginning in 1894, was a period in which Russian radical thought enjoyed superficial success. When examined more closely, however, it may instead appear as a time when radicalism passed a peak of popularity and influence and went into a decline.

A popular version of the events of the reign goes something like this: the ideas of Marxism and populism acquired a mass following, especially in the workers' strikes of 1895–1897 and 1903; peasant riots began to occur again in 1902 after decades of rural calm; student demonstrations beginning in 1899 had to be reckoned with as a sign of popular discontent; army and navy mutinies in 1905, combining with mass demonstrations and strikes including members of all previously mentioned groups, rose to a climax in the fall of that year in the so-called Revolution of 1905; the radical movement, temporarily muted by police repression and sham political concessions until 1914 and then kept quiescent by the conscription and governmental activity inherent in the World War I effort, broke through again to victory in 1917.

Note that such a view of the events of Nicholas II's reign lays less emphasis on the eleven-year period after 1905–1906 and more on the eleven years preceding it. Perhaps that may provide a key to a revised appraisal. On the surface, there seems no particular reason for slighting the later period in favor of the former; since the post-1906 period is later, it might even be of somewhat greater interest to the historian of recent events or to the intelligent layman who lives in the 1960's and would like to understand better how the world today came to be what it is. The emphasis, however, ought to depend on which factors and trends were most deeply rooted in Russian life, difficult as those may be to determine.

Suppose, then, that the same reign is approached through a different perspective, still taking as a starting point the fate of radical thought in Russia. I say "starting point," because radical or any other kind of political thought constitutes only a part of any culture, and culture itself is only part of the life of a people — even if a very important and, in the view of some, a fundamental part.

Our new version might run as follows: From 1894 onward the ideas of small, closed circles of radical intellectuals were increasingly exposed to the real needs and interests of large numbers of people from different social groups. This phenomenon can be observed in the workers' movement in the cities from the late 1890's, in student meetings and the organizations of professional men in the early 1900's, in the Revolution of 1905 and the Duma (1906–1917) which issued from it, and perhaps most of all in the manifold public committees, unions, and agencies that took shape during World War I. As this happened, the most cherished tenets of the radicals were modified or abandoned by many, including even some (though by no means all or most) of the radicals themselves. To the extent that various Russian social groups increasingly took it on themselves to advance their own demands for a better life, it became more difficult for the radicals to associate themselves with, identify, or predict the course of events. In 1905–1906 it was shown that the radicals had substantially misjudged the temper of the country, and after 1906 the price they paid for their miscalculation was the loss of much of the popular support which had seemed to be theirs during the revolutionary months. Between 1906 and 1917 the radical political parties that had burgeoned during 1905 reverted to

71

their former precarious status as tiny, isolated circles, and they lost any significant foothold they seemed to have gained in Russian life, either among the intellectuals or among the people as a whole. Thus, when 1917 came and the tsarist regime collapsed under the pressures of World War I, tsarism yielded not to radical or any other political ideas embodied in organizational or institutional form, but to anarchy.

♟ ♟ ♟

TO BE sure, the plausibility of such an analysis or the preferability of it to the previously mentioned one which concentrates on the pre-1905 period may not be established if one looks only at the reign of Nicholas II. Recent scholarship has advanced the view that from the late eighteenth century onward, Russian society may be shown to have been rapidly growing at the expense of the previously all-encompassing State. From the time of the emancipation of the gentry (1762/1785) and the emancipation of the serfs (1861), Russia's old single-centered social order was being replaced gradually by elements of a many-centered order more akin to that of the West. A new non–serf-owning gentry, a new industrial capitalist class hiring free labor, a new free laboring class, new professional classes, and the liberated peasantry showed in varying degrees a propensity to express interests and demands and to organize for such expression, in terms of both class interests and the needs of the nation.[1]

During the first half of Nicholas II's reign, the radical circles had apparent political successes that were not exactly in harmony with

---

[1] This is not the place to document this interpretation, but there is an ample literature which attempts to do so.

Victor Leontovitsch, *Geschichte des Liberalismus in Russland* (Frankfurt: Klostermann, 1957); Jacob Walkin, *The Rise of Democracy in Pre-Revolutionary Russia: Political and Social Institutions under the Last Three Czars* (New York: Praeger, 1962); Richard Pipes, "Communism and Russian History," in Donald W. Treadgold, ed., *Soviet and Chinese Communism: Similarities and Differences* (Seattle: University of Washington Press, 1967). For an approach that challenges this one, see Leopold Haimson, "The Problem of Social Stability in Urban Russia, 1905–1917," *Slavic Review*, XXIII (December 1964), 1–22, and XXIV (March 1965), 619–642.

the growth of social pluralism in Russia. In the half century between the 1840's and the 1890's, radical political ideas had become very influential among the intellectuals; it might even seem that they achieved a death grip on Russian intellectual life. To be sure tsarist censorship had dealt them severe blows, and prison and exile had claimed some of the leaders for long periods, from Alexander Herzen and Nicholas Chernyshevskii to Martov and Lenin. Nevertheless, among the educated or half-educated, the "censorship of the Left" was more powerful than the tsarist censorship. It could not prevent publication or seize issues of newspapers or printing presses; but it could effectively dictate what might and might not appear in the journals that formed educated opinion, and it could pronounce judgment on a novel, essay, poem, or official pronouncement, or on its author which was no less efficacious in forming opinion because it often had to be circumspect, veiled, and indirect. The "social command" of the dominant literary critics, such as Chernyshevskii and Nicholas Dobroliubov, insisted that no art or literature had value unless it served the cause of revolution. If an artist or writer was in fact not an advocate of revolution, he risked failing to find a publisher or at any rate the kind of one likely to yield him an audience; if, like Nicholas Gogol or Fedor Dostoevsky, he was too popular and gifted to be silenced, he was apt to find his works edited to produce a social and revolutionary message the author had not intended. (To this day the Western understanding of Gogol, for example, is distorted as a result.)

Only in the 1890's did the radical grip on Russian thought begin to weaken. Dmitrii Merezhkovskii's essay on the causes of what he saw as the ruinous contemporary state of literature in 1893 opened the way to real public discussion of the problem. Poetry, long moribund, experienced a revival whose initial phases were full of excesses and often deliberately unbalanced effects, but which soon earned widespread and deserved admiration. Painting struck out on new lines. The aim of synthesis of the visual arts and music was present in the new Russian ballet, which managed to escape the ideological and other limitations from which Richard Wagner's efforts at a fusion of the arts suffered. Much of Russia's cultural past was redis-

73

covered and studied with the resources of modern science; it began to be appreciated in both its medieval and timeless aspects. New trends in religious thought appeared side by side with the atheism and materialism of the radicals and challenged them, and an ever-growing if limited number of intellectuals were seeking a reconciliation with Russia's traditional Orthodox Christian culture if not necessarily becoming active participants in the life of the Church. If monism was yielding to pluralism in Russia's institutional life, the same was occurring in her high culture.[2]

Thus the story of radicalism from 1894 to 1917 is the story of only part of Russian thought of the time. It is the story of a period when the radicals' authority was being challenged and rejected by an increasing number of the educated men and women of Russia. And yet it is still true that the effort the radicals made, especially during the earlier half of the reign, to politicalize the discontent of various segments of Russian society and to channel all or most of it into direct revolutionary action seemed at the time to have good prospects of immediate success; moreover, in retrospect its impulses may be seen to have had a kind of ultimate victory, so that the Soviet claims to find partial antecedents in Russian nineteenth-century radicalism are by no means entirely unfounded.[3] The story of radicalism, then, needs to be told and to be understood.

♟ ♟ ♟

AMONG the politically conscious men and women of Russia in the 1890's, pluralism in thought, let alone political thought, seemed far away. This was the decade of the reception of Marxism

[2] See Wladimir Weidlé, *Russia: Absent and Present*, trans. by A. Gordon Smith (New York, London: Hollis & Carter, 1953); Camilla Gray, *The Great Experiment: Russian Art, 1863–1922* (New York: Abrams, 1962); Renato Poggioli, *The Poets of Russia, 1890–1930* (Cambridge, Mass.: Harvard University Press, 1960). Aside from Weidlé's brilliant but brief essay, however, the full story of these remarkable developments remains to be told in any language.

[3] No one ought to make the mistake of suggesting that such men as Chernyshevskii or Nicholas Mikhailovskii were Communists before their time, let alone of identifying them with the barbarities of Stalin. Neither the Soviet scholars nor any reputable scholars in the West, however different their starting points, neglect the differences.

in Russia (its reception by Russian exiles in the West came a good deal earlier), a time when Marxism was being received by many as the basis for a complete answer to all human problems — indeed, more or less consciously as a new "religion" (that is, as a complete substitute for a supernaturalist religious doctrine and for an organized church). The Russian exiles had already been interested in Marx's works and much influenced by Marxist ideas for decades: notably Michael Bakunin, Peter Tkachev, and Peter Lavrov, whom the books call "anarchist" or "populist" with but only partial truth. A few émigrés, led by George Plekhanov,[4] had in 1883 organized the first militantly and exclusivist Marxist circle, the Group for the Liberation of Labor.

In the 1890's, however, Marxist doctrines came flooding into Russia itself. In the Marxist historical scheme, the mode of production determined the character of history in a given epoch, social classes created by that mode clashed with one another and won or lost in more or less violent struggle, and all ideas other than Marxism itself were brushed aside as rationalizations of the position of exploiting classes — all this was widely accepted by many who had not read many of Marx's works or indeed even a line of them. (The same has happened in many other countries since then, including a number which have shown no signs of becoming Communist.) Among the politically conscious, that is, among the intelligentsia, it came to be widely accepted that Russia was on the threshold of entering the capitalist stage of history as analyzed by Marx. Plekhanov and the Marxists insisted that this was inevitable and a good thing: since Russia still had the institutions of what Marx had called a semi-Asiatic state, only a thoroughgoing bourgeois revolution could sweep it into the dustbin of history.[5]

In saying this the Marxists challenged the view sporadically ad-

---

[4] See Samuel H. Baron, *Plekhanov: The Father of Russian Marxism* (Stanford: Stanford University Press, 1963).

[5] The notion that Russian Marxists at this stage (or indeed, much later) thought Russia was "feudal" appears to be the result of a lamentable bit of deduction by a number of Westerners who failed to study the documents. The demonstration of this point is summarily presented in Karl A. Wittfogel, *Oriental Despotism: A Comparative Study of Total Power* (New Haven, Conn.: Yale University Press, 1957, 1963), but full exploration of the issue still awaits publication.

vanced for many decades before among the radicals and repeated in the 1890's by the populists — the idea that Russia could skip capitalism and establish socialism directly. Embarrassing for Marxists was the fact that some of the populists had written to Marx himself shortly before his death asking for a pronouncement on the subject, and had managed to elicit from him fairly strong support on this very point. But Marx had died in 1883 and Engels in 1895, just when the Russian debates were getting under way; the young men and women of St. Petersburg and Moscow were left to settle the issue as best they could.

Among Marxists, several took up with enthusiasm the idea of the inevitability of capitalism. They included Peter Struve (1870–1944), of partly German background, the son of the former governor of Irkutsk, and a teacher of law at St. Petersburg University; Michael Tugan-Baranovskii (1865–1919), who came from the Ukraine, had been educated at Kharkov University, and also taught in St. Petersburg; Sergei Bulgakov (1871–1944), who came from a family whose men had been Orthodox priests for six generations, rebelled against his background, and taught in Moscow; and Nicholas Berdiaev (1874–1948), of a gentry family, who had become a Social Democrat in Kiev. In the Imperial Free Economic Society (founded by Catherine the Great) and elsewhere, some of these men debated populists. Meanwhile, in St. Petersburg a series of strikes took place and mounted sufficiently in intensity to shake the Russian public, and indeed the government, which was led to enact a law limiting the working day to eleven and a half hours. During these strikes Lenin[6] — born Vladimir Ulianov in 1870, son of an ennobled school official, and newly arrived from Simbirsk — did his best to involve himself in the workers' movement, along with Julius Tsederbaum (known as Martov, 1873–1923), who came from a long line of Jewish scholars. Both men were arrested and sent to Siberia for several years, emerging into the emigration in 1900.

[6] There are several lives of Lenin; perhaps the most satisfactory, though its main strength does not lie in a discussion of Lenin's thought, is Louis Fischer, *The Life of Lenin* (New York: Harper, 1964). On Lenin's ideas, see Alfred G. Meyer, *Leninism* (Cambridge, Mass.: Harvard University Press, 1957).

By 1900 two things had happened: arguments, but also strikes had persuaded the populist leaders that they were wrong to keep on trying to avoid capitalism in Russia, for it had arrived in industry — though they continued to hope agriculture could escape it; and arguments, but also strikes had persuaded almost all the leading Marxists that orthodox Marxist dogma had been wrong, that capitalism had virtues in itself and not merely those of bringing the day of revolution nearer, and that improvement in the economic and political condition of the proletariat and the whole people of Russia was more urgent than dogmatic exegesis and preparation for the revolutionary apocalypse. Accordingly, the intellectual leaders of Russian Marxism abandoned it just at the moment it seemed to have overcome its ideological adversary. Struve became a liberal — and later a conservative; Bulgakov ended as an Orthodox priest like his forefathers; Berdiaev became a religious philosopher. As for the leaders of the workers' movement, though most of them remained in the ranks of Social Democratic organizations, they insisted that the most practical approach was to concentrate on raising workers' wages, decreasing their hours, and bettering their working conditions.[7]

Lenin labeled the former group as "Legal Marxists" and the latter "Economists"; or, more accurately, he took terms in contemporary usage and distorted their meaning to suit his purpose, which was not only to imply that both groups were heretics and he belonged to the ranks of Marxist orthodoxy, but also of course to suggest that they were wrong and he was right about the proper path for Russians concerned with progress to follow. In any event, he was generally right about who was orthodox and who was heretical in Marxist terms, but the fact that the heretics included the most gifted intellectuals from Marxist ranks on the one hand and the nearest thing the Marxists had to leaders of a genuine workers' movement on the other did not seem to suggest to him that it might be he who was on the wrong track. The orthodox party by the early 1900's

---

[7] See Richard Kindersley, *The First Russian Revisionists: A Study of "Legal Marxism" in Russia* (New York: Oxford University Press, 1962), and Richard Pipes, *Social Democracy and the St. Petersburg Labor Movement, 1885–1897* (Cambridge, Mass.: Harvard University Press, 1961).

consisted only of a few émigré writers of second-rank intellectual ability; only Plekhanov approximated the intellectual stature of those who were in the process of defecting (This includes Lenin; despite Lenin's greatness as a figure in world history and such mental qualities as a retentive memory and the capacity to judge men and events with considerable accuracy, he cannot claim towering intellectual stature.).

In 1898 a group of nine intellectuals assembled in Minsk and adopted a manifesto written by Struve, mainly for what was then already old time's sake. Almost all were promptly arrested, and all have since been forgotten except by specialists on the history of the Social Democratic Party.[8] The meeting called itself the First Congress of the Russian Social Democratic Labor Party, despite its utter failure, and was to be first in a series of congresses (the twenty-third was held in 1966) that did have importance in deciding the fate of the party as an underground network and then later as the ruling body of Russia. However, in 1898 there was not really any party, either in Russia or among Russian exiles in the West.

The Social Democratic Party came into existence only with the so-called Second Congress, held in Brussels and London in 1903. Lenin and Martov had been released, went abroad, together with Plekhanov and a few others wrote furious newspapers and pamphlets, and got together fifty delegates for the meeting in 1903. Not one party but really two were founded: the Bolsheviks and the Mensheviks, for a time officially "factions" of a single party but in 1912 giving up that pretense. On the Bolshevik side there was Lenin. On the Menshevik side there was everybody else of any stature remaining by then in Marxist ranks, either during the congress or soon after, including Plekhanov, Martov, Leon Trotsky, and others. Again Lenin's skill in using labels deserves note: he seized the term "Bolshevik," meaning "man of the majority," after

[8] On the rise of Russian Marxism, see J. L. H. Keep, *The Rise of Social Democracy in Russia* (London: Oxford University Press, 1963); Leopold H. Haimson, *The Russian Marxists and the Origins of Bolshevism* (Cambridge, Mass.: Harvard University Press, 1955); Bertram D. Wolfe, *Three Who Made a Revolution: A Biographical History* (New York: Dial Press, 1948); Leonard Schapiro, *The Communist Party of the Soviet Union* (New York: Random House, 1959).

DONALD W. TREADGOLD

a narrow vote in his favor at the congress; his opponents short-sightedly accepted his name "men of the minority," though the Mensheviks were in fact the majority for most of the time from 1903 to the fall of 1917 at least, and their predominance in Marxist ranks at the time of the February Revolution was to be overwhelming.

From 1903 to 1917 no Bolshevik other than Lenin was visible with any pretense of having ideas of his own, with the exception of A. A. Bogdanov (pseudonym of Malinovskii), who actually rejected much of Marxism for a new version of positivism called empirio-criticism, following Ernst Mach, and inspired the so-called "God-building" of Anatole Lunacharskii and the "winged Eros" notions of Alexandra Kollontai in the field of what has to be called sexology. Leinin attacked this group and read them out of the party, though they were willing to follow his leadership organizationally. Bolshevism consisted simply of Lenin's ideas, chiefly the notion that during the revolution which lay ahead Russia could pass quickly through the bourgeois revolution directly to socialist revolution — and thereby in effect skip capitalism, as the populists had said all along — by way of a very determined effort made by a tightly disciplined and carefully chosen small party, with a modicum of mass support produced by rallying the poor peasantry to the aid of a still small Russian proletariat (the poor peasant was to be made a sort of honorary proletarian).[9]

As for the Mensheviks, it is more difficult to identify their ideas clearly, since there were several prominent Mensheviks (and at different times, several Menshevik factions), who did not always agree and indeed recognized one another's right to disagree within the

[9] Trotsky is able to claim to have stated the idea of telescoping bourgeois and socialist phases in "uninterrupted revolution" (or "permanent revolution" as it was called on different occasions in application to Russia alone or on an international scale), but it is nevertheless true that Lenin never viewed the prospect of a genuinely "bourgeois revolution" with any enthusiasm and that from the first his strategy was to be couched in terms designed to carry Russia through such a phase as fast as possible. Trotsky joined the Bolsheviks in the middle of 1917, believing that Lenin had belatedly adopted his idea, but it is doubtful that he was warranted in this belief. See Donald W. Treadgold, *Lenin and His Rivals: The Struggle for Russia's Future, 1898–1906* (New York: Praeger, 1955), Ch. VIII.

limits of Marxism. Plekhanov, "father of Russian Marxism" and the most highly revered of the Mensheviks, was never really part of the Menshevik organizational effort. Perhaps the most prominent of the party leaders before the Revolution was Martov, who came to think that the Russian proletariat must not be ordered or dragooned into any given kind of revolution but needed to develop its own understanding of its position and its capacity for socialism. In the course of such a process, Martov was convinced, Marxists ought to strive for "bourgeois" freedoms and accept limited cooperation with liberals until the autocracy was overthrown and democracy achieved in Russia. Martov was, nevertheless, ambivalent toward Lenin's frank amoralism and single-minded insistence on the subordination of everything else to the victory of the party; and the close personal attachment of the two men helped to postpone or mask doctrinal disagreement. The Mensheviks in general fluctuated between angry condemnation of the Bolsheviks as Blanquists, Bonapartists, Jacobins, potential dictators, and so forth on the one hand and grudging admiration of Lenin's self-confidence and uncompromising denunciation of all who disagreed with him so much as an iota on the other.

Meanwhile the populists, worsted in the theoretical debate of the 1890's, took stock of their practical position.[10] They reluctantly accepted the fact that capitalism had come to Russia — not because they regretted the emergence of a proletariat, quite the contrary, but because they feared what would happen to agriculture. If the result was to be the polarization of the peasantry into rich and poor, the prospect was bleak. The populists wavered between declaring such a thing would never happen and trying feverishly to act in order to prevent its happening. Since there was an anarchist strain in populism, which led to distrusting the State and emphasizing the role of the individual in history and politics, organizing a populist political party was a task full of difficulty. Victor Chernov tried to solve the problem. Around 1900 there was constituted an organiza-

[10] On the rise of the S.R.'s, see Oliver H. Radkey, *Agrarian Foes of Bolshevism: Promise and Default of the Socialist Revolutionaries, March to October, 1917* (New York: Columbia University Press, 1958).

tion which would conduct the usual agitation and propaganda activities common to Russian revolutionary groups, but within it an autonomous subdivision called the Battle Organization would conduct terrorism, giving an outlet to those populists who wanted to act out their revolutionary convictions by killing tsarist officials. The new organization called itself the Socialist Revolutionary (S.R.) Party. It was less doctrinaire and less theoretically oriented than the Social Democratic (S.D.) Party, as shown by the fact that it did not get around to holding a congress and adopting a party program until 1906. But that did not mean that the S.R.'s lacked firm beliefs. They were interested in both the city and country, both the urban and rural poor, downtrodden, and exploited. What thus made their position distinctive within the revolutionary spectrum was their concern with the peasantry, not any absence of concern for the proletariat — their urban strength was quite comparable to that of the S.D.'s in 1905, when relatively few workers followed any particular revolutionary banner, and in 1917, when most workers came to adopt some more or less conscious party position. The S.R.'s refused to exclude the peasantry from their purview on doctrinal grounds, as the Mensheviks scornfully did, or to countenance any idea of class struggle among different groups of peasants such as that which the Bolsheviks preached. In their opinion the peasants, as well as the workers, were partly socialist already by virtue of their traditions and aspirations, and by means of S.R. propaganda and agitation, they could reasonably swiftly be prepared to shoulder their revolutionary responsibilities.

Should liberals be mentioned in the context of "Russian radical thought"? They were certainly not "conservative." Within the camp that called itself liberal, moreover, during the first half of the reign of Nicholas II, the leading strain could be at least as well described by the term *radical*.[11] The dominant spirits within the Union of Liberation, formed in early 1904 after two years of planning and preparation, clung to the old French slogan *pas d'ennemis à gauche*, and thought constantly in terms of solidarity with the revolutionaries

[11] See George Fischer, *Russian Liberalism: From Gentry to Intelligentsia* (Cambridge, Mass.: Harvard University Press, 1958).

81

against autocracy. Ahead, unquestionably, lay a revolution, preferably not a very violent or bloody one, but a revolution nonetheless, which would end autocracy, inaugurate a system of democracy, and permit the implementation of sweeping political and social reforms, including land reform, in Russia. The Union incorporated various social groups, from princes of ancient lineage to men from the middle classes; its members had various backgrounds of education and experience, ranging from those who were veterans of decades of administrative and political activity in the zemstva to young free-lance writers. Many of the liberals in the zemstva first had their own separate organization in the Union of Zemstvo-Constitutionalists. In the fall of 1905 the two unions fused to form a Constitutional Democratic (K.D. or Kadet) Party, but the Liberationists retained the upper hand. Their most capable leader, though not their most charismatic personality, was the historian Paul N. Miliukov, one of the most distinguished members of the whole Russian academic community. But there were numerous other men who were well educated, familiar with the parliamentary and constitutional practices of Western Europe and America, and at the same time devoted to the welfare of the Russian people as they conceived of it. It was said of more than one Kadet leader that if he had lived in England he would have been Prime Minister. One of the expected by-products of the revolution to come was that it would permit such men to be cabinet members and parliamentary leaders.

♰ ♰ ♰

THE radicals — Marxists, S.R.'s, and Kadets — were encouraged by the popular ferment occasioned by the Russian defeats at the hands of Japan in 1904–1905 to escalate their demands.[12] The riots and demonstrations which reached their climax in the general strike of autumn 1905 saw the radical leaders publicly unanimous in aiming at a constituent assembly elected according to the "four-tailed" formula of universal, secret, direct, and equal suffrage. Such a body would mean the end of autocracy and most likely the over-

[12] On the Revolution of 1905, see Sidney Harcave, *First Blood: The Russian Revolution of 1905* (New York: Macmillan, 1964).

throw of the dynasty, since the Tsar was not expected to entrust the determination of the future of the Russian State to any popularly elected assembly. The radicals, in effect, staked everything on one throw of the dice. Russia did not emerge from 1905 with a constituent assembly, but instead with a new political system which offered sufficient promise of change to cause the rioters and demonstrators to hesitate and to frustrate the radical leaders. Under the new system every law was supposed to be approved by a lower house, or Duma, elected on the basis of a very broad though not "four-tailed" suffrage, and by a partly appointive upper house, or State Council, before being sanctioned by the Tsar and promulgated.

The S.D.'s and S.R.'s would not at first have anything to do with the new system. Since the Kadets won a plurality of delegates in the elections to the First Duma in the spring of 1906, their leaders determined to use what they had won. Instead, however, of trying to use the Duma to make laws, the Kadets decided in effect to try to turn it into a constituent assembly, as the French States-General had been turned into such a body. The government dissolved the Duma after a few months of inconclusive wrangling. The Second Duma, in 1907, turned out no better. Now the government, which had come to be headed by P. A. Stolypin, decided a change had to be made. Technically violating its own laws, the government changed the electoral regulations; the result was the Third Duma, which came into being at the end of 1907 and lasted its full term of five years. It was moderate enough to work with the government, and Stolypin was, with some reservations, willing to work with it. A period of relative equilibrium seemed to have been reached.

During the four years which elapsed before Stolypin was assassinated in 1911, the radicals' position came to seem desperate. The S.R. Party virtually disintegrated, as a result of the failure of revolution and also because one of its top leaders, Evno Azef, was exposed as a police spy. The S.D.'s lost most of their mass following, and their leaders returned to exile in Western Europe or America. The Kadets were still numerous in the Duma, but had nothing like the preponderance or influence they had enjoyed in 1906.

In such circumstances the radicals had leisure, either in Russia or abroad, to examine the abortive Revolution of 1905 and the lessons, if any, to be learned from it. What was most bitter to them was the gradual realization that the mass of the Russian people — especially the peasantry — had failed to follow them to the barricades. Of the thousands or even hundreds of thousands who had seemed to do so here and there and for a time, in what was apparently one of the great successes in history for revolutionary leaders in politicalizing mass discontent, most had wavered at the crucial moment and drawn back from what at least a large share of the radicals might have considered victory. The radicals were not alone in their alarm at what 1905 had shown. The government was also shocked to find that the peasantry was no longer the bulwark of autocracy and dynastic loyalty it had been assumed to be, and Stolypin's policy was to a large extent based on an effort to harness governmental action to the peasants' desire for independence, private property, and more productive agricultural methods. But the radicals, hostile to private property and unsure of their rapport with the peasantry, could only nurse their impotence and frustration and hope that somehow something would happen to improve their prospects.

A few of the intelligentsia did conclude from the failure of 1905 that the whole radical camp (and in some cases, they themselves) had been wrong. The men who had been Marxist leaders in the 1890's and had left Marxism for liberalism and other positions in the 1900's, headed by Struve, in 1909 issued a volume called *Signposts* (*Vekhi*), whose essays shared this conclusion.[13] It was argued that the intelligentsia had missed the opportunity for healthy constitutional development in 1906, since they had thought only of the destruction of the bad State and had ignored the impossibility of creating some kind of instant perfection to replace it. Theirs had been a failure of moral responsibility, rooted in atheism and the erection of a cult of the "people" in place of the fallen God. The authors of *Signposts* did not seek any reconciliation with the

[13] See Leonard Schapiro, "The *Vekhi* Group and the Mystique of Revolution," *Slavic and East European Review*, XXIV (December 1955), 56–76.

DONALD W. TREADGOLD

autocracy, and continued to demand that a rule of law replace arbitrariness, including what remained of the latter under the quasi-constitutional system (whether because or in spite of it) during the post-1905 period. However, the message of *Signposts* was taken to be chiefly an indictment of the radicals for mistaken beliefs and mistaken acts and a call to them to abandon many of their cherished nineteenth-century positions.

The radicals did not hasten to acknowledge the truth of the indictment or to answer the call to change. Some continued to wait for the next revolution, without any great or immediate hope. Others, however, whether or not they read *Signposts*, were taking a different tack. They quietly abandoned politics for active professional life or assumed positions in the Duma, the zemstva, the courts, and so forth (for the most part, not in the central bureaucracy). In so doing these men found themselves out of touch with their old radical friends and in the company (if not necessarily in intimacy with them) of the growing number of younger nonpolitical intellectuals who thought it important to do their best in art or science or journalism today rather than staking their lives and fates on the remote chance of a utopian tomorrow. Such men, who saw both autocracy and the nineteenth-century intelligentsia as relics of a Russian past receding into history, cannot be said, of course, to have constituted the wave of the immediate future.

♟ ♟ ♟

THE revolution of February 1917 gave the old-style intelligentsia a few months in which to cherish the heady illusion that they had won and would rule the new Russia. That is, it proved an illusion for all except the Bolsheviks, some of whom, despite their lack of influence during those few months (and despite the radical disassociation from the Provisional Government Lenin demanded of them, though that was only in April), identified to some degree with the revolution that had taken place. The Bolsheviks in October 1917 proceeded to sweep their old fellow radicals aside as thoroughly as they eliminated the old bureaucrats, landowners, and middle classes. The system they established in many

85

ways combined the worst features of both the autocracy and intelligentsia of the past. It became an utterly arbitrary, uncompromisingly centralized system in which it was state policy to demand that all artists, writers, and intellectuals of all kinds serve the cause of revolution — no longer the revolution to come, but the revolution in power — the manner of their so doing being dictated down to the last ideological comma.

And yet the nonpolitical intellectuals of the reign of Nicholas II, especially its second half, may have the last laugh. The events of the last few years, disturbingly for the Soviet regime, in many ways hark back to the pre-1917 period.[14] The recent attempts to challenge "Stalin's heirs," the rediscovery of the poets and painters of the early 1900's by the dissident youth, the attempt to take up where those men left off, the demand for "freedom of art" (from political dictation) that was the foremost demand of the student demonstrations of April 1965 — these and related phenomena suggest that the ideal of the free human personality is not dead in Russia. Many of the radicals of Nicholas II's reign cherished this same ideal, and their fundamental criticism of autocracy stemmed from its denial of individual human dignity. The most serious indictment of them that can be made, leaving aside the fact that their fate might be thought to expiate even much worse sins, is that in their impatience they believed that conditions could be changed if only good men (supported, to be sure, by "the people") could replace the bad men in power. The necessity for institutional underpinnings which could secure the real victory of a democratic revolution was something they were slow to acknowledge, seeing in the allusion to such problems a veiled defense of the old order. The ideal of the free human personality is difficult to approach, however, except through the security afforded by social and cultural pluralism. It is, at any rate, a noble ideal, an ideal that has roots in Russia's ancient Christian culture, an ideal that has survived Lenin, Stalin, and Khrushchev, an ideal that may yet play a role in Russia's future.

[14] See James H. Billington, *The Icon and the Axe: An Interpretive History of Russian Culture* (New York: Knopf, 1966), Ch. VI, p. 3, "Fresh Ferment."

THOMAS RIHA

Constitutional Developments
in Russia

♰ ♰ ♰

ON APRIL 27, 1906, the Emperor and Autocrat (for he
retained that title even in the new Fundamental Laws issued four
days earlier) of All the Russias addressed, in the Winter Palace,
the assembled deputies of his First Duma. "With ardent faith in
the radiant future of Russia," he told them, "I greet in you those
best men whom I ordered my beloved subjects to choose from their
midst . . . May this day be henceforth remembered as the day of
the rebirth of the moral fibre of the Russian land, the day of the
rebirth of her best forces."[1] Many in that great hall must have
remained skeptical — not only among the deputies, but also among
the notables and courtiers — for they must have remembered that
only a decade earlier the Emperor had spoken very differently.
Addressing representatives of the zemstva on January 17, 1895,
the Emperor, at the very outset of his reign, had said in the same
Winter Palace: "Of late, in some zemstvo assemblies, there have

---

[1] Gosudarstvennaia Duma, Pervyi Sozyv, *Stenograficheskie Otchety* (St.
Petersburg), April 27, 1906, no pagination (cited below as *Otchety*). There
is an English translation of the speech in Vasilii A. Maklakov, *The First
State Duma: Contemporary Reminiscences* (Bloomington: Indiana University Press, 1964), pp. 44–45; it is, however, inaccurate, as are many passages in this unsatisfactory English version of an important book.

been heard voices of persons who have been carried away by senseless dreams of the participation of zemstvo representatives in the affairs of internal administration. Let it be known to all that I, while devoting all my energies to the good of the people, shall maintain the principle of autocracy just as firmly and unflinchingly as did my unforgettable father." [2] Which of the two sentiments more clearly represented the Emperor's conviction: the speech of 1906, or that of 1895? The record of the eleven years between his two pronouncements seemed to suggest that Nicholas II was more sincere when he spoke of "senseless dreams" than when he met his elected parliamentarians.

The Emperor's negative attitude toward representative institutions was shared by most of his officials. They believed, with Vladimir I. Gurko, Deputy Minister of Interior in 1906, that "the state apparatus had absorbed all that was best in Russia in the way of talent, of loyalty in the rational execution of duty, and especially of ability to understand state problems. Outside this apparatus, with minor exceptions, the only remaining active forces were fanatics befogged with Utopian dreams and theories . . ." [3] It was only because that state apparatus had been unable to cope with the crisis brought about by the Russo-Japanese War that the Emperor was willing to consider summoning the "best men." But the first Russian parliament was assembling in a country in which very little had been done to prepare the ground for constitutionalism. In the twelve years since the accession of Nicholas, the government had placed every obstacle in the road of healthy public initiative.

The only school for constitutionalism in Russia was local government. But, Count Sergei Witte admitted in 1899, "the zemstvo institutions are now deprived of almost all independence, and placed under strict administrative wardship . . . Our local government finds itself in the most abnormal, most pitiful condition." [4]

[2] Cited in George Fischer, *Russian Liberalism: From Gentry to Intelligentsia* (Cambridge, Mass.: Harvard University Press, 1958), pp. 74–75.

[3] *Features and Figures of the Past: Government and Opinion in the Reign of Nicholas II* (Stanford: Stanford University Press, 1939), pp. 361–362.

[4] *Samoderzhavie i Zemstvo* (St. Petersburg, 1908), pp. 200, 183.

THOMAS RIHA

Despite the fact that the Zemstvo Statute of 1890 gave the nobility an artificial predominance, the local governors retained the right of approving all elections and could annul any zemstvo decision as "unsuitable." This led to apathy and, despite rare meetings (the provincial zemstva met only once a year for a few days), there was low attendance.[5] Nevertheless the zemstvo, in times of crisis, such as the period 1904–1906, did honor to the capacity of Russia's educated classes to participate in public affairs. It was this capacity for participation that Sir Paul Vinogradov was recognizing when he spoke of "the necessity for the state of appealing to the help of the self-governing institutions on all occasions when the country was in trouble."[6]

"The self-governing institutions" included, in addition to the zemstva, the municipal dumas. Here the limits imposed by the government were even graver than in the zemstva, resulting in the same apathy and low attendance at meetings. Only one per cent of what was, in any case, a small urban population, had the franchise for the city government, and only half of this tiny group exercised it. One of Moscow's city fathers, Nikolai Astrov, reported that the central government treated the municipalities "with the same hostility with which it would have regarded foreign elements in the country." From 1900 to 1914 the elections of 217 mayors and of members of municipal boards in 318 towns were annulled by the government. The narrow-minded Municipal Statute of 1892 was a noose around the city government's neck, and Astrov spoke of "its failure to provide for the growth of the political instinct."[7] Still, some former city councillors achieved national prominence;

[5] Fischer, *Russian Liberalism*, p. 13.

[6] *Self-Government in Russia* (London: Constable, 1915), p. 94. That fairly large numbers of persons were involved in zemstvo operations is evident from the fact that, in 1912, there were 85,000 members of the so-called "Third Element" at work in the provinces with zemstvo institutions (see Alexander Vucinich, "The State and the Local Community," in Cyril E. Black, ed., *The Transformation of Russian Society: Aspects of Social Change since 1861* (Cambridge, Mass.: Harvard University Press, 1960), p. 204).

[7] Astrov is quoted from N. I. Astrov and P. P. Gronsky, *The War and the Russian Government* (New Haven, Conn.: Yale University Press, 1929), pp. 134–137.

the best known was Moscow's Sergei Muromtsev, elected chairman of the First Duma.

Municipal and rural self-government remained weak plants in autocratic Russia. The same was true of the Russian middle class, the seedbed from which representative institutions grew in the West. The Russian language, one historian noted, "has no appropriate term to express the concept of the middle class." [8] The commercial classes, Boris Chicherin stressed, "had long been accustomed to bow before authority." [9] The same was true of the industrialists. The chairmen of the annual congresses of industries were appointed by the Ministry of Finance (by the Ministry of Trade and Industry after 1906), and their agenda had to be approved beforehand by the government. The political passivity of those who should have been in the forefront of Russian constitutionalism prompted the famous outburst of the Russian Social Democrats in 1898. "The farther east one goes in Europe," the party's first program had charged, "the more the bourgeoisie becomes in the political respect weaker, more cowardly, and meaner, and the larger are the cultural and political tasks which fall to the share of the proletariat. On its broad shoulders the Russian working class must bear and will bear the cause of the fight for political freedom." [10]

Political parties — another school for constitutional training — remained illegal, and worked underground until 1906. Even the liberals had to resort to subterfuges like the Union of Liberation, and the revolutionaries, in their turn, practiced politics by assassination, liquidating two Ministers of the Interior, one Minister of Education, and a Grand Duke between 1902 and 1904. Officials, for their part, were convinced that the population was indifferent to constitutionalism. "The peasantry simply do not care about politics," said Premier Peter Stolypin to Bernard Pares. The latter, too, believed that the peasants were not attached to the existing political parties, since one hundred deputies of the First Duma preferred to

[8] Michael T. Florinsky, *The End of the Russian Empire* (New York: Collier, 1961), p. 115.

[9] *Vospominaniia* (Moscow, 1934), Vol. IV, p. 255.

[10] Quoted in Robert V. Daniels, ed., *A Documentary History of Communism* (New York: Random House, 1962), Vol. I, p. 7.

be identified as "non-Party" men.[11] Even in 1905–1906 the bureaucracy refused to recognize the existence of political parties. "I do not know of any parties," said Minister of the Interior Peter Durnovo, and his deputy Sergei Kryzhanovskii admitted, "In general I never recognized any parties." At the time of the First Duma there were, in Russia, only three legal parties: the hoodlum Union of the Russian People, the Octobrists, and the tiny Party of Peaceful Reconstruction. The mass parties – such as the Socialist Revolutionaries, the Mensheviks, the Bolsheviks, and even the Kadets – remained unregistered, and, therefore, illegal. When they attempted to register, as the Kadets did on numerous occasions, they were always turned down. [12]

Despite the promises of the October Manifesto there was, in the spring of 1906, no guarantee of political freedom. The jails of St. Petersburg were filled with political prisoners, who waved at the deputies on their way to the Duma meeting in the Taurida Palace. No wonder the Duma's first demand was for an amnesty. Between October 17, 1905, and January 15, 1906, alone some forty-five thousand persons had been sent into administrative exile.[13] Of course, one must not confuse those milder days with the later horrible concentration camps of another regime. Nadezhda Krupskaia recalled that Lenin's administrative exile in Siberia in 1898 had been rather comfortable: [14]

Vladimir Ilyich's monthly allowance of eight rubles procured him clean lodgings and meals, and paid for laundry and mending . . . True, the dinner and supper were simple enough meals. One week a sheep would be slaughtered, and Vladimir Ilyich would be fed with it day in and day out until it was all gone . . . But there was milk and cream enough for both Vladimir Ilyich and his dog, a fine Gordon setter named Zhenka.

[11] Bernard Pares, "Conversations with Mr. Stolypin," *Russian Review* (London), II, No. 1 (1913), 105; see also his *Russia and Reform* (London: Constable, 1907), p. 448.

[12] V. Nabokov, "Polozhenie Politicheskikh Partii," *Pravo* (St. Petersburg), No. 27 (1907), pp. 188–193; S. Kryzhanovskii, in P. E. Shchegolev, ed., *Padenie Tsarskogo Rezhima* (Moscow, 1926), Vol. V, p. 435 (cited below as *Padenie*).

[13] A. Lopukhin, *Otryvki iz Vospominanii* (Moscow, 1923), p. 93.

[14] *Reminiscences of Lenin* (Moscow: Foreign Languages Publishing House, 1959), p. 36.

The regime, despite its many shortcomings, had made room for some fairly effective safeguards against total arbitrariness. One of these was the existence of courts and lawyers who were not utterly at the administration's mercy. The more than eleven thousand Russian lawyers were, on the whole, a brave and conscientious company, and many made a name fighting on behalf of political causes. The court was a place where individual freedom of expression was possible. Alexander Kerensky, the future Premier of Russia, was one of these men who got their political training in the courtroom. Vasilii Maklakov, deputy of three Dumas, was another, and exercised the lawyer's privilege of speaking freely. Defending peasants who looted and pillaged in 1905 he told the court: [15]

Our customs are cruel, but they are cruel both at the top and at the bottom. We reap in cruelty what we have sown ourselves . . . They [the defendants] are such as you have yourselves made them, and you have as little right to blame them for rudeness as to blame, for illiteracy, the people whom you deprive of the possibility of getting an education.

There was freedom of speech at least for the Russian lawyer. The press too was not entirely muzzled. The censorship attacked the work in question, not the author, who remained free to continue his work against the regime. Though this was not true of the periodical press, the institution of feigned editors, prepared to go to jail in place of the real ones, protected many an outspoken critic of the system. After 1905 Aesopian language became largely unnecessary, and, for a brief period, the Russian press enjoyed a real renaissance. At a press conference on October 18, 1905, Witte recognized its unique role: "You know," he told the assembled editors, "that in Russia, thanks to special conditions, public opinion was expressed only through the press, as there were no other organs which could clarify the opinions of the majority, the minority, and the extreme elements. In view of this the Russian press has always had exceptional significance." [16] Despite the new severity

---

[15] Quoted in Samuel Kucherov, *Courts, Trials and Lawyers under the Last Three Tzars* (New York: Praeger, 1953), pp. 237–238, p. 316, n. 43.

[16] "Interviiu S. I. Vitte s Predstaviteliami Pechati," *Krasnyi Arkhiv* (Moscow), XI–XII (1925), 100.

of the censor after 1906, the growth of Russian newspapers was phenomenal: the total number of newspapers increased from 123 in 1898 to 800 in 1908, and to 1,158 immediately before World War I, in 1913.[17]

♟ ♟ ♟

INTO this uncertain atmosphere of both promise and denial Russian constitutionalism was officially born in 1906. There was hope among those few who had tasted the promise of freedom, but there was also much hostility in the air based on old prejudices, archaic traditions, and bitter experience. The Dowager Empress who had been present at the Winter Palace opening of the Duma recognized this when she told Finance Minister Vladimir Kokovtsov of the deputies: "They looked at us as upon their enemies, and I could not make myself stop looking at certain faces, so much did they seem to reflect an incomprehensible hatred for us all."[18] In the Duma the Cossack deputy Timofei Sedel'nikov recalled the Winter Palace scene with bitterness: "That luxury, that gold, the diamonds which I saw there, those huge buildings of the capital, where have they all come from, if not from the labor, the sweat, the property of the masses?"[19] This heritage of anger and resentment did not augur well for the smooth functioning of the Russian parliament.

The electoral law of December 1905 had been quite generous, for the government, at that time, had been frightened. Among the deputies were 191 peasants (39 per cent of the total), as against 123 deputies representing the nobility. In addition, the non-Russian nationalities were well represented. As Pares remembered the colorful body:[20]

[17] K. Noviskii, "Pechat' v Rossii," *Malaia Sovetskaia Entsiklopediia* (Moscow, 1930), Vol. VI, p. 500.

[18] *Out of My Past: The Memoirs of Count Kokovtsov, Russian Minister of Finance, 1904–1914* (Stanford: Stanford University Press, 1935), pp. 130–131.

[19] *Otchety*, April 29, 1906, 29.

[20] The Duma's membership is analyzed in Warren B. Walsh, "The Composition of the Dumas," *Russian Review* (New Haven), VIII (1949), 112–113; the description is from Pares, *Russia and Reform*, pp. 550–551.

93

It would be difficult to imagine a more picturesque gathering. Each man wore the costume of his class. The country gentry and the Intelligents dressed very simply, but there were Russian priests with long beards and hair, a Roman Catholic bishop in skull-cap lined with red, finely accoutred Cossacks from the Caucasus, Bashkirs and Buryats in strange and tinselled Asiatic dress, Polish peasants in the brilliant and martial costumes of their people, and a whole mass of staid, bearded, and top-booted Russian peasants.

"The Duma of National Hopes," as it was called, was full of expectations, but it was also most impatient: reforms had been delayed too long. The government, no longer so frightened as it had been in 1905, chose the worst possible tactics to deal with this immature legislature. To replace the agile Witte, the Tsar chose Ivan Goremykin, a bureaucrat of the old school, without imagination or initiative. His address to the Duma was an insult — he deemed most of the Duma's demands "inadmissible," and instead of a program, submitted to the Duma two bills providing, respectively, for the creation of a hothouse and a laundry at Derpt University. No legislation was likely to come from an encounter between an overly eager Duma and a resentful Cabinet. The seventy-two days of the Duma's existence were heroic, but unproductive. Still, no less a traditionalist than the great historian Vasilii Kliuchevskii remained impressed. "Observing this Duma's activity," he wrote a friend in July 1906, "I was forced to admit two facts which I had not expected: the speed with which the people came to regard the Duma as the most promising legislative organ, and the unquestionable moderation of the Duma's dominant mood." [21]

That moderation was absent at Vyborg when, after the Duma's dissolution, many deputies signed a manifesto urging a boycott of the government, As a result, 169 signers of the manifesto were deprived of their political rights, and Russian constitutionalism lost some of its ablest spokesmen. This impoverished the Second Duma, in which only 6 per cent of the deputies were members of the First. Peasants kept the percentage they had had earlier, and the nationality ratio was preserved — 38 per cent of the deputies

[21] A. Koni, *Na Zhiznenom Puti* (St. Petersburg, 1912), Vol. II, pp. 189–190.

were not Great Russians. This Duma, known as the "Duma of Popular Anger," was more radical than its predecessor. The Kadet center had been weakened, and the Socialist wing strengthened. The large Social Democratic delegation was a thorn in the government's side, and a most unconstitutional method was found to remove it. The new Premier, Stolypin, though he had a comprehensive program of legislation, proved to be no more tolerant of the Duma than his predecessor, and dissolved the Second Duma before it had passed any bills, or made any permanent impact on Russian life.[22]

So far the record of both government and legislature was largely negative. Russian constitutionalism had had a strange impact. The Emperor and his officials interpreted the record in their own way. The peasantry, whom they had considered conservative and politicalically indifferent, had betrayed their confidence. The fault, they reasoned, lay in the electoral law, which they now proceeded to change, in direct violation of the Fundamental Laws of April 1906. Neither the regime nor its opponents wished to abide by the law, when it did not suit them. It was a vicious circle. The electoral law of June 3, 1907, ensured that the elections would be neither universal, direct, nor equal; nor were they altogether secret. The nobility was to dominate the Duma, as they did the zemstva. "If you took an assembly which represented the majority of the population," Stolypin told Pares in 1908, "sane ideas would not prevail in it . . . We want not Professors but men with roots in the country, the local gentry, and such like."[23] Also wanted were Russians, not the national minorities, though they formed 45 per cent of the population. Poland now had 14 instead of 37 seats, Central Asia lost all its 21 seats and the Steppe Region its 10, Siberia had 15 instead of 21 seats, and the Caucasus had 10 in place of its former 25 deputies. Only seven instead of the former twenty-five cities now

---

[22] For the Second Duma's composition, see Walsh, "The Composition of the Dumas," pp. 113–114. See also the thorough study of Alfred Levin, *The Second Duma: A Study of the Social-Democratic Party and the Russian Constitutional Experiment* (New Haven, Conn.: Yale University Press, 1940).

[23] Pares, "Conversations with Mr. Stolypin," p. 106.

elected their deputies directly. Now only 19 per cent of the deputies were peasants, and 44 per cent were nobles. Fully 40 per cent of the deputies had experience in local government (compared with less than a third in the previous Dumas), but these were the zemstvo conservatives rather than the liberals. Only 3.5 million persons had voted in the elections to the Third Duma (this in a population of 140 million). It was thus apparent that a very small number of Russians were getting the experience needed for the growth of constitutionalism.[24]

Stolypin had opted for economic rather than political solutions to the Russian crisis. He was convinced that Russian constitutionalism could only grow if a new class of Russian citizens were created. Stolypin therefore told the assembled Third Duma on November 16, 1907,[25]

As long as the peasant is poor, does not possess individual landed property, and is held by force within the vise of the commune, he will remain a slave, and no written law will give him the benefits of civil liberty . . . The small landed proprietor . . . will introduce into the village culture, enlightenment, and prosperity. Only then will paper freedom be transformed into real freedom.

Stolypin was right from a long-range point of view, but Russia was not to be granted the decades of peaceful development which his plan took for granted. Armed with the hindsight not available to him, it is hard to disagree with Pares when he says that "in 1917 if Russia had possessed a Duma elected by universal suffrage it seems almost impossible that events would have followed the course

[24] On the 1907 electoral law see Samuel N. Harper, *The New Electoral Law for the Russian Duma* (Chicago: University of Chicago Press, 1908). See also Walsh, "The Composition of the Dumas," pp. 114–115. Statistics on the elections are in Ministerstvo Vnutrennykh Del, *Vybory v 3-iu Gosudarstvennuiu Dumu* (St. Petersburg, 1911), Vols. VI–XXIII *passim*. They show that 3,528,378 persons voted, representing 16 per cent of the male population above the age of twenty-five. Many of those eligible chose not to vote. The peasant curia had the best showing with 65 per cent of those eligible actually voting; the percentage dropped to 42 per cent in the landowners' curia, 37 per cent in the first city curia, 33 per cent in the second city curia, and a mere 25 per cent in the workers' curia.

[25] Quoted in Jacob Walkin, *The Rise of Democracy in Pre-Revolutionary Russia: Political and Social Institutions under the Last Three Czars* (New York: Praeger, 1962), p. 267, n. 36.

which they actually took after the March Revolution."[26] The dangers inherent in the artificial suffrage of 1907 were apparent even to its own creatures, the deputies elected under it, who, in their majority, were hardly radicals. In 1913 the Fourth Duma voted that "it acknowledges the need for a revision of the electoral law of June 3, 1907, in the direction of broadening the suffrage, and ensuring the freedom of elections from administrative interference."[27]

The Third Duma became a strange constitutional oasis in the Russian political desert. Its parties led a hothouse existence, while the rest of the country slumbered in a form of political anesthesia. The revolutionary experience of 1905–1907 was now a matter of the past, and the country lived under what was, facetiously, described as a demi- or semi-constitution. The Emperor had ceased being an autocrat, and yet the *Almanach de Gotha* which, before 1906, had described Russia as "a hereditary monarchy" now called it "a constitutional monarchy under an autocratic tsar."[28] The Third Duma, destined to live out its full five constitutional years, would live them in the shadow of the Emperor's considerable rights.[29] It could do nothing about the Fundamental Laws of April 1906, passed before the First Duma was called, which could be revised only on the Emperor's initiative. He possessed an absolute veto on all legislation. He retained complete control of foreign affairs and special rights in the field of defense legislation. He could promulgate exceptional decrees (the famous Article 87) that had, temporarily, the force of law, and could proclaim the "exceptional measures" in any part of his realm. Such a proclamation, in fact, suspended the operation of most laws in the given area, and gave full reign to the arbitrariness of the local administration. That this was no empty threat is attested by the fact that, in 1912, only five million Russians did not live under the jurisdiction of

[26] Bernard Pares, *The Fall of the Russian Monarchy* (New York: Vintage, 1961), p. 102.

[27] *Otchety*, March 13, 1913, 2223.

[28] See *Almanach de Gotha* (1906), 1032; (1907), 1040.

[29] The English text of Articles 1–82 of the Fundamental Laws is in Walter F. Dodd, *Modern Constitutions* (Chicago: University of Chicago Press, 1909), Vol. II, pp. 181–195. For a brief analysis see Astrov and Gronsky, *The War and the Russian Government*, pp. 3–25.

THOMAS RIHA

some form of "exceptional measures."[30] The Emperor appointed half the membership of the State Council, the upper chamber of the Russian legislature, which had veto power over any Duma bill. Even the elected half of the Council was hardly progressive, since it was chosen on the basis of a suffrage even more restrictive than that for the Duma. The appointed members could and were removed if they did not please the government, and the Council turned into "the cemetery of the Duma's hopes," defeating most of the progressive legislation which managed to pass the Duma.

The Emperor had a strange concept of what constituted legal and respectable political activity. It was not surprising that he abhorred the radical parties. But he was almost equally suspicious of the Octobrists who, after all, wished to put into effect the October Manifesto which he, himself, had issued. He, who should have stood above parties, clearly favored the Right, and became a member of the ultrareactionary Union of the Russian People to whom, in 1907, he sent a much-quoted telegram: "Let the Union of the Russian People be my support, serving in the eyes of all and in everything as an example of legality and of order."[31] This could hardly encourage Russia's constitutionalists.

♟ ♟ ♟

HOWEVER, Russia now had an instrument by which the popular will, even if much filtered by the restricted suffrage, could be expressed in legislation. The Octobrists, with their respect for the constitution, dominated the chamber. The Kadets, who had been almost reckless in pushing for political reform, and who had tainted their reputation by a tacit alliance with the Left, were now only a respectable minority. The Third Duma, known as "The Masters' Duma," was docile compared with its predecessors. The Octobrist center, if it wished to accomplish anything, had to find allies in either wing. Since, on principle, they would not turn to the

[30] For a map showing their operation see *Utro Rossii* (Moscow), January 1, 1912; an analysis is in Samuel N. Harper, "Exceptional Measures in Russia," *Russian Review* (London), I, No. 4 (1912), 92–105.

[31] Cited in *Vestnik Partii Narodnoi Svobody* (St. Petersburg), June 21, 1907, 1362 (cited below as *Vestnik*).

Left, they had to swallow some bitter political pills from the Right.[32] The government now flooded the Duma with legislation, both of the so-called "spaghetti class" (minor bills of local importance), and major reforms such as the Stolypin land bill, which aimed at breaking up the commune and transforming the Russian village.

An examination of the Third Duma's legislative performance reveals both the positive and the negative features of the Russian constitutional structure. The Duma improved the Stolypin land bill, and passed it despite Left opposition. In the field of popular education the Duma led a reluctant government on the road to universal literacy by repeatedly increasing the allotments to primary schools. Between 1907 and 1913 the expenditures on elementary schools grew from 19 million rubles (1.8 per cent of the government budget) to 76 million (4.2 per cent of the total budget). This was a genuine Duma accomplishment.[33] The government alone would have never done as much, for, as a critic put it, the Ministry of Education "was less a ministry for public instruction than a ministry for the prevention of it."[34] Ministers Aleksander Shvarts (1908–1910) and Leo Kasso (1910–1914) were both on bad terms with the Duma, and did much to restrict the autonomy of Russian schools, particularly the universities, which had been granted almost unlimited freedom in 1905. But after the University of Moscow repressions of 1911 there was a haven for academic refugees from bureaucratic terror — the newly founded Moscow Shaniavskii Popular University, not under the Ministry's thumb, which absorbed most of those persecuted by the government. A new oasis of political and academic freedom had been created in Russia, with the Duma's participation and consent. Literacy, too, grew from 27.8 to 40.2 per cent in the period 1897–1914. There was

[32] The Third Duma was divided almost equally into a right wing, with 145 deputies (of several conservative parties), a center (with 133 Octobrists), and a left wing (consisting of several parties with 146 deputies) (see Paul N. Miliukov, "The Representative System in Russia," in J. D. Duff, ed., *Russian Realities and Problems* (Cambridge: Cambridge University Press, 1917), p. 32).

[33] Nicholas A. Hans, *History of Russian Educational Policy* (London: P. S. King, 1931), pp. 229–330.

[34] Pares, *The Fall of the Russian Monarchy*, p. 110.

99

progress in that department of Russian life, essential to any growth of constitutionalism.[35]

The Duma extended local self-government by providing zemstva for nine additional provinces, raising the total from 34 to 43. To be sure, these new zemstva had the negative feature of national curias to ensure a dominance by Russians in the West Russian areas where they were instituted. Still, it was a step forward, as was the passage of the much more important volost zemstvo bill, unfortunately vetoed by the State Council. It would have provided the foundation for the zemstvo structure, which, with the Duma, now had a roof. The zemstvo institutions did not go below the county level, and thus the Russian village had no real self-government — this drawback would never be removed under the old regime. The Duma also extended Russia's religious freedom with several bills concerning Old Believers and the citizens' right to pass from one faith to another. Here, too, the State Council interfered, and reduced the net gains made. The Duma established new justice-of-the-peace courts in the localities, which reduced the powers of the hated land captains.

In the field of budget control, the Duma's record was mixed. The Russian legislature possessed only a limited power of the purse; its budget competence was regulated by the rules of March 8, 1906, which provided that if the Duma did not approve a given budget, the budget of the previous year would remain in effect. Furthermore, the Duma could not legislate on railway rates and tariffs, import and export tariffs, or the price of vodka. Even the moderate Third Duma was dissatisfied with such limitations and, in May 1911, passed a bill widening its budget rights. The measure, however, was rejected by the State Council, and the situation remained unchanged until 1917.[36] Large parts of the budget were closed to Duma inspection and control. Thus, by 1912, despite all its efforts,

[35] On Shaniavskii University, see Alexander Kizevetter, *Na rubezhe dvukh stoletii: Vospominaniia, 1881–1914* (Prague, 1929), pp. 470–495; literacy statistics are from Walkin, *The Rise of Democracy in Pre-Revolutionary Russia*, p. 101. See also Evgrav Kovalevsky, "The Duma and Public Instruction," *Russian Review* (London), I, No. 3 (1912), 64–79.

[36] The history of the Duma's budget bill is in an editorial in *Riech'* (St. Petersburg), October 29, 1913.

the Duma controlled only 26 per cent of the Ministry of Interior budget, 36 per cent of the Ministry of Education budget, and 65 per cent of the Ministry of War budget. In the period 1907–1912 the Duma had succeeded in raising the share of the total state budget subject to its control from 53 to 62 per cent. The Russian legislature still had a long road to travel in this field,[37] but the bureaucracy had had to learn to limit its appetites, and even the Emperor found that he could no longer dispense state funds arbitrarily. "One thing is difficult," he wrote his mother in 1909, "to persuade Kokovtsov to get money without the Duma; but we will do it one way or another, never fear." [38]

In the field of defense, the Duma did much to help reorganize the army and navy after the shameful defeat in the Russo-Japanese War. The Octobrist leader Alexander Guchkov made this his special concern, and minced no words in his criticisms. He dared to raise his voice even against the various grand dukes holding high positions in many defense departments, and protested against their negative role. If Russia's defense establishment was not so prepared as it should have been in 1914, it was not the Duma's fault; the legislature had repeatedly appropriated more funds than the defense departments managed to spend. This, it should be noted, was done over the protests of the Duma Left, which, until 1915, was not even admitted to the Duma's Defense Committee on the charge that it could not keep state secrets. On the whole, the deputies were well informed about defense matters, and Pares noted that "the Duma's budget committee gets much more inside information on the military spending departments put before it than ever reaches the private members of the House of Commons." [39] The Emperor, for his part, did not like to share defense information with

---

[37] *Zakonodatel'nykh Palat* (St. Petersburg, 1910), and Samuel N. Harper, "The Budget Rights of the Russian Duma," *Journal of Political Economy* (Chicago), XVI (1908), 152–156. Also of interest is Michael Alexeyenko, "Five Years of Budget Work," *Russian Review* (London), I, No. 3 (1912), 14–44.

[38] E. Bing, ed., *The Secret Letters of the Last Tsar; Being the Confidential Letters between Nicholas II and His Mother, Dowager Empress Maria Feodorovna* (New York: Longmans, 1938), letter of September 27, 1909.

[39] "Onlookers at the Duma," *Russian Review* (London), I, No. 3 (1912), 85.

101

the Duma, and dismissed two of his Ministers of War, Aleksander Rediger and Aleksei Polivanov, for being too cooperative with the legislature. In 1909 he forbade his new Minister of War, Vladimir Sukhomlinov, to appear in the Duma. "Why should you argue with them," he told him, "you are my Minister . . . I created the Duma not to have it instruct me, but to have it advise me."[40] Sukhomlinov stayed away from the Duma for five years.

The making of foreign policy remained in the Emperor's exclusive jurisdiction. Nevertheless the Duma had a yearly chance to debate Russian foreign policy on the occasion of its examination of the Ministry of Foreign Affairs budget. Beginning with 1908 an increasing number of deputies of all persuasions, from ultraconservatives to Social Democrats, took part in these debates and usually criticized the conduct of Russian foreign affairs. It was probably true, as the Octobrist deputy Mikhail Kapustin asserted, that "the majority of Duma members are not qualified to examine our foreign affairs."[41] Nevertheless, a small number of voices could be heard — some of whom, like Paul Miliukov, enjoyed international repute, and were listened to even in the chancelleries of foreign governments. When, in 1911, Foreign Minister Sergei Sazonov failed to deliver the yearly Duma report (for which he had to secure, in each instance, the Emperor's permission), the Octobrists stated their regret "that the Minister of Foreign Affairs, instead of making his customary presentation on foreign policy, is absent . . . The government will remain isolated if it does not lean on public opinion."[42]

The Duma, for its part, was most sensitive to public opinion, at least to its nonrevolutionary manifestations. Its best weapon was that of public criticism and of interpellation. The First Duma had resorted to interpellations in a kind of frenzy, and the Second Duma too had been most eager to embarrass the government. The Third Duma exercised its rights in this domain most moderately,

[40] A. Polivanov, *Iz dnevnikov i vospominanii* (Moscow, 1924), pp. 67, 69, 130; see also Alexander Zvegintsev, "The Duma and Imperial Defense," *Russian Review* (London), I, No. 3 (1912), 49–63.
[41] *Otchety*, April 4, 1908, 1798.
[42] See the foreign policy debate in *ibid.*, March 2, 1911, 3301–3344.

and made the passage of interpellations a rather complicated affair. Once an interpellation was approved, it was certain that a real grievance was at hand. In the first thirty months of its existence the Duma approved only twelve of sixty-seven interpellations.[43] Of the twelve three were answered in only nineteen months (though the government was obligated to give an answer in thirty days), two in fifteen months, and the rest in periods up to nine months. Duma wits warned that, at that rate, future generations would read the government's answers in historical journals.

☩ ☩ ☩

THE most important cause for interpellations was the government's continued disregard for individual liberties. This exasperated not only the revolutionaries and radicals, but even the moderates. During the 1910 debate on the Ministry of Interior budget, the Octobrist spokesman Prince Aleksander Golitsyn charged that "the inviolability of person promised by the October Manifesto appears now simply as a myth."[44] To be sure the days of mass field court martials were now safely gone, and the number of executions declined rapidly.[45] Nevertheless, the police remained arbitrary, and armed by special powers under the "exceptional measures," they raised havoc with political liberties. They exceeded their powers on numberless occasions, and even the tolerant Third Duma finally passed a bill on "the criminal responsibility of civil servants." It provided a humble beginning, for it covered only the lower echelons of officialdom, and provided no compensation for losses caused by administrative error: the Ministry of Finance claimed that the

[43] For purposes of comparison, the British government, in 1903 alone, answered 2,554 questions in Parliament. For the data cited here see L. Nemanov, "Pravo zaprosov v 3-ei Dume," *Pravo*, No. 1 (1910), pp. 14–20. Sergei Levitskii, "Interpellations According to the Russian Constitution of 1906," *Etudes Slaves et Est-Européennes* (Montreal), I (1957), 220–231, is much too optimistic in his conclusions.

[44] *Otchety*, February 2, 1910, 1763.

[45] Between August 1906 and April 1907 more than a thousand persons were executed on grounds of sentences passed by field court martials: see Kucherov, *Courts, Lawyers and Trials*, p. 206. Thereafter, the number declined rapidly; there were 782 executions in 1908, 543 in 1909, 129 in 1910, and 58 in 1911: see S. F., "Repressii," *Ezhegodnik* (1912), p. 517.

government lacked sufficient funds for the purpose. Even this weak measure was rejected by the State Council, which vetoed the measure a second time when it was repassed by the Fourth Duma.[46] Even so, there was a sharp decline in the number of those affected by police measures; the number of political exiles dropped continuously, and drastically.[47] The Duma Left played a conspicuous part in this process by drawing public attention to the government's abuse of civil liberties.

In the process of gathering data for its interpellations the Duma ran into endless government obstacles. Article 40 of the Duma Statute gave it the right to obtain information for legislative purposes. But officials would not appear before Duma committees to testify, the guards would not admit outsiders whom the Duma had invited to submit testimony, inquiries to government departments would not be answered. If the Duma obtained needed information in some roundabout fashion, the government spoke of "illegal methods," and Deputy Minister of the Interior Kryzhanovskii said that "the government will protest against references to documents not submitted to the Duma by the government." "The government," he told a Duma committee, "considers political materials to be its property, and cannot submit them to the Duma committee."[48]

Deputies, too, were treated as a form of government property which was not to be made available to the population except by special permission. Duma deputies' speeches to their constituents, like all meetings, required official permission, which was granted rarely, and reluctantly. The Kadet deputy Kiril Chernosvitov was prevented from addressing his constituency in Vladimir on the grounds that his appearance "might arouse undesirable conse-

[46] The history of the bill is in *Riech'* editorials for November 28, 1911, and March 21, 1914.

[47] In 1909 there had been 22,568 political exiles; the number dropped to 10,972 in 1910, and to 5,682 in 1911; see *Riech'*, September 3, 1909, January 1, 1911, and September 7, 1911.

[48] D. M., "K voprosu o primenenii st.40 nakaza Gosudarstvennoi Dumy," *Pravo*, No. 52 (1911), pp. 2955–2966, and *Riech'*, November 27, 1909. It should be noted that, with the exception of the budget committee, the Duma committees did not print their accounts, and thus much interesting information about the Duma's functioning can be found only in Soviet archives.

quences," and that the Duma's activities were "well-known to everyone from the more objective stenographic accounts." The governor of Viatka forbade a meeting between a deputy and his electors fearing that the police "might not show enough respect" for the nation's representative.[49] But Duma deputies did see their constituents, who expected something of them. Thus, the non-Party peasant deputy Peter Dvorianinov told the Duma during the debates on the Stolypin land law: "Gentlemen, when we leave here after the adjournment you intellectuals will stay in the cities, protected by the police, but we must return to our village, to our neighbors, who will look at us with hatred and say — you are getting a salary but doing nothing."[50] The mail brought the deputies letters from men and women of all walks of life who turned to the Duma for help. In the First and Second Dumas there had been flaming petitions, signed, in some cases, by thousands of irate citizens. Now there were letters about an infinite variety of individual grievances, sometimes petty, but always important to the individual petitioner.[51]

The individual citizen was beginning to learn that he had recourse against the all-powerful government. But he was also beginning to realize that he could not get redress for everything that bothered him, and immediately. In that sense a much-needed sense of patience was being developed, surely an essential ingredient of constitutionalism anywhere. As Sir David Mackenzie Wallace put it in 1912:[52]

No one now imagines, as many imagined in 1906, when the First Duma was opened, that it is possible to cure, in the short space of a few weeks, by the indignant denunciations and untried statesmanship of four or five hundred national representatives, the administrative and political evils from which Russia has been suffering for centuries.

[49] *Vestnik*, January 6, 1908, p. 26, and *Riech'* editorial of August 20, 1909.
[50] Cited in A. Avrekh, "Agrarnyi vopros v 3-ei Dume," *Istoricheskiia Zapiski* (Moscow), LXII (1958), p. 51.
[51] The Paul Miliukov Papers in the Archives of Russian History and Culture at Columbia University contain hundreds of letters to Miliukov as a member of the Third and Fourth Dumas. They come from all over Russia, and concern every subject imaginable. None of them have been published, and they constitute a fascinating subject for research.
[52] "Looking Back over Forty Years," *Russian Review* (London), I, No. 1 (1912), 17.

Had the temper of the popular masses remained patient, particularly the temper of the urban workers and the parties which led them, there would have been a better chance for Russian constitutionalism. As it was, too few were learning to move slowly. The Kadet leader Paul Miliukov, for one, was being "conquered" by this temper. He told a London audience in 1909: [53]

No one will of course expect me to praise the constitutional establishment in Russia. We, representatives of the Opposition, would like the Duma's rights greatly enlarged, the electoral law democratized, and the system of political institutions brought into harmony, to make productive legislative work possible. But so long as Russia has a legislative chamber with the right to control the budget, the Russian Opposition will remain His Majesty's Opposition, and not opposition to His Majesty.

"To make productive legislative work possible," it would have been necessary to curb the State Council, which, during the Third Duma's lifetime, did much to undo its most useful work. Maksim Kovalevskii, an elected member of the upper chamber, recalled that "when both chambers assembled, and the members of the Imperial Council invited those of the Duma to tea, the latter sulked and refused the invitation. In one way or another this boycott has gone on to the present day." The relations between the two chambers could not but have a negative effect on the resulting legislation. "Towards the Duma," Kovalevskii continued, "even as at present elected principally from the landowners, the attitude of the Council is one of unconcealed animosity." The State Council, as we have already noted, defeated the volost zemstvo bill, the bill enlarging the Duma's budget rights, and the bill on criminal responsibility of civil servants. It also defeated a bill improving labor conditions for trade employees, bills extending the zemstvo institutions to Siberia and some Southern provinces, and a bill lowering the tax on sugar. It spoiled the bill on Old Believers, some of the elementary education bills, a university admissions bill, and others. It sometimes kept measures from passing for years, and even defeated legislation favored by the government. It quite often restored

[53] The speech is in *Riech'*, September 10, 1909.

the cuts made in the budget by the Duma. Still, as Kovalevskii pointed out, the record was not altogether negative: [54]

There are also laws which would perhaps hardly have passed without the greatest difficulty such an aristocratic chamber as the English House of Lords. We have equalized the rights of men and women teachers; we have doubled the share of the woman's inheritance in real property and have secured for her equal rights in the inheritance of movable property. We are creating a fairly broad system of insurance for workmen, in which almost the whole of the financial burden lies on the employer.

The results of five years of legislating were modest, but not insignificant. There was progress in several directions, and there was surely no stagnation in the growth of political awareness. The conservatives had reconquered some privileges lost during the revolution, but there was no wholesale retreat. One dangerous product of the Third Duma, however, was the increase in national animosities and chauvinism. Before 1905 this could have been blamed on the government and the ultraconservatives alone. Now the Duma shared in the blame and, in the process, tarnished the name of the Russian legislature. Its bills limiting the rights of Finland were clearly not forced upon it by the government; there was, in fact, a great deal of enthusiasm for the measures in the Third Duma.[55] The Poles were antagonized by the Russification of the Kholm province, and by measures against them in the new Western zemstva. The Jews were offended by discriminatory clauses against them in a variety of bills. The Duma participated in the Russification of Turkestan and of the Caucasus, and passed measures against Ukrainian cultural autonomy. Several Duma deputies made a national reputation by their vociferous and blatant chauvinism. These were poisonous seeds, and, through them, the Duma tribune served negative ends. But it remained an open forum for all points of view, and was used by the Left as vigorously as by the Right.

[54] "The Upper House in Russia," *Russian Review* (London), I, No. 2 (1912), 60–70; see also I. Idin, "Trudy Gosudarstvennogo Soveta," *Ezhegodnik* (1912), pp. 132–147.
[55] For an analysis of the Duma legislation regarding Finland, see John H. Hodgson, "Finland's Position in the Russian Empire, 1905–1910," *Journal of Central European Affairs*, XX (1960), 158–173.

♟ ♟ ♟

THE Fourth Duma, elected for a five-year term in September 1912 seemed, outwardly, to be even more conservative than its predecessor: 51 per cent of the deputies were nobles, the highest percentage in any Duma; the forty-eight deputies who were clergy were entirely too conservative for the good of the Church; the Right was strengthened (it now had 153 deputies), the center weakened (130 deputies), and the Left gained (152 deputies).[56] The moderate Octobrists had been weakened at the expense of the two extremes, though it was only in the artificial situation of Russian politics that the Kadets, or the Progressives, could be called extremists. The country's mood had become more radical, and the government's interference in the elections had only made it worse. Now even the Octobrists, who had been harassed by the government in the elections, joined the opposition. Their motion, passed by the Duma after Premier Kokovtsov's government declaration, made this clear: [57]

Normal legislative activity is possible only as a result of the joint work of the government and the legislative bodies in the direction of the sincere realization of the principles announced by the October Manifesto, and by the establishment of strict legality. The Duma calls upon the government to take this step openly, and decisively.

The government, however, deprived of Stolypin and any real leadership, and beginning to give in to the Tsarina and Rasputin, seemed to elect the very opposite course. The country was doing reasonably well economically, but its political temperature was rising, because the government's course was turning to open reaction. Only "spaghetti" bills were being introduced into the legislature, which was being treated more and more as simply another government department. In the spring of 1913 the ministers, offended by a deputy's remark, engaged in a singular "ministerial strike," refusing to attend meetings until the entire Duma should apologize for its member. The "strike" continued into the autumn

[56] Walsh, "The Composition of the Russian Dumas," p. 115; Miliukov, "The Representative System in Russia," p. 32.
[57] Quoted in *Riech'* editorial of December 15, 1912.

of 1913, and further undermined the reputation of the bureaucracy.[58] Minister of the Interior Nikolai Maklakov was an open reactionary, a member of the Union of the Russian People, and a Great Russian chauvinist. When the budget of his Ministry was being debated, the Duma passed the following resolution, worth quoting in full:[59]

Taking into account: (1) that the Ministry of the Interior, by continuing the use of exceptional measures after order has been restored in the country, arouses in the people general dissatisfaction and a legitimate feeling of revolt against unnecessary restrictions; (2) that a strong authority, necessary in every state, can be really effective only if it is based on law, and that in supporting by its illegal acts the prevalence of arbitrary power and in refusing to introduce into the legislative bodies Bills on the long necessary reforms set forth in the Imperial Manifesto of October 17, 1905, and in other Imperial Edicts, the Ministry prevents the establishment of legal order in Russia, and destroys in the population respect for law and authority, and thus strengthens the feeling of opposition in the country; (3) that in delaying the reform of local self-government, which has been recognized as necessary by the Government itself, and the extension of this reform to all of Russia, the Government hinders the cultural development of the population and the betterment of its economic conditions; and (4) that the administrative authorities, in applying the existing laws with regard to separate nationalities, are disintegrating the population and weakening Russia — the State Duma calls the above-stated facts to the Government's attention, and insists on the immediate realization of extensive reforms.

It was a strong bill of indictment drawn up by men who could hardly be suspected of revolutionary intentions.

Minister Maklakov took up the challenge and, in October 1913, suggested to the Emperor that he

deliver from the Duma tribune a calm, clear, but decisive warning to the effect that the path which the Duma is attempting to take is dangerous, and impermissible . . . If the character of the Duma's work does not change the government will have to ask for Your Majesty's instructions to dissolve this Duma.

[58] For details see *Riech'*, June 20 and November 2, 1913.
[59] Translated in *Russian Review* (London), II, No. 3 (1913), 170.

The Emperor, who had watched his legislature with distrust from the very outset, harbored plans for a new coup d'état. A Duma which persisted in trying to teach him a lesson was to be turned into an advisory body such as the so-called Bulygin Duma of 1905, which had never been summoned. He approved Maklakov's suggestions, and revealed his plans for the Duma's future: "The submission of majority and minority opinions for the Emperor's decision will be a praiseworthy return to the former peaceful course of legislative work, and will be in the Russian spirit." The Emperor's plan was considered by a special cabinet meeting of June 1914 at which, Minister of Justice Ivan Shcheglovitov testified, "we were asked to give our judgment on whether to return to the unrealized situation of August 6, 1905 — namely, whether the State Duma could be changed from a legislative to a consultative institution." [60] The ministers unanimously advised against any changes, and the matter was permitted to drop. Nevertheless, it is highly significant that, on the eve of the war, the Emperor was less of a constitutionalist at heart than in earlier years.

This was clear also from his appointment, in January 1914, of old Goremykin as the replacement for Kokovtsov who, despite his loyalty to the Emperor, was also loyal to the laws. The new Premier was chosen by the Empress because, according to Pares, he "was acceptable to both the sovereigns for his attitude of a butler taking instructions to be communicated to the other servants." [61] He had shown his mettle during the First Duma, and he came back to his old post with the same contempt and disregard for the legislature, and for the new order of things. The government even ceased to respect the deputies' freedom of speech when, in the spring of 1914, it brought suit against deputy Nikolai Chkheidze, of future Soviet fame, for a statement he made from the Duma tribune. The Duma was quick to protect its freedom, and even the Nationalist deputy Demchenko, one of the Duma's reactionaries, objected: "We have seen," he said, "attempts by the government to violate the Duma's

[60] The correspondence between the Emperor and Maklakov is in *Padenie*, Vol. V, pp. 194–196; Shcheglovitov's comments are in *Padenie*, Vol. II, pp. 435–437.
[61] *The Fall of the Russian Monarchy*, p. 157.

rights and even our freedom of speech without which we are quite useless." Such attempts, he added, "explain the dissatisfaction among even the most moderate elements of the population." The Emperor finally ordered the discontinuation of the case only days before the outbreak of World War I.[62]

In the last months before the great holocaust, government and society were again at loggerheads. The regime seemed unable to live with a legislature which had any self-respect, even a legislature elected under a limited suffrage, and hedged with all manner of restrictions. In the strongest motion on record in either the Third or Fourth Duma the legislature voted, in May 1914, the following resolution against the government: [63]

The Ministry of Interior systematically scorns public opinion and ignores the repeated wishes of the legislature. The Duma considers it pointless to express any new wishes in regard to internal policy. The Ministry's activities arouse dissatisfaction among the broad masses who have hitherto been peaceful. Such a situation threatens Russia with untold dangers.

The "untold dangers" were to become explicit only three years later. The war intervened, and temporarily saved the government from the approaching storm. The outburst of patriotism which followed the declaration of war seemed to wipe out the old animosities, at least on the surface. The Duma, so hostile only a few weeks earlier, united behind the government, and promised its enthusiastic support in the war effort. The opposition quieted down, and only the Social Democrats and the Trudoviks refused to join in the patriotic manifestations. They seemed a tiny minority at the time, and no one took them very seriously.

They also refused to participate in the new coalition which now ran the Duma, the Progressive Bloc led by the Kadets, which included all parties except the two extreme wings which had never accepted any constitutional regime as permanent, or satisfactory.[64]

[62] For details see *Riech'*, April 26 and July 12, 1914.
[63] Quoted in *Riech'* editorial of May 4, 1914.
[64] See Thomas Riha, "Miliukov and the Progressive Bloc in 1915: A Study in Last Chance Politics," *Journal of Modern History* (Chicago), XXXII (1960), 16–24.

These two wings, unfortunately, continued to represent the real power in the country. The Right, with its support among the bureaucracy, the army, and the Court, had behind it the organized might of the Russian State which, at least until the first defeats of 1915, was still formidable. The Left had shown its strength in the Revolution of 1905, and continued to display its potential in the strikes of 1912–1914, many of which were political. Its true capacities would only be revealed in the fateful year 1917.

The monarchy, which, that year would demonstrate, was a vital prerequisite for the existence of a constitutional Russia, did everything to discredit itself in the public eye. Instead of cooperating with his nation, which had, unexpectedly, offered its hand to the monarch for the last time, the Emperor drew farther than ever away from Russian realities. Neither the Duma, nor the zemstva, nor the unions of Russian cities, nor the committees of industrial leaders, all of which did essential work on behalf of the war effort, were deemed worthy of trust or support. The bureaucracy, taking its cue from the Emperor, displayed more arrogance than ever, and did its best to stifle public initiative wherever it could. The most moderate Russians began to lose all hope that a real settlement could be reached peacefully, especially as the military failures revealed the regime's weakness and incompetence. When the population stopped supporting a war which seemed increasingly senseless, there appeared only one way out — a change of regimes.

When it occurred, in early 1917, it seemed as if constitutionalism would win in Russia after all. The Tsar and his brother both abdicated without any bloodshed, and the country was governed by a Provisional Government composed of men for whom constitutional democracy was an article of faith. Russia suddenly enjoyed more political freedom than almost any land in the world. Its fate was to be settled by a freely elected Constituent Assembly based on universal suffrage of both sexes. But like the Duma, the Provisional Government had only paper power. The real authority belonged to the Soviet, representing only Socialist opinion, but exercising more and more sway over the nation's destiny. The Dumas had ignored the wishes of the socialists. Now the latter

112

would dismiss all claims of the bourgeoisie. The local government, which had never been given political authority, was now unable to exercise power locally, and the soviets replaced the zemstva in the localities too. A zemstvo leader, Prince George Lvov, was Premier, but he illustrated the limitations which the old regime had placed on the training of political leaders — he was full of good intentions but, in the political arena, completely naïve. Nor could the former Duma deputies, so many of whom were now ministers, be expected to be resolute and experienced, when they had never had anything but the shadow of real authority. Once the monarchy disappeared, the old bureaucracy went with it; it had no more claim on anyone's respect. In Russia political freedom meant political chaos, and the country submitted to the party which promised to re-establish order and went about its business ruthlessly. Order did not require a constitutional structure, and the Constituent Assembly was dismissed without much fear of popular resistance. What the masses wanted oould be granted to them without an elaborate constitutional process, for they had never learned to look to any parliament for real solutions. The First Duma was the only legislature which the masses ever trusted, and it had never done anything for them. Subsequent Dumas, and the zemstva too, had never been willing or able to come to grips with those economic problems that were of utmost concern to the large majority of the population.

♟ ♟ ♟

IT HAS recently been asserted that "there was no chance for a liberal-constitutional Russia whatsoever." [65] This claim is made in a context of both economic and foreign policy developments which have not been examined in this essay. Within that context the claim is not only tenable, but justified. What remains to be said here is something else. Even granted that economics and world politics would not permit Russia to try out constitutionalism long enough to make it viable, we should ask whether the experi-

[65] Theodore H. Von Laue, "The Chances for Liberal Constitutionalism," *Slavic Review*, XXIV (March 1965), 46.

ment had been entirely unsuccessful, and had left no traces in the Russian body politic. The more pessimistic among Russia's moderates had, already before 1914, admitted that Russian constitutionalism had failed. Thus, Guchkov charged at an Octobrist conference in November 1913 that "the attempt made by the Russian public, as represented by our party — the attempt to effect a peaceful, painless transition from the old, condemned system, to a new order — has failed." [66] But in the bitterness of those days Guchkov could not have assessed the progress that had been made in the short time available.

For it must be remembered that Russian constitutionalism had at its disposal a grand total of eleven years (1906–1917). Of these, three years were lost in a debilitating war which made all Russian economic and political problems almost insuperable. The centuries that preceded 1906, and the decades that have passed since 1917, seem to make the short interlude a mirage, an insignificant blot on the huge canvas of Russian history. And yet, one cannot fail to be impressed by some of the accomplishments of that brief era, modest though they may be in contrast to what was wanted. We have, after all, learned to be modest in our hopes for political freedom in Russia, and judged by such standards, the period described in these pages has a good deal to recommend it. For the first (and so far, last) time in Russian history, Russians came close to enjoying certain political freedoms. There was freedom of speech for some Russians, and there was a tribune from which all points of view could be heard. As Miliukov described it: [67]

[66] "Types of Russian Political Oratory. The General Political Situation and the Octobrist Party," speech at the Octobrist Conference on November 21, 1913, *Russian Review* (London), III, No. 1 (1914), 152.

[67] *Russia Today and Tomorrow* (New York: Macmillan, 1922), p. 7. For English translations of some Duma speeches, see Alexander I. Guchkov, "Types of Russian Parliamentary Oratory, Speeches on the Naval and Military Estimate of 1908 by Alexander Guchkov," *Russian Review* (London), II, No. 1 (1913), 111–121; "Speeches on the Address of the First Duma," *ibid.*, No. 2, pp. 165–179; "Mr. Michael Stakhovich on Terrorism," *ibid.*, No. 3, pp. 154–161; and "Speech on the Armed Attacks on Jews by Prince Sergei Urusov," *ibid.*, No. 4, pp. 121–126. See also "Excerpts from the Speech of Markov the Second," in Frank A. Golder, ed., *Documents of Russian History, 1914–1917* (New York, London: Century, 1927), pp. 24–28; "Speeches at the Duma, August 8, 1914," *ibid.*, pp. 32–37; "Miliukov's

Public debates on questions of the budget, legislation, foreign politics, military and naval defense, contributed to lift the veil which until then had kept back the unqualified layman from the sanctuary of government practice. Due to the Duma, political discussion was becoming common property.

Not only the Duma but also the press spoke loudly about matters which bothered many Russians. And when the government wanted to take action against its outspoken critics, it felt increasingly unable to do so — not because it did not have the power, but because, owing to the new habits of thought, it felt unable to use it. This is perhaps best illustrated by a remark made to Kokovtsov by the Emperor in 1912: "I have decided to part with [Aleksandr A.] Makarov. He has let the press get completely out of hand, and has absolutely refused to proclaim a law which would give the government authority to check the excesses in which the newspapers have been indulging." [68] A Minister of the Interior was being dismissed because he could no longer deal with the press in the manner to which the government had been accustomed. His replacement was no more successful.

It would be encouraging to be able to report that some of these gains have not been lost since. This, unfortunately, is quite impossible. The best one can say is that the gains were still understood in the early 1930's, as reported by Philip Mosely: [69]

In those years, which now seem so far away, there was no need to explain to educated Russians . . . the meaning of individual freedom, the right of personal judgment, or the institutions of repre-

Speech in the Duma, November 14, 1916," *ibid.*, pp. 154–166; "Purishkevich' Speech in the Duma, December 2, 1916," *ibid.*, pp. 166–175.

[68] Kokovtsov, *Out of My Past*, p. 326. For more on the Russian press, see Thomas Riha, *"Riech'*: A Portrait of a Russian Newspaper," *Slavic Review*, XXII (1963), 663–682, and Jacob Walkin, "Government Controls Over the Press in Russia, 1905–1914," *Russian Review* (New Haven), XIII (1954), 203–209.

[69] "1930–1932. Some Vignettes of Soviet Life," *Survey* (London), LX (April 1965), 54. Written about a period immediately preceding the great purges when numberless thousands of innocent persons perished for political reasons; it seems proper to recall in this connection that, in 1915, the Ministry of Justice reported that it had arrested, in 1910–1914, a total of 35,353 persons on political charges, of whom 10,006 were released as innocent (*Riech'*, December 27, 1915).

sentative democracy. Whether they rejected them, or cherished them from a hopeless distance, Russians knew what they were, and what they meant. Twenty and thirty years later a visitor to the Soviet Union had to go back to elementary notions of high school civics to explain the nature of free political competition, freedom of association, the role of pressure groups, and all the other institutions and customs the West takes for granted.

THEODORE VON LAUE

Problems of Industrialization

♟ ♟ ♟

IN THE contemporary discussion of the destiny of nations, industrialization is one of the most prominent topics. For the "developing" countries, in particular, it seems to hold the key to the advance that will bring them equality, power, and self-respect in the global community. Furthermore, whatever sense of global community has emerged thus far, whatever hope we have of deepening it by providing for greater equality seems based on technological and industrial progress.

Like the global community itself, the concept of industrialization is of rather recent origin. The word was not used in its present sense during the period with which this volume is concerned (which, however, does not rule out its usefulness in this essay). It made its official debut in Russia at the Plenum of the Central Committee of the Communist Party in early April 1926,[1] a gathering much concerned with the penalties of backwardness. Despite some earlier English references recorded by the *Oxford English Dictionary*,[2] it started its worldwide career as a by-product, no doubt, of what

[1] *KPSS v rezoliutsiakh i resheniakh s'ezdov, konferentsii, i plenumov TsK* (Moscow, 1954), Pt. II, p. 259. Unofficially, however, the term was used long before — for instance, in a report of the Congress of Mineowners in 1915 which called "the Russian people a people of ploughmen only to a small degree touched by the processes of industrialization" (quoted by P. V. Volobuev, *Ekonomicheskaia politika vremennogo pravitel'stva* (Moscow, 1962), p. 28).

[2] *OED*, Vol. 13, Supplement and Bibliography, p. 500.

Edward H. Carr has called "the Soviet impact upon the Western world."[3] By now it has become a universal shorthand for the deliberate forcing of industrial growth in pre-industrial societies, for willfully diverting the course of economic development from its natural — or spontaneous — direction into a preconceived channel, cutting athwart all or most of the existing pathways of custom, habit, or tradition.

Yet, despite our free use of the term *industrialization*, one may doubt whether we understand the concomitant processes of social change, even though they are central to all experiments of fusing the technological accomplishments of Western, and above all, English-speaking civilization with non-Western (or non-English-speaking) civilization. We are all watching these experiments in Japan, India, Ghana, or Venezuela, in all four corners of the world. We have perhaps been watching them for several generations, without knowing it, in Germany, Italy, or France. The longest of these experiments, one might argue, is that of Russia, if we begin with the reign of Peter the Great (some historians begin even earlier). Ever since, the Russian government has been caught in a power race with technologically more advanced countries. There were moments when it seemed as if Russia had caught up; but defeat, famine, or other setbacks always followed upon such delusions of grandeur. Even now, despite totalitarian compulsions (or partly, maybe, because of them), the Soviet regime finds it impossible to match the precipitous pace of industrial progress set up by "the leading capitalist countries." Why has it been such a difficult race for the Russians? Why do most of the contemporary experiments in industrialization seem to falter? Why is the gap between the "developed" and the "developing" countries still widening rather than narrowing?

I venture at the outset a bald hypothesis: The answer lies in the fact that all experiments in industrialization (or even modernization) try to fuse elements that have no natural affinity for one another. The naive assumption among most industrializers has been

[3] *The Soviet Impact on the Western World* (New York: Macmillan, 1947).

that they need but take over the gadgets of Western civilization ready-made and free of all the expenses that have led to their development and graft them, somehow, onto their dearly cherished native traditions. Invariably, the graft does not take, because — apart from the determination or necessity to make it stick — it does not find the nutrient conditions under which it was originally grown. There is, in other words, a consanguinary sustaining framework of social, political, and economic institutions; of education, basic values, ultimate aims; of the country's position in the world; of visible and invisible ingredients — an organic congruence, in short, of the totality of state and society into which technology and industry must fit. If they do not fit and yet are to prosper, the sustaining tissues must be rebuilt around them, artificially, by a prolonged Promethean effort, in a vast if not hopeless undertaking utterly ruinous to native tradition or welfare.[4]

This hypothesis lies at the base of the analysis set forth in the following pages. It emphasizes the complexity and all-inclusiveness of the topic and suggests a compass for the many detailed investigations that must be undertaken not only by historians and economists, but also by sociologists, anthropologists, psychologists, and even psychiatrists. The hypothesis also calls attention to the fact that the study of Russia (as of other even less developed countries[5]), if it is to be fitted into the contexts of American thinking, must proceed from a comprehensive theoretical framework permitting valid comparison; we must devise common denominators for American and

[4] This is not the place, even in a footnote, to argue the unique case of modern Japanese development, except to point out the following assets of Japanese society: (1) the relative external security of Japan, as compared with that of Russia; (2) the smallness and compactness of territory; (3) the persistence of essential forms of social and individual discipline which, by accident, turned out to be highly useful for an imported industrial economy.

[5] Bracketing modern Russia with the underdeveloped countries accentuates the essential inadequacy and injustice of the term. The practice is justified solely by the fact that the standards of Western urban-industrial society have become, for better or worse, the measure of all things throughout the global world; it is a global world to the extent to which it has been Westernized. The unfairness of the term is implicit also in Hegelian and Marxist dialectics. Even Soviet writers, when dealing with Imperial Russia, comply with this usage, as did Lenin in his day. The author would apply the concept of backwardness to Lenin's and Stalin's Russia as well.

Russian development – indeed, for the whole of global modernization. Unfortunately, for the tsarist regime, historical facts even in
the traditional sense are exceedingly scarce, and worse: they are
still at the mercy of ideological conflict and dogma, which makes
true comparison highly difficult. The following discussion, therefore, is merely a thumbnail sketch of an elusive and baffling phenomenon.

♟ ♟ ♟

GIVEN the difficulties of bridging two distinct polities, a
contemporary American might best approach Imperial Russia at
the turn of the century by way of Indianapolis (as a Bostonian goes
west by way of Worcester, Massachusetts). Indianapolis was the
home of an up-and-coming member of the United States Senate,
Albert J. Beveridge, a farm boy who had started to work at the
age of twelve and earned his way through college by winning prizes
at oratorical contests.[6] His command of words made him not only
a distinguished senator but also a well-known writer and biographer
in whose memory the American Historical Association gives an
award to this day. In 1901, two years after his election, Senator
Beveridge crossed the Pacific to the Far East and traveled over
the Siberian railroad, then in the last stages of completion, to St.
Petersburg; he kept his eyes and ears wide open and made notes
for a book that he published after his return, entitled *The Russian
Advance.*[7]

The book begins with the clarion call, "Russia has arrived on
the Pacific." Those were the days, one must remember, of Great
Power competition for the Chinese treaty ports, the Chinese market, and global power in general. John J. Hay was about to proclaim
the Open Door, and Captain Mahan called attention to the importance of seapower and the survival of the fittest in the great race
called history. Senator Beveridge was much impressed by the views
of Captain Mahan; he was one of the first Americans to apply them

[6] See the article on Beveridge by James A. Woodburn in the *Dictionary
of American Biography*, Vol. III, p. 231.
[7] New York, London: Harper, 1904.

120

to Russia. Everywhere during his trip he observed the elemental outward surge of Russian power. After he reached St. Petersburg, he found his estimate confirmed in the words of Pobedonostsev, who told him that Russia was not a country, but a world. As Beveridge commented with characteristic hyperbole: [8]

This was the voice of Russia — Russia that ever waits, Russia that is ever patient, Russia that ever advances, Russia that never hurries, Russia that looks upon other peoples as disorganized communities and dying races, and considers herself the heir of all ages, Russia that believes and feels that she is not a state but the world.

Senator Beveridge was also curious about Russia's economy. A hard-nosed, practical Midwesterner who had no trouble in striking a similar vein among his Russian acquaintances, he talked with all manner of businessmen and officials. Two of his comments are of particular interest here, the first dealing with the "racial slowness" of Russian labor that made it so much less efficient than American labor; obviously, that lethargy had to go if there was to be economic progress: "The customs of centuries which are so deeply embedded in the lives of the people . . . must be replaced by popular practices distinctly and characteristically non-Russian . . . Most important of all, the very spirit of the Slav itself must undergo a transformation . . ."[9] so as to create what Stalin later called "a new man."

The other comment stemmed from Beveridge's observation of the various forms of collectivism in Russian life and government. "The influence of the government is always favorable to every form of communistic industry. Indeed, the Russian state may be said to be at the bottom communistic."[10] And even more emphatically a few pages later: "No student or observer of Russian character with whom this writer ever talked believes that the time will ever come

[8] *Ibid.*, p. 461. The reader will notice the unconscious enlargement of Russian power — Pobedonostsev's characterization of Russia as "*a* world" becomes, in Beveridge's text, an identification of Russia with *the* world. The distortion, alas, has been an almost constant factor in American-Russian relations. Something of that sort takes place, probably, in any people's interpretation of an enigmatic and powerful competitor.

[9] *Ibid.*, pp. 263–264.

[10] *Ibid.*, p. 331.

when the Russian people will proceed upon anything but communistic lines either in their social living or in their industrial efforts." [11] These were prophetic forecasts (Beveridge's middle name, incidentally, was Jeremiah).

This is not the place to inquire how these two observations of the Senator may be reconciled with each other — how the new Russian man of energy and hard work might be fitted into the communistic future of Russia. We shall, rather, return to the starting point of his thought, his preoccupation with global power and the place of the United States in the world. Beveridge, who at a later stage in his career was the author of the slogan, "America first, and not only America first but America only," had drunk deeply, like Theodore Roosevelt or Henry Cabot Lodge, of the doctrines of Captain Mahan. These men took the British Empire for their model. Like the British Empire, the United States was engaged, in their view, in "necessary, irrepressible expansion," as Mahan had phrased it, and this expansion was bound to lead to dangerous but electrifying collisions. "Conflict," to quote Mahan again, "is the condition of all life, natural and spiritual. . . . Time and staying power must be secured for ourselves by that rude and imperfect but not ignoble arbiter, force, which so far has won and still secures the greatest triumph of good . . ." [12]

From the United States of Theodore Roosevelt, John D. Rockefeller, Andrew Carnegie, J. P. Morgan, and the coming Henry Ford, we now turn to Germany, the Germany of the Krupps, the great chemical and electrical firms, and the giant industrial banks. While Senator Beveridge was touring Russia, Chancellor Bülow was claiming for his country a place in the sun. We will not call at the Wilhelmstrasse in Berlin, however, but proceed to a humbler place, the professorial study of Max Weber, a student of economics, history, law, and of the new discipline called sociology. Max Weber, like Mahan and Beveridge, was deeply concerned with the global competition for power. But, living in a country more profoundly rent by social conflict and class war than the United States, he was

[11] *Ibid.*, p. 336.
[12] A. T. Mahan, *The Interest of American Sea Power* (Boston: Little, Brown, 1897), pp. 268 and 245.

THEODORE VON LAUE

more worried about the vigor of common citizenship that sustained a people in the battle for global ascendancy — How could it be created if it did not exist? The British, whom Max Weber also took for his model, had been lucky. For centuries they had been through "the political excitement, the vibrations of world politics which impose on the state great political tasks and put the individual through a continuous political education." [13] The Germans, on the other hand, still had to achieve such education — by a deliberate government policy of creating social unity. "Not happiness or welfare is the objective of our social policy," Max Weber told his students in 1895, "but the social consolidation of our nation . . . in view of the bitter struggles looming ahead" in the world.[14] There was profound trouble brewing for the future, and the morale of the German people had to be prepared.

But there was more at stake than a common loyalty. As a sociologist, Max Weber saw the deepest cause of British greatness in a spiritual force, the Puritan ethic. "The fact that our nation has never passed through the hard school of asceticism in any form," he once confided to a German friend, "is the source of everything that I find hateworthy in my country and in myself." [15] He laid bare, in a celebrated essay, the Calvinist roots of British industry, enterprise, and global power, an inner-directed drive that contrasted strongly with the "racial slowness" of the Russians that Beveridge had noticed.[16]

These digressions on the way to St. Petersburg must suffice to indicate the scope and magnitude of the power competition that had come to prevail at the end of the nineteenth century. The race was to the swift, and it imposed a ruinous strain on every polity in Europe (the Western Hemisphere and the United States will hence-

[13] Weber, *Gesammelte Politische Schriften* (Tübingen: J. C. B. Mohr, 1958), p. 23.
[14] *Ibid.*
[15] W. J. Mommsen, *Max Weber und die deutsche Politik, 1890–1920* (Tübingen: J. C. B. Mohr, 1959), p. 106.
[16] The point here is not to plead for the accuracy or soundness of Max Weber's analysis in his essay on the Protestant ethic and the spirit of capitalism, but — as in the case of A. J. Beveridge's observations — to emphasize the various dimensions of human relations that have to be considered in any inquiry into industrialization.

123

forth be left out of consideration in this context).[17] The traditional European state system was giving way to a yet undefined and unlimited global state system. Bismarck was the last great European statesman deliberately holding fast to the old framework and its checks and balances, yet it was through him that Germany acquired a colonial empire and a taste for a place in the sun. Even before he stepped down in 1890, the competition for global expansion was on, chaotically, through innumerable diplomatic crises and two world wars until at present, the great political vacuums in the non-European world having been filled, a precarious global balance appears to be in the making.

The great political vacuums created at the end of the nineteenth century by the expansion of European technology and communications, and by the weakness of native societies, had to be filled, one might say, in a double sense: first, by laying out new political boundaries (or by the rise of local powers in Asia and Africa) and, second, more subtly and vastly more important, through a new balance of the cultural and spiritual aspirations of the major competitors. In what measure, in other words, was putting the White Man's Burden on nonwhites to be an English show, or a French, German, or Russian show? Which national culture with all its variegated ingredients was to put its imprint on the global future? And what was the gist of such influence — technology, the ideals of government and social justice, a style of life, the innermost structure of man's psychic energy as Max Weber implied, or all of these combined? In short, the competition of the various models of human development, of right and wrong, was as fierce and complex as the clash of armies.

The new spirit of global competition in its political and cultural dimensions was manifested not only in the handful of American and German writers quoted here but also in hundreds more English, French, Italian, even Indian writers. The great variety of these testimonials underscores the fact that we deal with a historic phenomenon transcending individual nations or classes. *All* peoples, *all*

---

[17] This does not imply that the American development was not closely watched in Imperial Russia in these years. Already then it was serving as a model or as a symbol of modernization (however undesirable).

classes were caught in a sudden widening out of the framework of their political existence; *all* were forced to reconsider their place and their ambitions in the world. To be sure, one could ignore, at one's peril, the new challenge to human order or ascribe it to the machinations of capitalists or militarists; but one could not wish it out of existence. Or, conversely, one could fall in with it or even aggravate it, at one's peril, by acts of aggression and expansion. Yet the titanic struggles of the first half of the twentieth century lay beyond the control of any statesman, class, or country; they reached the magnitude not of a self-fulfilling prophecy but of a transcendant objective reality. This point — and it seems to represent the essence of the age of imperialism — can hardly be overstressed in any analysis of recent and contemporary history; it is particularly crucial in the study of twentieth-century Russia.

Now that we have arrived within sight of the tall spires of St. Petersburg, we shall at once proceed to the British Embassy, where, at the time of Beverldge's journey, the reasons for Russian vulnerability in the twentieth-century were succinctly described in March 1901 by the Secretary of the Embassy, Charles Hardinge, one of Britain's most distinguished younger diplomats: [18]

With the dawn of the new century, in spite of much material progress . . . the dark sides of Russian life are only too apparent, among which may be noticed the general material insecurity of the population as a whole, the absolute want of even a low level of education, the excessive gambling and speculative nature of industrial life, the insufficiency and inferiority of the judicial system, the excessive crippling of individual and corporative initiative or enterprise, and the absence of all freedom of the press, which are factors that cannot but influence the general welfare of the country *and leave it heavily handicapped in the sharp competition with other countries* which are all devoting more and more attention to subjects of moral and intellectual improvement, while in Russia these are at present altogether neglected.

Hardinge said, in other words, that Russia was backward and that Russia's backwardness corroded her position as a Great Power.

This is not the place for submitting detailed proof of Russian

[18] Public Records Office, London, Foreign Office Series 65, Vol. 1620. Italics added.

backwardness in the decades before 1914. But a few observations are in order, if only to provide the proper perspective and to counteract a tendency among some Western scholars to discount the adversities facing Russia in her Silver Age. These years, it is sometimes said or implied with a view to the gifted writers and artists of those days, give no evidence of backwardness — as though the arts could uphold state and society in the age of steel and mass politics! These crude foundations of the modern world counted all too little among the Russian intelligentsia — that, indeed, was one of the symptoms of Russian backwardness. There is no reason, however, for Western historians to adopt the same blinders.

Rather than dwell on the material poverty of Russian life, which was obvious to all, I shall deal with the more elusive political infirmities, above all the lack of a sense of citizenship and political community far more critical than in Max Weber's Germany. The peasants, the bulk of the population, were legally and socially segregated from the educated minority; they lived in a state of endemic rebellion. Their kin in the factories labored in similar deep estrangement from the regime and from all educated society. Large segments of the privileged Europeanized minority also were alienated from the regime, among them: *obshchestvo*, the so-called "public" — intolerant, emotional, faultfinding, and profoundly ignorant of the basic problems of government in their country; within *obshchestvo*, the intelligentsia — ill disciplined, divided in itself among rival schools of ideology and under attack by a radical fringe of professional revolutionaries; the liberal landowners — with the constitutional ambitions of the British gentry, but without its standing in the community or its tradition of independent public service. Russian society — even if we disregard the non-Russian nationalities and ethnic groups bitterly at odds with the Great Russian elite — lacked what Miliukov once called in characteristic distortion "the cement of social hypocrisy," by which he meant the natural cohesion and mutual goodwill born of centuries of profitable and spontaneous cooperation.[19] How would autocracy fare in

[19] *Russia and Its Crisis* (Chicago: University of Chicago Press, 1905), p. 15. It is unfortunate that so many Western historians have ignored this

an age when all depended on the willing and well-regulated cooperation between governed and governors, and on the fullest employment of the popular energy for common purposes in peace and war?
How would the Tsar, Nicholas II, with his weak will and shallow
political understanding, react in an age when the population was
becoming politically conscious and claimed its democratic rights
for suffrage and self-determination? Poor Russia, we muse as we
now move from the British Embassy to the Winter Palace — poor
Russia, having to solve the basic problems of mass politics from
scratch during the critical transition from the European to the global
state system, and the problems of rapid industrial development to
boot! [20]

A visitor to Russia in 1901 would soon learn that the most powerful minister of the Tsar was the Minister of Finance, Sergei Witte,
a railroad tycoon drafted into government service by Alexander III.
Needless to say, Senator Beveridge called on him and came away
immensely impressed. As he wrote subsequently, Witte was "the
incarnation of the practical, the personification of the business and
commercial spirit of Russia . . . the first modern, up-to-date
financier and administrator Russia has yet produced . . . the man
who is determined that Russia shall herself manufacture everything
the Russian people need . . . silent, relentless, immovable . . .
no man in America so busy as he . . . the man who 'does things'
in Russia, with an expression of patience and weariness about [his
eyes] which reminds you of what you read about the eyes of Lin-
coln." [21] The Senator was as effusive in his prose as in his praise.

evidence, falling into the same illusions as the run of Russian liberals and
socialists who would not give themselves an honest account of the profound
fissures in the Russian polity.

[20] It is well to remember at this point Max Weber's prediction, written
shortly after the failure of the revolution of 1905: "The traditional autocracy, i.e., the centralized police bureaucracy, has in all human likelihood
no choice but to dig its own grave. There cannot be in its own self-interest
a so-called 'enlightened despotism.' . . . For the sake of its indispensable
prestige it must ally itself with those economic forces which under Russian
conditions are the bearers of 'enlightenment' and decomposition. It is in-
capable of attempting the solution of the great social problems without
injuring itself fatally." (*Gesammelte Politische Schriften*, p. 63.)

[21] *The Russian Advance*, p. 439.

127

Yet in essence, his view was correct: Witte was the first modern financier and administrator in Russia, in some aspects of his work and personality closer perhaps to the later Bolsheviks than to his fellow ministers. In any analysis of Russian industrial development before the Soviets, he is the dominant figure.

⚜ ⚜ ⚜

A SURVEY of the basic problems of Russian industrialization during the time in which Witte was Minister of Finance, 1892–1903,[22] must begin by citing Witte's view of Russia's place in the global world. In 1893, he spoke the language of Beveridge and Mahan:[23]

In possession of the lands between the shores of the Pacific and the heights of the Himalayas Russia [is destined] to dominate not only the affairs of Asia but of Europe as well . . . Standing on the confines of two such different worlds, in close contact with both of them, Russia nonetheless represents a world apart . . . with a mission of cultural enlightenment in the spirit of those principles which have given special character to her own development [i.e., of orthodoxy, autocracy, and nationality].

Subsequently, when the trials of a Russian minister of finance had taught him the limitations of Russian resources, he added a note of caution and even alarm when he addressed the Tsar in 1899:[24]

At present the political strength of the Great Powers which are called to fulfill great historical tasks in the world is created not only by the spiritual valor of their peoples but also by their economic organization. Even the military preparedness of a country is determined . . . by the degree of its industrial development. Russia with her vast multinational population, her complex historical tasks in international relations, and her many-sided interests [the Tsar was reminded] needs perhaps more than any other country a proper economic foundation for her national policy and her culture . . .

[22] For the following pages on Witte, see Theodore H. Von Laue, *Sergei Witte and the Industrialization of Russia* (New York: Columbia University Press, 1963).

[23] *"Za kulisami tsarizma" (Arkhiv Badmaeva)*, ed. V. P. Semennikov (Leningrad, 1925), p. 78.

[24] "Dokladnaia zapiska Vitte Nikolaiu II," *Istorik Marksist*, Nos. 2–3 (1935), pp. 30ff.

Political greatness, in short, called for a proper industrial base. But, alas, "in relation to the needs of the country, and in comparison with foreign countries," so Witte's report concluded, "our industry is still very backward."

These passages, one might argue, reveal the deepest source of the modern Russian drive for industrialization. It was fed, on the one hand, by the familiar imperialist arrogance – Russia was one of those countries called to fulfill great historic tasks in the world – and on the other hand, by the realization that Russia, in her present economic organization at least, was backward. Something had to be done, and quickly, to remedy the discrepancy between ends and means, between ambition and resources. At the end of the nineteenth century, this meant developing modern industries artificially – not waiting for their natural growth but forcing them, through government action, according to some grand design or plan. It is not surprising, therefore, to observe in Witte's economic and financial policy a growing emphasis on long-range economic planning.

The blueprints, to be sure, remained vague enough. In theory Witte made little progress beyond Friedrich List, the German prophet of the nationalist ambition to catch up with the British model, whose book *The National System of Political Economy* had made a lasting impression on him. Like most other promoters of industrialization, List was an optimist: given the advantage of copying the advanced models of technology, there was no reason why those who had fallen behind should not catch up quickly with the help of a proper commercial policy, by which he meant tariff protection. List, however, was a liberal as well as a nationalist: the British model, in his view, combined economic development with political liberty; parliamentary institutions favored economic progress. Witte, by contrast, adhered to the conservative triad of orthodoxy, autocracy, and nationality. He – like many other European conservatives before him – assumed that one could readily graft the instruments of technological power onto any native tradition and thereby strengthen the existing form of government. "Western technology plus Russian autocracy equals Russia's imperial greatness in the world" roughly ran the formula that Witte held out to a Court forever in search of miracles. What he offered, and what all thinking Russia wanted, was rapid modernization without change. What a miserable and tragic fallacy — and one of the most widespread even in the contemporary world!

In practice, however, Witte went considerably beyond List's theories. As a former railroad magnate he conceived a plan of industrial and economic development centered around a vigorous expansion of Russia's railway network. It was he who was primarily responsible for the construction of the Siberian railroad; but the European lines were built up even more assiduously. Large-scale railroad construction could not but encourage the expansion of heavy industry in general. The demand for rails and locomotives called for steel mills, and steel mills for coal and pig iron. All sorts of metallurgical works and machine shops would arise. In turn, they would stimulate the growth of auxiliary industries producing cement, bricks, instruments. Their progress would be recorded also in the stimulation of consumers' industries, and all industrial advance would in turn prod agricultural production. In the end Russia would manufacture everything that her people needed, and the coffers of the State would be filled with increased tax receipts, public health and education more amply endowed, the army modernized, and the mounting government debts paid off. Thus, railroad construction and Russian greatness were linked in one comprehensive vision of economic development.

It is not the purpose of this essay to describe the phenomenal industrial boom of the 1890's, which was Witte's pride. It is more important to turn to the failures, for from them we can learn something about the complex processes of change that were involved. Problems certainly sprang up right and left as Witte tried to carry out his vision.

Extensive railroad construction, obviously, cost money. How was it to be financed, and, more generally, where was the capital for the build-up of industry to come from? Russia, by every count, was a poor country. Traditionally, her resources had been poured into maintaining and expanding the power of the Russian State.

130

There had been no accumulation of native capital in private hands sufficient for capital construction of any major proportion. Therefore, the government virtually had to take over the responsibility for financing railroad construction (and much else besides) as a burden on the budget and, indirectly, on the "paying powers of the population," to use the official phrase. All accounts agree that the tax screws were turned as tightly as possible — too tightly, as even Witte conceded in 1899.[25] The accounts further agree that the heaviest burden fell on the poorest sections of the population, whereas the rich were spared; indeed, their position under the Witte regime was spectacularly rising. But there were good reasons for sparing them: If the government was ever to be relieved of the unwanted responsibility for economic development, there had to be sufficient accumulation of capital in private hands — and in the most competent hands available. Let the businessmen get rich, the argument ran, so that they could take over the job of economic development. Whether, of course, they were capable of doing that job, was another question, as will appear shortly. Anyway, one can imagine the sneers with which the revolutionary elements of the Russian intelligentsia or the agrarian spokesmen received this line of thought.

Besides taxes, Witte had another and more important source of funds for railroad construction and industrial development — foreign loans. They furnished the bulk of the capital investment responsible for the boom of the 'nineties. But foreign loans were hardly an unmixed blessing. In the first place, their supply depended largely on the peace and the goodwill of the world. When the wars and rumors of wars at the end of the 'nineties drove the money from the market, Witte's boom came to an end, with highly adverse consequences. Foreign loans, moreover, channeled, as they were in the case of Russia, through the government were subject to all sorts of political intrigues. Both these aspects took the effective control over Russia's economic advance out of Russian hands: when

[25] "A Secret Memorandum of Sergei Witte on the Industrialization of Imperial Russia," *Journal of Modern History*, XXVI, No. 1 (March 1954), 67.

the money was needed most, it might not be available. This constituted a severe limitation on Russian sovereignty.

Even when foreign loans were available, they created a number of unpalatable problems. For instance, Russia had to pay the interest and carrying charges for her growing foreign indebtedness by earning foreign currency (that is, gold) through her exports. This meant that the government had to force exports, grain and foodstuffs, even at the risk of starving its people — there was no escape from poverty even through the use of foreign loans. The government, furthermore, had constantly to worry about its credit. It had to create a favorable impression abroad, on Western terms, which meant, among other things, that the Tsar could not freely indulge his anti-Semitism. It also meant that the government had to pay high or extortionist commissions to foreign bankers, subsidies to newspapers, and bribes to blackmailers.

In addition, it had to make every effort to build up Russia's gold supplies for the sake of a free and stable convertibility for the ruble — and what a nettle that was! When in 1896 Witte put Russia on the gold standard, he incurred the profound hatred of all agrarian pressure groups. The measure was enacted, indeed, only by an unusual assertion of the autocratic prerogative. Acquiring and preserving a sufficient gold reserve also required curtailment of imports; hence, the continued need for an exorbitant tariff designed to protect Russia's balance of payments rather than her industries. Both the tariff and the gold standard antagonized all those who put agriculture and popular welfare first in their scale of social and political priorities. The "cross of gold" under which the Russian peasantry was said to groan was perhaps an even more potent political slogan in Russia than it was in the United States. But even from a purely economic point of view, the long-range prospects were clouded. After all, what guarantee was there that Russia's productive capacity would rise more rapidly than her foreign debts?

The bitter fact was that the spontaneous multipliers of economic progress which economists take for granted in Western society, did not exist in Russia. Who were the Russian counterparts of the

Krupps and Siemens or Carnegies and Fords? Witte never ceased to deplore the absence of initiative and enterprise among the Russian business community. It was by all accounts a conservative lot, organized in guilds under a segregated legal category of Russian subjects called the *kupechestvo*, traditionally dependent on the government and unused to competition. To be sure, Witte boosted as much as he could their opportunities and their profits, for of all the available social groups in Russia the *kupechestvo* alone was capable of moving Russia forward toward industrialization through private enterprise; the *kupechestvo* and the kulaks were Witte's natural allies. But the alliance suffered from a paradox. In his anxiety to produce results, Witte prodded the business community and at the same time circumscribed its freedom of action by extensive government regulation. Some of this regulation he would gladly have chucked except for the opposition of the Tsar and the Ministry of the Interior. But he remained adamant about the tariff, government regulation of railroads, factory legislation, or above all, the ascendancy of State interest over private profit. Nothing, for instance, alarmed the business community, particularly in Moscow, more than Witte's eagerness to introduce foreign enterprise as an effective multiplier of economic activity. There was, as Beveridge had sensed, a communist ingredient in his policy; the logic of his ambition favored ever more extensive State control. At the same time Witte, like List, realized that there is no more effective guarantee of progress than the untrammeled creativity of free citizens. Thus, he found his task confused by a basic dilemma of forced economic progress.

Education is fundamental among the natural accelerators of economic growth. Here Witte, realizing the penalties of illiteracy and lagging technical training, revealed himself a true revolutionary. He succeeded in taking under his control much of the technical education connected with industrial and commercial development. But with popular education he ran into the deep-seated fear of his fellow ministers. Their hesitation prompted one of his most embittered — and revealing — outbursts. Perhaps education was corrupting the people, he informed Nicholas II in 1899, but even so, it had to be promoted, lest Russia be left behind. "A dark people cannot be perfected. He who does not go forward will, for that very reason, fall back as compared with countries that do move forward." [26] One cannot help noticing the dreadful, almost Stalinist implication: even if the loyalty of the population would be undermined by education, so be it. In the competition of modernization, education was more important than anything else — the inherited form of government, tradition, religion . . .

An even bigger obstacle to the liberation of enterprise in Russia lay in the organization of agriculture. In the economic chain reaction started by railroad construction, agriculture too, it will be remembered, was to be quickened. Food production was to be stimulated, farming skill improved, the price of land to rise, rural surplus population to be absorbed, and the countryside infused with a new sense of opportunity. Capitalist enterprise was to flourish in agriculture as it prospered in industry. Yet as Witte — and his successors to the present — soon discovered, the stimulation of industry does not automatically carry over into agriculture. Although one could find signs of improvement in the 'nineties, the overall conditions of the Russian agricultural population remained stationary or even deteriorated. In part, this was due to factors beyond the government's control, such as the worldwide agricultural depression, the rapid population increase in rural Russia, and, of course, the weather. But it was also due to the organization of Russian agriculture and the attitudes of landowners and peasants. Of the Russian landed nobility, Witte, like Lenin, had the lowest possible opinion; they were parasites on the body politic. As for the peasants, their energies were stifled by the collective organization of the *mir*. Long before Stolypin, therefore, Witte advocated the dissolution of the peasant commune. He also favored complete legal equality of the peasants with the rest of Russian society — a measure accomplished only by the Provisional Government. Needless to say, calling for such drastic recasting of rural Russia was

[26] The letter is reprinted in Witte, *Vospominaniia: Tsarstvovanie Nikolaia II*, 2 vols. (Berlin, 1922), Vol. II, p. 468. This work was also published in Moscow in 1923, in three volumes, with a preface by M. N. Pokrovskii.

a major political move: the very foundations of Russian autocracy were questioned. It was no wonder, then, that the last years of Witte's career as Minister of Finance were devoted more to the reorganization of the countryside than to the promotion of industry. There was, indeed, a chain reaction from railroad construction to agriculture, but not in the manner Witte had originally intended.

Rural Russia influenced the development of industry in still another fashion. Even a little research into the subject leads to the conclusion that workers and peasants were very much akin and of the same mold of mind.[27] Their ideal in regard to politics and economics was self-determination with a strong egalitarian bias. Although working at the factory — in some cases for the second or even third generation — the millhands still considered themselves a part of the village. Even when their ties with the village were severed, their instincts were those of rural rather than of urban Russia. Inevitably, they carried over into the factory the village resentment of the *barin* and the government, and with industrialization more of them came into the factories and towns or cities. There grew up, in other words, a novel type of industrial labor force, hardly a proletariat in the Marxist sense, for the most part sullen, resentful, and like the peasants standing outside urban-industrial and privileged society in Russia at this time. How could this labor force be integrated into the emerging industrial Russia that Witte envisaged and, more generally, into the tsarist regime?

This essay, unfortunately, cannot discuss the social policy of the tsarist government in these years. Let it be merely pointed out that in this field, too, Witte's policies created a major problem. Unlike the peasant problem, however, it did not receive the full attention of his energies. He congratulated Russia's employers (and himself) for the good fortune of having an abundant supply of cheap and docile labor as an asset for rapid industrial growth, and he thereby tacitly accepted the fact that rural poverty was carried over into industry and city. This burdened his policies with yet another politi-

[27] The relevant publications on Russian labor in the Witte period may be found in Von Laue, *Sergei Witte and the Industrialization of Russia*, Bibliography.

cal liability, for the workers viewed the factories as their village kin eyed the landlords' lands.

That indeed was the bane of Witte's program: there was no foreseeable end to the need for regulation. Under Russian conditions a policy of rapid industrial development called for far-reaching rearrangements in the entire social and political household of autocracy. There was an expansionist logic in Witte's work driving him ever further afield. It led from finance to economics, and from economics to agriculture, education, domestic and foreign policy; from relatively simple matters to the most complex; from the Ministry of Finance to the very prerogatives of the Tsar. By 1901, when Beveridge interviewed him, Witte was caught in a welter of political intrigues.

Of all the servants of the Tsar Witte undoubtedly was the most mindful of public opinion. He knew that he needed full public support for his policies. And yet, in his efforts to arouse public support, he had driven himself into a corner. He had greatly raised popular expectations by holding out a promise of prosperity, national self-sufficiency, and political greatness. But he also had to preach the need for austerity and hard work, for French loans and foreign enterprises, for drastic changes in Russian traditions, for retrenchment in foreign policy, for endless toil without palpable rewards. He wanted Russia to catch up, yet he held her back. One can imagine the slashing criticism among the intelligentsia that fed on this contradiction. How was Witte to stand up against the mounting opposition to his policy among landed interests, the intelligentsia, and even the advisors of the Tsar? How was he to face the rising constitutional movement?

Without going into details, it is fair to say that Witte's policies, both by their successes and failures, contributed to the growing political activation of the Russian population that led to the Revolution of 1905. The new mobility created by the railroads, the expanded opportunities for social contact and comparison, the increased intercourse with Western Europe, the Westernized level of expectations, as well as the famines, strikes, high taxes, and after 1899, the depression — all helped to stir up the population as it

136

THEODORE VON LAUE

had never been stirred up before. No doubt, the government's repressive policies (which Witte deplored), its lack of a sense of public relations or of leadership in times of rapid change, and the defeats of the Russo-Japanese War had their share in swelling the revolutionary tide; but the resentment of the strains of rapid industrialization also played a significant part.

Needless to say, these developments came as a great shock to Witte, who was anything but a liberal by conviction. His policy of industrialization, indeed, deepened his devotion to autocracy. The Russian people, he could see, were not ready to accept the necessary sacrifices; they were not convinced by his most cogent arguments. If Russia was to be saved from the perils of backwardness, which remained acute whether or not the people perceived them, autocratic leadership had to be strengthened. For Witte as much as for Pobedonostsev, the idea of constitutional government for Russia was a fraud.[28]

But here Witte was trapped by his second major political problem: the personality of the autocrat. The fact was that Nicholas II feared his Minister of Finance, an administrative empire builder who aspired to control the entire government. Worse, he did not even share Witte's apprehensions about the perils of backwardness. Nicholas II, a narodnik on the throne of Peter the Great, looked backward toward Muscovy rather than forward into the twentieth century; he himself was a period piece among the furniture of Russian backwardness. When after the outbreak of the depression Witte's policy became a liability, he unceremoniously dropped its author. Autocracy as exemplified by Nicholas II obviously was not strong enough to carry a long-range plan of rapid industrial development against the opposition of its uncomprehending subjects; the tsarist regime as it was then constituted could not become the vanguard of modernization.

This probably was the deepest cause of Witte's patent hostility in later years toward Nicholas II. Sometime after the turn of the century, the ardent adherent of autocracy became disillusioned with

[28] This is the chief point in Witte's pamphlet, *Samoderzhavie i zemstvo*, 2nd ed., with an introduction by Peter Struve (Stuttgart, 1903).

137

the autocrat, although there is some evidence that he continued to nourish an ideal of autocratic leadership suited to industrialization. This is how, many years later, the journalist, Emile J. Dillon, a close friend, characterized Witte's goals: [29]

Witte had long the feeling that the social and political molecules of which the Tsardom was composed and which were forever forming and reforming themselves into fleeting shapes, might be attracted and held permanently together by the central force of a grandiose economic transformation and by the interests that it would foster and create, seconded by educational influences properly systematized.

The biographer of Witte, however, is in no position to document in detail Witte's vision of a modernized autocracy. The dominant impression which one carries away from a study of Witte's later years is one of bewilderment: belief in autocracy mingled with a realization that constitutional government was inescapable. This tragic confusion crippled Witte's effectiveness in the Revolution of 1905 and subsequent years; it may account for the vehemence of his memoirs.[30]

The confusion was indeed tragic, for it was in no man's power at the time to overcome it. As this analysis so far has tried to make clear, in Russia the two mighty currents of the age — mass participation in politics and industrialization — ran counter to each other. There could be no spontaneous democratic process of industrialization enabling Russia to overcome the handicaps of backwardness in time for the struggles that Max Weber saw looming ahead. Or, to put the matter differently, there could be no effective industrialization until the problems of mass politics in the vastnesses of the Russian Empire had been solved. And solving these problems was a historic task far beyond the capacity of an imperial nonentity like Nicholas II or even his most brilliant Minister of Finance.

[29] The Eclipse of Russia (New York: Doran, 1918), p. 113. It is difficult to obey the historicist injunction not to view this summary of Witte's intentions in the light of Soviet experience.

[30] For an interpretation of Witte's state of mind in 1904–1906, see Theodore Von Laue, "Count Witte and the Russian Revolution of 1905," *American Slavic and East European Review*, XVII, No. 1 (February 1958), 25–46.

♟ ♟ ♟

HAVING had a look at some of the basic problems of Russian industrialization in the decade before 1905, we now turn to the years that followed. How did Russian industrial development fare at the eve of World War I?

I shall first consider the changes in the basic framework that resulted from the Revolution of 1905. The October Manifesto represented a decided retreat from autocratic tradition; it implied the acceptance of at least a minimum of public support. This was apparent not only in the creation of the legislative Duma, but also in the shift of domestic policy from industrial development to rural reform and the stimulation of agriculture, which was still the livelihood for the great majority of Russians. This shift, prepared by Witte and enforced, in the last analysis, by the agrarian revolts of 1905–1906, laid bare one of the major pivots around which Russian domestic politics in modern times has revolved. There exists, visible to the present day, a close affinity between autocracy (or dictatorship) and industry on the one hand, and popular government and agriculture on the other. The promotion of industry, particularly heavy industry, has always been a strongly antidemocratic pursuit. Russian liberalism and constitutionalism, by contrast, were predominantly agrarian in orientation. The zemstva, one of the sources of liberalism in Russia, had protested from the start against the tariff, the gold standard, or any other favors to the commercial and industrial community. Miliukov's Kadets also looked toward the peasants, who, like much of the liberal intelligentsia, were anticapitalist and anti-industrial in their outlook. And for the further Left, democracy in any form was bound to release the most deepseated anti-industrial habits and instincts in Russian life. But even the most conservative form of representative institutions, the Third and Fourth Dumas, were highly unsatisfactory bodies from the point of view of the representatives of Russian trade and industry.

Thus, by turning its solicitude to agriculture the tsarist regime in its pseudo-constitutional phase assured itself of a measure of popular backing. In the new setting Witte's plans for capitalist agriculture and the encouragement of the kulaks were carried out by Stolypin, perhaps more vehemently than Witte might have done (had he had a free hand), and certainly too impatiently for their ultimate success.[31] Plans were also laid for universal elementary education, another concession along one of the lines of Witte's vision.

By the same token the government's role in industrial development was curtailed and the alarm about falling behind muted. The Ministry of Finance, the economic cockpit in Witte's day, was split into two ministries. Trade and industry were entrusted to a new ministry that never counted for much in the councils of the empire. It possessed, to be sure, an excellent staff of technical experts, but no forceful leadership at the top; to this day nobody bothers to remember the names of the Ministers of Trade and Industry.[32] The Minister of Finance, on the other hand, still retained the overall direction of financial policy and, thus, the keys to industrial development. Yet he found his hands tied by routine priorities: maintaining the gold standard after the crises of the Russo-Japanese War and the Revolution of 1905, preserving the tariff, upholding Russia's credit abroad, negotiating new loans, and balancing the

[31] One of the Provisional Government's concessions to peasant pressure was the repeal of Stolypin's agrarian laws and the abolition of the machinery created to enforce them. See Launcelot A. Owen, *The Russian Peasant Movement, 1906–1917* (London, New York: Russell, 1937, 1963), pp. 185, 210.

[32] The Ministers of Trade and Industry were Dmitrii A. Filosofov (1906–1907), Ivan P. Shipov (1908–1909), Vasilii I. Timiriazev (1909), Sergei I. Timashev (1909–1915), and Prince Vsevolod N. Shakhovskoi (1915–February 1917); the office was vacant during 1907–1908. How low the Ministry of Trade and Industry had fallen in these years may be gathered from the following episode. When in January 1914 the complaints about shortages of fuel and metal reached the Council of Ministers, the Minister of Trade and Industry argued that the condition of Russian industry was sounder than it had been in Witte's day and that he saw no reason, therefore, to force industrial expansion. Thereupon, the Council of Ministers (it is not clear from the official record who acted as its spokesman) replied that obviously the present condition of industry was abnormal, since it could not satisfy the increased demand — only 8 per cent of the present supply of pig iron came from domestic sources — as against 20 per cent in 1910. The Council of Ministers then urged the Minister of Trade and Industry to investigate possible restrictions imposed by the cartels. (M. Ia. Gefter, "K istorii toplivno-metallurgicheskoi 'goloda' v Rossii nakanune pervoi mirovoi voiny," *Istoricheskii arkhiv*, VI (1951), 78–79.

budget. In addition, of course, he had to finance Stolypin's agrarian reforms.

The man who carried out these complex and thankless tasks from 1906 to early 1914, Vladimir Nikolaevich Kokovtsov, was no mean figure, even by comparison with Witte. He was a model bureaucrat, a man of compromise, tact, and honesty at a time when these qualities were as badly needed as firmness. After the assassination of Stolypin he was given the additional and equally thankless task of presiding over the Council of Ministers. If he lacked the sense of mission that had given wings to Witte, he could still boast of considerable accomplishments. He managed to balance the budgets without increases in taxation, a difficult feat after the redemption payments of the peasants had been abolished, and he still increased government expenditures for cultural and other productive purposes, as he claimed, by 143 per cent.[33] He also could point with pride to the growing prosperity of Russian agriculture, which provided the foundation for a "sound and rational development of all the productive forces of the country." He reminisced years later: "On these firm foundations had it not been for the Bolshevik catastrophe, [the progress of Russian industry] would have continued its swift and powerful development in perfect harmony with other manifest developments in the country's economic life and with the parallel growth of public prosperity."[34] In other words, the growth of the market and the rise of industry were proceeding side by side, whereas under Witte industrial development had been artificially pushed far ahead of the needs of the Russian consumers.

The detailed story of Russia's economic development in these years is still to be unravelled by historians.[35] But there can be no doubt that, thanks to a renewed spurt of railroad construction, Russia's heavy industries boomed between 1910 and 1913. The statistics

[33] *Out of My Past: The Memoirs of Count Kokovtsov, Russian Minister of Finance, 1904–1914* (Stanford: Stanford University Press, 1935), p. 462.
[34] *Ibid.*, p. 465.
[35] The best account, despite all manner of distortions, is still P. I. Liashchenko's *Istoriia narodnogo khoziaistva SSSR* (2nd ed.; Moscow, 1950), Vol. II, especially Pt. II, Chs. X–XVIII. A translation by L. M. Herman is available, *History of the National Economy of Russia to the 1917 Revolution* (New York: Macmillan, 1949).

of industrial growth, as they have been computed in recent years, are as impressive as those for the Witte years.[36] Furthermore, in this expansion the share of private initiative through Russian banks and entrepreneurs was greater than before; Witte's tax policies were bearing fruit: native capital was now more abundant, native enterprise more prominent.[37] Whether, however, the expansion of Russia's productive forces was as rational as the national interest demanded or at least as circumstances permitted, or whether it was artificially curtailed by wicked "capitalists" and "monopolists,"[38] as the agrarian critics said at the time and Soviet historians have reiterated since, is a question that calls for further historical investigation.[39] Let the point stand, at any rate, that the industrial advance and the rate of economic development in general was impressive in the years before 1914 and that, thanks to excellent harvests and voluminous exports, the prosperity was fairly widespread. But do these facts justify Kokovtsov's optimistic conclusion that except for the Bolshevik catastrophe, Russia's economic growth would have continued "its swift and powerful development"?

Before coping with that question, it is necessary to look at the one agency in Russia which continued to sound Witte's alarms, the Association of Trade and Industry. This institution served, according to its recent American historian,[40] as the principal representative and defender of large-scale industrial interests before governmental ministries, within the Duma, and in the press, from its foundation in 1906 to its involuntary liquidation in 1917.

[36] Alexander Gerschenkron, "The Rate of Industrial Growth in Russia since 1885," *Journal of Economic History*, Supplement VII, 1947, 144–174.

[37] One must keep in mind, however, that foreign capital still played a predominant role in heavy industry and in the most modern branches of industry anywhere. Furthermore, Russia's foreign indebtedness continued to increase in this period.

[38] The terms *monopoly* and *monopolist* are used very loosely by all anticapitalist writers in Russia and the Soviet Union. In the strict sense of the term no monopolies existed in Russia. In most cases the term is almost synonymous with what in American usage is called "Big Business."

[39] This applies particularly to the much-discussed "hunger" for iron, coal, and oil during 1911–1913. See Liashchenko, *Istoriia narodnogo khoziaistva SSSR*, pp. 226, 239, and Gefter's article (cited in n. 32).

[40] Ruth A. Roosa, "Russian Industrialists Look at the Future," in John S. Curtiss, ed., *Essays in Russian and Soviet History* (New York: Columbia University Press, 1962), p. 198ff.

Echoing Witte, the spokesmen of this organization continually harped on the need for a proper economic and industrial basis for Russia's global greatness. Like other Great Powers, so its spokesmen said, Russia must have her economic center within herself (an ambition, incidentally, which does *not* call for complete autarchy); like them, she must liberate her productive forces to the utmost. There was no dearth of projects, such as using the Magnitogorsk iron deposits, digging the Volga-Don canal, or expanding the irrigation of the Turkestan desert — projects familiar to all students of Soviet economic achievement. Needless to say, such ambition demanded effective central planning with plans of five, ten, or even fifteen years' duration; planning would also overcome the vagaries of the trade cycle. Such comprehensive planning, however, would fail without adequate statistical information. Inevitably this called for greater government action and the creation of a central economic agency: [41]

The government must have an organ that can continually gather and synthesize all the data of current economic life, deriving from this synthesis practical directives for legislation and for the administrative functioning of the various departments of government . . . The creation of such an organ under the soviet of ministers . . . is a measure . . . capable . . . of having an enormous and useful influence on the entire economic life of the country in the sense of giving it greater stability and consciousness, those necessary conditions of economic progress.

This, it is well to remember, was written in 1914, not in 1920 when Gosplan was established.

As one scans the records of the Association, one finds again Witte's emphasis on austerity: production was to have precedence over consumption, with due consideration for entrepreneurial incentives. The emphasis, however, was not on profits but on productivity, of the employer and the employee alike. As a spokesman for the Association stated in 1910 (without acknowledgments, incidentally, to Senator Beveridge, Max Weber, or Karl Marx): "Among us the time is not far distant when work will become the cult it ought

[41] *Ibid.*, p. 210. Notice the term *consciousness*, so familiar from Lenin's writings.

143

to be, when that solid rule that only he who works and produces has the right to consume will become universal property."[42] Let it be noted, however, that it was only work, not the means of production, that was to become universal property. For, needless to say, the Association stood by the rights of the entrepreneur. He was to be heard and respected as never before. The development of a rich, cultured, and powerful Russia, in the opinion of this group, called for an influential business community and for a free hand for it. This implied, in the terms of those days, the freedom to create cartels, syndicates, even monopolies, if that seemed best for Russian industrial development. Cartels and syndicates had, of course, been part of Russian industrial life since the turn of the century, but they were under constant attack by the agrarian spokesmen.[43] In 1908, for instance, the Duma helped to thwart the conversion of the chief cartel in the metal industries (Prodamet) into a full-blown trust, which showed how relatively powerless big industry was.[44] However, large-scale organization was the order of the day in heavy industry, and it seems that the government agencies most concerned were not unresponsive to the desire of the leading industries.

Needless to say, the relations between industrialists and the government were of continuous concern to the Association. From its publication, one senses an expectation of a gradual convergence of interests and an eventual fusion. The logic of its arguments left little choice: since the Association favored ever more detailed planning through organs of the State, it had to integrate its views and its own agencies with those of the government — in a line of development that fitted well into some of Lenin's theses.[45] The ideal

[42] *Ibid.*, p. 206.
[43] The zemstvo of Ekaterinoslav in the industrial south took the lead in antitrust agitation. See Roger Portal, *La Russie industrielle de 1881 à 1927* (Paris: 1927; Centre de Documentation Universitaire, 1956), p. 132.
[44] Liashchenko, *Istoriia narodnogo khoziaistva SSSR*, p. 326; also Portal, *La Russie industrielle*, p. 134. One should add that heavy industry was by no means a solid or united pressure group. It was divided regionally, by size and variety of operations, and by its financial ties and foreign connections.
[45] As pointed out by K. N. Tarnovskii, *Formirovanie gosudarstvenno-monopolisticheskogo kapitalizma v Rossii v gody pervoi mirovoi voiny* (Moscow, 1958), *passim*.

that emerged in the discussions of the industrialists was some sort of corporate state. Because of their agrarian bias, the Duma and the zemstva could hardly appear as suitable parliaments.

But to return to the crucial question, Was the prewar rate of Russian economic and industrial progress rapid enough to overcome Russian backwardness? The Association of Russian Trade and Industry would have answered with a resounding no. It would have strongly protested a recent opinion that "from the point of view of the industrial development of the country war and revolution or the threat thereof may reasonably be seen as extraneous phenomena."[46] Witte and the Russian industrialists knew better: the realities of the political and diplomatic power struggle did not permit separation of economics from politics. They dreaded the political consequences of economic weakness both in domestic and in foreign policy; this was why they turned industrializers. And if further proof was needed for the justification of their impatience, World War I furnished it all too painfully.

There is no need here to recite the Soviet statistics that illustrate Russia's industrial backwardness on the eve of the war.[47] Rather, I shall quote the conservatives or even reactionaries, among whom Witte was usually included in the last years of his life. It is no exaggeration to say that those most intimately concerned with economic and financial policy were most alarmed by the prospects of war. Kokovtsov, whatever his views after the Revolution of 1917, was dismissed from his posts in large part because of his warnings about Russia's economic weakness[48] (which made him automatically appear pro-German in those mixed-up days). Witte, as chairman of

[46] Alexander Gerschenkron, *Economic Backwardness in Historical Perspective* (Cambridge, Mass.: Harvard University Press, 1962), p. 141.

[47] Besides Liashchenko, *Istoriia narodnogo khoziaistva SSSR*, see I. V. Maevskii, *Ekonomika russkoi promyshlennosti v usloviakh pervoi mirovoi voiny* (Moscow, 1957).

[48] See, for instance, Paleologue's report to Doumergue: "The Emperor [Nicholas II] reproached Kokovtsov for subordinating general and foreign policy to the interests of the Treasury" (M. N. Pokrovskii, ed., *Die internationalen Beziehungen im Zeitalter des Imperialismus*, German ed. Otto Hoetzsch (8 vols.; Berlin: R. Hobbing, 1931–1936), Vol. I, Pt. I, p. 242). Kokovtsov, according to his memoirs, does not seem to have been aware of this aspect of his dismissal, although his own account lends substance to it, particularly p. 359.

the Imperial Finance Committee, pleaded that Russia was in worse state, financially and economically, than at the eve of the Russo-Japanese War in 1904.[49] The most compelling testimony, however, came from the clairvoyant memorandum written by P. N. Durnovo, former Minister of the Interior, which called the Tsar's attention to "the insufficiency of our ammunitions . . . the embryonic condition of our industries and the dependence of our defense on foreign industries."[50] A few paragraphs later it predicted that "the technical backwardness of our industries does not create favorable conditions for our adoption of new inventions," to which war usually gives rise. The political forecasts of this amazing document were, of course, even gloomier.

On the issue, then, of Russian industrial backwardness at the eve of World War I, one finds the unusual case of agreement between conservatives and Communists.[51] For the benefit of doubting middle-of-the-roaders, however, the argument calls for a quick sortie into the period of the war itself. I must limit myself to two points. The first is that although after the initial defeats the government and the nongovernmental agencies created by the "public" succeeded in superficially solving the munitions crisis by 1916, they did so only by starving the metal industries of transport and raw materials. Every shell that exploded on the battlefield helped to reduce the production of more shells back home in the munition factories. In other words, the Russian economy could not support both war production and the railways, steel mills, factories, and mines that made war production possible (not to mention the continuing needs of the civilian sector of the economy, particularly of agriculture). The industrial collapse was inevitable and fully foreseen by the end of 1916.[52]

---

[49] Die internationalen Beziehungen, Vol. I, Pt. II, p. 94.

[50] F. A. Golder, Documents of Russian History, 1914–1917 (New York: Century, 1927), pp. 11, 18.

[51] On second thought, the agreement is perhaps not so unusual, since on the subject of economic and industrial progress in Russia in these years, Lenin and the Bolsheviks often drew on the views of the agrarians in order to discredit the tsarist regime. The identity of outlook is perhaps greatest in regard to the influence of foreign capital.

[53] Tarnovskii, Formirovanie gosudarstvenno-monopolisticheskogo kapitalizma v Rossii, particularly Chs. II and IV.

The second point is that, as one might expect, the clamor for rapid industrialization became more intensive. After the great military defeats of the spring and summer of 1915, the gap between resources and political ambition was wider than ever — not only in view of the immediate emergency, but for the long pull as well. Said one spokesman for the Association of Trade and Industry with a touch of prophecy: "Probably not one decade after the conclusion of the present struggle of the nations of Europe the entire civilized world will again live under the threat of a great war." [53] Russia, in this perspective, faced a protracted, almost apocalyptic danger. More than ever she must be able to rely only on her own resources. (We usually do not associate such Stalinist pessimism with Russian capitalists — this is, maybe, why we overlook basic continuities.)

In view of such urgency, the emphasis among many economists and industrialists lay more than ever on rigorous and detailed planning. By 1915 the spokesmen for trade and industry were ready to include in the plan all aspects of Russia's economic life, and even integrate foreign policy into it. In short, if the war taught one lesson to Russian economists, it was that a gradual and balanced economic policy, which Kokovtsov held out as the ideal, was too slow for the overall needs of the country; and there is evidence that the lesson had a wider public appeal than in Witte's day.[54]

The stage was set for the Soviet regime and its most drastic and revolutionary determination to push industrialization at any price whatsoever.

✢ ✢ ✢

IT IS not the purpose of this essay to lead up to a discussion of Stalinist industrialization. I shall, rather, search the evidence here submitted for some fundamentals. This essay has dealt with a pre-

---

[53] Roosa, "Russian Industrialists Look at the Future," p. 214.

[54] When S. N. Prokopovich, Minister of Trade and Industry, remarked at the Moscow State Conference in August 1917 that "the whole nation is interested in the development of industry," he was greeted with "stormy applause" (Robert P. Browder and Alexander F. Kerensky, *The Russian Provisional Government, 1917: Documents* (3 vols.; Stanford: Stanford University Press, 1934), Vol. III, p. 1467).

paratory phase of Russian industrialization, with the build-up, in some circles at least, of a sense of urgency, of a set of concepts and attitudes essential to rapid industrial expansion in an underdeveloped country *that also claimed to be a Great Power.*[55] Moreover, the alternative of letting Russian industry imitate the British model — that is, proceed in harmony with the well-being of agriculture and the expansion of the consumers market and without upsetting too deeply the traditional balance of social, political, and spiritual forces — was ruled out because such a policy did not prepare the country rapidly enough for the crisis of political survival which Witte had predicted and which became a reality in World War I. But Witte's policy of deliberately forcing industrial growth had opened an abyss: there would be no end of turmoil and change, all of it contrary to established tradition and human preference, for all cherished values except the crude political ambition of the Russian State (and its leaders) to ensure Russia's survival as a Great Power. Industrialization, so the foregoing analysis implied, meant revolution, a revolution led by a small minority, a revolution from above and potentially a permanent revolution if full equality as a Great Power was to be achieved. The logic of artificial stimulation of industries was apt to culminate in the continuous creation and re-creation of an artificial society, alien to the spontaneity of the peoples inhabiting the vast Russian Empire.

It is well to outline, for a moment, the tragic arrogance, the hybris, of rapid industrialization by looking back at the place of industrial development in the evolution of modern Britain. In the British case, as in the American, we cannot properly speak of industrialization at all. We cannot find in British or American history a period dominated by a deliberate policy of developing industries. Industries, on the whole, grew up like Topsy. Granted, government often lent a helping hand, but only in a limited sense. The industrial revolution in England followed no blueprint, no preconceived goal. Its very turbulence was the result of the total unexpectedness of all

[55] This clause sets Russia off from all other underdeveloped countries, even Communist China or Japan. None of them have been situated, by geographical accident, so close to the crucible of European power politics in the modern age.

the phenomena that we usually associate with industrialization. Ever since the middle of the eighteenth century, industrial development has been woven into British life and society. It was permeated from the start with British supremacy and insular security; integrated with parliamentary tradition; favored by the lack of firm class barriers and other obstacles to an "open society"; propelled by the habit of self-help and individual initiative; disciplined by the ethics of the most zealous of religious movements; profiting from the wealth accumulated not only by the brutalities of what Marx called "primitive capitalist accumulation" but also by grace, skill, and hard work; taking advantage of both the keenness of competition and the highly developed arts of social cooperation. One could go on for many pages listing all the visible and invisible ingredients that anticipated and produced the British model of industrialization.

What matters here is not the infinite number of ingredients but the fact of their happy congruence. As Francis Bacon put the essence of the argument a long time ago: [56]

It is true that what is settled by custom, though it be not good, yet at least it is fit; and those things which have long gone together, are as it were confederate within themselves; whereas new things piece not so well, but though they help by their utility, yet they trouble by their inconformity. Besides, they are like strangers, more admired and less favored.

By 1914 there were few strangers on the British scene. The revolutionary change from the European to a global state system mentioned at the outset of this essay did not affect the British Empire; it was a global institution from the start. The revolution of mass politics, utterly unsolved in tsarist Russia, had been worked on in England since the seventeenth century; by 1911 it was essentially solved. And finally, in 1900 when Russia had barely started, the industrial revolution had transformed Britain into the foremost urban-industrial nation. British society, despite considerable trouble on the surface, was, as Bacon put it, "confederate within itself." How was Russia to achieve such confederacy of industry with life

[56] *Essays*, "Of Innovation."

149

and tradition, with state and society, and with an appropriate station in the global world?

If we answer *by time* — which, in Bacon's words, "indeed innovateth greatly but quietly, and by degrees scarce to be perceived" — we are wrong, for time, as the foregoing has indicated, was of the utmost essence. Russian industry had to develop on the double, and forced industrialization could never be quiet. Witte had tried to substitute a new framework for all the traditions that stood in his way, and had aroused a great noise. The answer which recent history seems to have given, then, to this question is substitution, noisy substitution.

Economic development in backward countries has sometimes been interpreted as just that: [57]

A series of attempts to find — or to create — substitutes for those factors which in more advanced countries had substantially facilitated economic development . . . Such substitutions are the key to an understanding of the way in which the original disabilities were overcome and a process of sustained industrial growth was started.

This is the view of Professor Gerschenkron, who unfortunately limits his analysis to economic factors only. But why stop there? The lessons of Witte's experience would seem to be that if rapid industrialization was to have any chance in Russia, the process of substitution must be carried over into State and society, and into the deepest motivation of every individual as well. There had to be created confederates, effective leadership, the fluidity or openness of society, a sense of unity and citizenship, a guarantee of common purpose, close ties between the individual and the community, a spiritual commitment of every individual to hard seemingly self-denying work, and a willingness to share the burden of common effort and protection against external danger — to mention but a few key ingredients. The social solidarity that Max Weber had admired among the English had to be introduced into Russia, and the "racial slowness" of Russian labor that Beveridge had observed had to be replaced by American efficiency. Since these sub-

[57] Gerschenkron, *Economic Backwardness*, p. 123.

stitutions were not happening spontaneously, they had to be brought about by compulsion. Rapid industrialization of Russia, in short, required the effective substitution of compulsion for a lacking spontaneity.

This process of substitution places an endless burden upon the government. It has to take over functions that were performed, in the British model, by the plurality of groups, agencies, and voluntary organizations, and by the private citizen thanks to an internalized self-discipline that needed perhaps the Church but not the State for reinforcement. It is clear from recent Russian experience whither this extension of state power was tending: it expanded in inverse proportion as the spontaneous prerequisites of industrial growth were lacking. One might almost formulate the relationship in terms of a law (applicable, to be sure, only to an elite of Great or would-be Great Powers): the more underdeveloped a country, the more lacking in the proper individual and social discipline, the more communistic (in Senator Beveridge's terms) or the more totalitarian (in our own) it was apt to be — up to a limit. For there are limits, as the failure of the "Great Leap Forward" in Communist China would indicate.

But there is an even more effective limit than the elemental, last-ditch resistance of any society to drastic change: the inherent contradiction of the very process of substitution. Compulsion can never take the place of the free creativity of an inner-directed individual. The communistic society which Senator Beveridge predicted for Russia and the new man free of the "racial slowness" of the Slav for whom he called do not piece together, except in permanent inefficiency. Moreover, organized compulsion diverts scarce energies from more directly productive pursuits. In short, there can be no substitute for the inwardly conditioned individual initiative, as John Stuart Mill long ago made clear: [58]

A state which dwarfs its men in order that they may be more docile instruments even for beneficial purposes will find that with small men no great things can be accomplished. . . . The perfection of machinery to which it has sacrificed everything will in the end avail

[58] Essay, "On Liberty."

151

itself nothing, for want of the vital power which, in order that the machine might work more smoothly, it has preferred to banish.

In the suppression of that vital power lies the inherent tragic flaw of all compulsory industrialization: the process of substitution offers no real solution. It cannot fuse the Western ingredients of modern industry with native society even by uprooting native tradition, for the command and the hurry always discourage or blunt spontaneous creativity.

ŧ ŧ ŧ

THIS essay has submitted, in a sketchy and tentative form, a pessimistic theory of industrialization based on the course of modern Russian history. However, given our lack of experience in these matters, it cannot claim to be more accurate than the numerous optimistic theories in the field. It merely suggests that in the present generation nobody can say for sure what the outcome of these experiments in industrialization and compulsory substitution will be. Recent events would seem to give at least a temporary advantage to those observers who, at the time of the greatest apprehension in the United States over Khrushchev's grandiloquent predictions of Soviet economic superiority by 1970 or 1980, maintained that the Soviet economy, taken as a whole, would catch up to the American economy only by the Roman calends. The current slowing down of Soviet economic growth, however, calls not for exultation but for sorrow. The American example needlessly incites Russian ambition and perpetuates both the cause and effect of all Russian efforts to catch up with and overtake the global pacesetter.

We must always remember that in discussing industrialization we deal not primarily with machines, factories, or even a higher standard of living measured statistically, but with the subversion of unprepared societies by alien influences and necessities — with stark tragedy. All of us in the United States are imposing, half willingly, half unawares, our highly imperfect, tentative, and exceedingly complex society upon men and women living by norms and values that are simpler but not necessarily inferior to ours in what they originally set out to accomplish. We have left these native societies, now rendered hopelessly "backward," to cope with our intricate accomplishments through unsuitable and primitive tools. As citizens of the most phenomenally successful and prosperous (yet still mortal) society of this time, it may well turn out in the larger perspectives of global history that we too are guilty of the crimes and atrocities that have been committed in the name of rapid industrialization — in Russia and anywhere else in the world.

ALEXANDER VUCINICH

Politics, Universities, and Science

♟ ♟ ♟

SEVERAL months before Nicholas II ascended the throne, the Ninth Congress of Russian Naturalists and Physicians convened in Moscow to take inventory of the national effort and achievements in science. The 2,170 persons attending the Congress heard the eminent plant physiologist Kliment Timiriazev deliver the keynote address entitled "The Holiday of Russian Science," in which he declared that [science was an intellectual pillar of Russian culture and, together with the great literary works of Pushkin, Gogol, Turgenev, and Tolstoi, a most meaningful expression of the realistic bent of the Russian mind.[1] He placed particular emphasis on the continuous blossoming of Russian scientific thought since the 1860's, the decade in which ideological challenges and social ferment inaugurated a vigorous search for a wider base of scientific wisdom.]

At the beginning of the twentieth century, another Russian scientist asserted that "many extraordinary ideas, and often entire branches of natural science, came as results of the labors of Russian naturalists — a fact which was generally acknowledged."[2] The in-

[1] *Nekotoryia osnovniia zadachi sovremennogo estestvoznaniia* (Moscow, 1895), p. 20.
[2] V. L. Omelianskii, "Razvitie estestvoznaniia v Rossii v poslednuiu chetvert veka," in *Istoriia Rossii v XIX veke* (St. Petersburg: Granat Brothers, n.d.), Vol. IX, p. 143.

tensity, scope, and cultural background of Russian science during the waning decades of the *ancien régime* are the main topic of this paper.

⚜ ⚜ ⚜

THE best way to trace and analyze the development of scientific thought in Russia under the last tsar is to examine the growth of Russian universities, for the main function of these institutions was to serve as centers of scientific investigation, to meet the challenge of rapidly growing needs for scientifically trained personnel, and to blend science and official ideology. They were the social and cultural base of Russian science. In addition, the universities were the most sensitive institutional component of the Russian polity. The critical spirit cultivated in universities extended far beyond the sciences and deep into the mainstream of Russian politics. As institutions of higher learning, they played the leading role in the advancement of science in Russia; as political tribunes they accelerated the downfall of the autocratic system.

When Nicholas II ascended the throne, the universities were governed by the Statute of 1884 and dominated by an uncompromising denial of academic autonomy. The Russian university was never a truer "barometer of social pressure" — to use a phrase of Nikolai Pirogov, the grand old man of Russian medicine — than during the reigns of the last two tsars; yet at no other time was the government so determined to destroy the critical spirit and independence of university life. In inaugurating the Statute of 1884 the government was concerned with its own survival and not with the welfare of the universities.[3]

The government viewed the universities as the prime movers of

[3] For details on various aspects of this statute see V. M. Friche, "Vysshaia shkola v kontse veka," in *Istoriia Rossii v XIX veke*, Vol. IX, pp. 150–153; Omelianskii, "Razvitie estestvoznaniia v Rossii v poslednuiu chetvert veka," pp. 118–119; S. V. Rozhdestvenskii, *Istoricheskii obzor deiatel'nosti Ministerstva narodnogo prosveshcheniia, 1802–1902* (St. Petersburg, 1902), pp. 615–622; M. N. Tikhomirov, ed., *Istoriia Moskovskogo universiteta* (Moscow, 1955), Vol. I, p. 273; B. B. Glinskii, "Universitetskie ustavy (1755–1884 gg.)," *Istoricheskii vestnik*, XXI (1900), 729ff.; I. Miklashevskii, "K voprosu o professorskom gonorare," *Obrazovanie*, XXII (1897), 1–20.

political and social unrest and felt obliged to tame them. It could not follow a straight and simple course of repressive measures because the need for professional personnel with higher education was never before so acute. The country was going through accelerated industrialization, and the growing complexity of international relations and the increased role of power politics forced it to harness modern mechanics, chemistry, and metallurgy for the modernization of the armed forces.

The Statute of 1884 made the subordination of universities to the Ministry of National Education direct and absolute. The rector ceased to be an elected official and a symbol of academic autonomy. The Minister of National Education was authorized to determine the organization of each university, to institute various procedures for controlling the classroom activities of every instructor, and to appoint, promote, and dismiss professors. The work of the elected academic councils was reduced to handling routine curricular matters.[4]

The Statute defined only the general policies affecting the students. The Rules for Students, issued in 1885, deprived the students of any right to form independent associations. No measure was resented more by both professors and students, and none did more damage to the universities than the establishment of special state commissions to conduct examinations in major courses. By controlling the examination, the government hoped to establish full control over the information incorporated by professors into their lectures. To make control easier, professors were required to submit their lectures to appointed agents of the Ministry of National Education for examination and approval. The paradox of the new system was that the examination questions were written before the courses were given, and the lectures were tailored to fit the examinations. The new regulation took the dignity and originality out of teaching. It created an apathetic and demoralized faculty and kept the students away from the classrooms.

Most professors, student organizations, and newspapers inter-

[4] Rozhdestvenskii, *Istoricheskii obzor deiatel'nosti Ministerstva narodnogo prosveshcheniia*, p. 617.

preted the new regulations as a tragic defeat for the universities. Even Konstantin Pobedonostsev, the artificer of official conservatism, expressed disapproval of its uncompromising and cruel attack on the cherished tenets of academic autonomy.[5] A famous chemist expressed the sentiment of the academic community by stating that the Statute of 1884 erased all the great institutional gains made by Russian universities during the preceding fifty years. He said that the frequent changes of statutes disrupted the normal growth of universities and that they often expressed the passing mood of the politicians rather than the long-range needs of the academic community.[6]

The practical effects of the Statute of 1884 were far-reaching. Some professors sought employment in nonacademic professions and some became the first Russian academic emigrants. From 1885 to 1890 the major schools of higher education recorded a decrease in enrollment. In 1887 the government raised the tuition and ordered that no person be allowed to register before he submitted a loyalty affidavit issued by the police. The university became a place of ominous silence. Traditional informal contacts between professors and students were drastically curtailed. Most student organizations survived the crisis by going underground and continuing to work quietly but steadily to alleviate the educational and financial plight of their members.

The silence lasted less than a decade. During the 1890's the country was swept by all kinds of manifestations of a profound social and ideological ferment. Endless polemics between the Marxists and populists in and outside the universities sharpened the ideological conflict and broadened the demand for basic reforms. The enlightened segments of zemstvo leaders sought to overcome the traditional atomism of rural politics by creating representative bodies — the zemstvo congresses — covering larger territorial units.

[5] Sergei I. Witte, *Vospominaniia* (Moscow, 1960), Vol. I, p. 302.

[6] V. V. Markovnikov, "Istoricheskii ocherk khimii v Moskovskom universitete," in *Lomonosovskii sbornik: materialy dlia istorii razvitiia khimii v Rossii* (Moscow, 1901), p. 7. See also Glinskii, "Universitetskie ustavy," pp. 329ff., and A. S., "Organizatsiia srednei shkoly v Rossii v sviazi s usloviiami gosudarstvennoi i obshchestvennoi zhizni," *Obrazovanie*, XII (1903), 105–106.

The succession of congresses of various professional groups — typified by the so-called Pirogov congresses of physicians — demanded basic social reforms, and the proliferating literacy committees disturbed the tranquillity of the countryside by flooding it with literacy courses and popular literature. The trade union movement, tinged with socialist ideals, contributed tangibly to the rapid crystallization of a revolutionary movement in urban centers.

These and similar developments spurred the student associations to mass action in favor of academic and administrative improvements in the university community. Student leaders began to hold national congresses in search of united action. The plight of the students and the university crisis were best depicted by the idealistic philosopher S. N. Trubetskoi in 1897:[7]

During the thirteen years of the new Statute the university has begun to look like a sick person who can maintain a rather unsteady rhythm of work only under external pressure. The university has produced a group of Young Turks in the form of centralized student organizations. These Young Turks have indeed organized their own university, with its own leadership, its own activities, and its own science — a free and reckless university with its own peculiar, but sufficiently solid, organization that follows completely anti-academic principles.

At the end of the century mob disobedience became a daily occurrence, and the government, in a state of panic, could turn only to more repression and threats. In 1899 it decided to induct all students participating in disorders into military service. During the next three years more than a thousand students were expelled from the universities. It took the general revolutionary conditions of 1905 to force the government to void the Statute of 1884: the Provisional Regulations of August 27, 1905, re-established academic autonomy and tacitly recognized the right of students to organize independent associations. The academic community re-

[7] *Sobranie sochinenii* (Moscow, 1907), Vol. I, p. 263. For a similar statement by the historian Paul Vinogradov, see Paul N. Ignatiev *et al.*, *Russian Schools and Universities in the World War* (New Haven, Conn.: Yale University Press, 1929), pp. 136–137. For a general picture, see A. A. Kizevetter, *Na rubezhe dvukh stoletii: Vospominaniia 1881–1914* (Prague, 1929), pp. 211ff.

ceived the Provisional Regulations with great enthusiasm. Kliment Timiriazev interpreted the changes as an official recognition of the full citizenship of the students and of the inseparability of science from society.[8] As the new rector of Moscow University, S. N. Trubetskoi, stated, "The victory for academic autonomy for which we waited such a long time means not only a moral victory for the university, but also a triumph for Russian society."[9] However, in the larger society, caught in an insurrection of revolutionary proportions, the university reform went virtually unnoticed. The conservative circles close to the government argued that the autonomy of university life could not survive for long because the Russian academic world — both professors and students — had not reached the stage of maturity essential for a sound use of freedom.

By 1907 peace and order were restored in the country, the Provisional Regulations were an academic reality, and the principles of autonomy became an integral part of the university. This was a period of relative tranquillity in the institutions of higher education. Stimulating philosophical and sociological debates in circles of various ideological orientations became much more common than the shouting of slogans and mob actions. The students took their course work more seriously, and the professors felt a relief from protracted tension and disruptions in the normal flow of academic life. The universities quickly reasserted themselves as the guiding lights of Russian scholarship.

Peace was restored, but the political crisis was not eliminated. As the university was settling down and was well on the way to a full resumption of its many functions, it became a target of vicious attacks by ultranationalist organizations, one of which was the Union of the Russian People. The Minister of National Education then embarked on a policy of gradual retreats from the liberal commitments to the university. In the autumn of 1908, he announced that the autonomy granted to the institutions of higher education should be interpreted only as a privilege extended to university councils to

[8] *Nauka i demokratiia* (Moscow, 1963), pp. 41–44.
[9] *Sobranie sochinenii*, p. 140.

159

elect rectors and prorectors and as a right of the faculty to participate in regulating the curricular and instruction plans.

The smoldering fire in the universities was gradually rekindled; in the late autumn of 1910, Moscow University, the country's largest institution of higher education, burst into a conflagration of revolutionary scope. The initial explosion occurred on November 8, 1910, following a student meeting in commemoration of the death of Leo Tolstoi. The students paid homage to the great novelist, but they also used the opportunity to condemn the ominous threats to the legal rights of academic councils and student organizations. The rebellious mood of the convocation led to intensified government threats and police surveillance of student activities. The students responded by calling new protest meetings in rapid succession and by disregarding established constraints and university administrators' appeals.

The university began to crumble under the mounting pressure of student disorders and government reprisals. By the time the storm subsided in February 1911, the rector and his two chief assistants had been dismissed, and 130 professors — about one third of the entire faculty — had resigned in protest. Many leading scholars, including the famous physicist P. N. Lebedev, found themselves not only without employment but also without access to laboratories.[10] Another period of promise and excitement in Russian universities came to an end.

When peace was restored in the ravaged university, L. A. Kasso, Minister of National Education — the man largely responsible for the conflagration — claimed that it would take a long time before the university healed its wounds. Russian universities, he said, did not need a new statute but a gradual cure for their chronic ills. After existing for more than a century and a half, Moscow University found itself with over a hundred vacant teaching positions and faced the grim task of replenishing its staff. Kasso expressed the fear of the government rather than the weakness of Russian universities when he worked out a preposterous plan for the establishment of

[10] Timiriazev, *Nauka i democratiia*, pp. 67ff.; P. P. Lazarev, *Ocherki po istorii russkoi nauki* (Moscow, 1950), p. 220.

special "seminars" at the universities of Berlin, Heidelberg, and Paris for the training of future Russian professors.[11] World War I froze the liberal plans of P. N. Ignatiev, Kasso's successor as Minister of National Education, to reform the universities. It brought academic life to a standstill.

⚵ ⚵ ⚵

HOW did the Russian universities fare in their dedication to the advancement of science in the face of mounting political crisis, irreconcilable ideological conflict, and repressive educational legislation? Science is a mode of inquiry and a world view. As a mode of inquiry it is pre-eminently a part of secular culture; as a world view it profoundly affects sacred culture. In post-reform Russia, it enriched secular culture by contributing to the growth of industrial technology, agricultural production, public health service, and military power. It also challenged sacred culture — the system of values intolerant of change and sustaining the autocratic system. Both the ideologists and the foes of the autocratic system adopted the view that the values of autocracy and the ethos of science were incompatible. The philosopher Nicholas Berdiaev stated laconically but meaningfully that "we have always equated the scientific spirit with progressive politics and social radicalism." [12]

The authorities were afraid not of science but of the scientific spirit — of the probing and ever-challenging mind trained to be in constant search of truth. Most Ministers of National Education made crude efforts to purge science of the scientific spirit — and in the process they hurt both. However, their ideological warfare, reinforced by repressive legislative measures, did not threaten the very existence of scientific thought; these merely slowed its development. The compounded ideological and political difficulties did not prevent scientists in the universities from making measurable progress, which was a result of the beneficial influence of several historically significant developments. By the end of the nineteenth century, the

[11] N. Speranskii, *Krizis russkoi shkoly* (Moscow, 1914), pp. 128–129.
[12] Berdiaev *et al., Vekhi: Sbornik statei o russkoi intelligentsii* (4th ed.; Moscow, 1909), p. 11.

universities were not only modern educational institutions but also vital centers of scientific investigation. As I noted earlier, when taking an inventory of his country's scientific achievements during the nineteenth century, V. L. Omelianskii observed that Russian scholarship contributed to every branch of natural science and that "many extraordinary ideas, and often entire branches of natural science, came as results of the labors of Russian naturalists." [13] K. A. Timiriazev, noted the fulfillment of Lomonosov's prophecy that Russia will produce its own Platos and Newtons and claimed that in some areas the Russian scientists not only caught up with the work of their Western European peers but surpassed it.[14] At the turn of the century, Russian scientists had two things in common: an almost romantic faith in science as a vital index of Russia's cultural advancement, and a very realistic awareness of the growing role of universities as the centers of scientific investigation.

The forces that helped the universities surmount the oppressive measures of the government and other unfavorable conditions came from many sides and in many forms. Some came from the impetus generated by young industry, and others from the cultural needs of a society caught in the irreversible process of modernization. Some had their source in the growing private support for scholarship, and others in increased government funds for laboratories and institutes. The growing membership of learned societies, the stimulating waves of new scientific developments in the West, and the spontaneous response of professors to the inner momentum of science — all these combined to assure the university and university science of tangible progress.

What the government took away by oppressive legislation, it gave back by its readiness — not always wholehearted — to help universities modernize instruction and expand scientific work. The government provided funds for the development of auxiliary educational and research facilities in the universities as part of the plan to keep students so busy with their studies that little time was left for undesirable extracurricular activities. The official policy to ex-

[13] "Razvitie estestvoznaniia v Rossii v poslednuiu chetvert veka," p. 143.

[14] *Nasushchnyia zadachi*, p. 6. See also V. Modestov, "Russkaia nauka v posledniia dvadtsat piatilet," *Russkaia mysl'*, XI, No. 5 (1890), 91.

162

pand the universities' control over the students did not alleviate the constant threat of mass disorders, but it did exercise a beneficial influence on the growth and modernization of institutionalized research facilities. After 1906 the emphasis in the university shifted from general courses to specialized studies in clusters of related subjects in which the lectures were supplemented by practicums of various types. Modern laboratories emerged in all universities. Whereas the preceding generation witnessed an accelerated transformation of specialized natural history collections into working laboratories, the present generation saw the growth of more advanced laboratories into research institutes — the clusters of related laboratories and scientific workshops. For example, the Physical Institute of Moscow University, founded at the end of the nineteenth century, consisted of four distinct research units, including the laboratory in which Peter N. Lebedev made his famous measurement of the pressure of light.[15]

Enlarged and modernized laboratories — still meager by Western standards — helped established scholars embark on more complex and challenging research problems and provided a sound apprenticeship for the increasing ranks of young scientists. The liveliest and most influential of the new scientific workshops were I. P. Pavlov's physiological laboratory, N. E. Zhukovskii's aerodynamic laboratories, and P. N. Lebedev's physical laboratory. The laboratories became the real nurseries of scientific thought, in which the formal academic atmosphere was fraught with the informal comradeship of science circles. It was in the laboratories that dedicated scholars found a refuge in times of political crisis, and that young professors and advanced students learned to appreciate the limitless potential of science and its growing social value.

Eager to keep as many young men as possible away from the universities but not from higher education in general, the government paid much attention to the development of professional schools of university rank. It was interested not only in meeting the modern economic and military needs of the country but also in making the

---

[15] For the results of this measurement see Peter Lebedev, "An Experimental Investigation of the Pressure of Light," *Smithsonian Institution: Annual Report, 1902* (Washington, 1903), pp. 177–178.

specialized schools the institutional core of higher education. Speaking in defense of the universities, V. I. Vernadskii stated bluntly that "without the universities the Russian society could not develop the much needed respect for pure knowledge." [16] He added that the universities had a deeper tradition in academic freedom and autonomy than most other schools and that their pivotal position in the system of higher education should be consolidated and improved. He emphasized theoretical exploration as the primary function of universities, and the freedom of inquiry as the basic condition for successful scientific inquiry; the government stressed technological application of scientific knowledge and a drastic limitation of academic autonomy. The German educational system provided most of the models for new Russian schools and for the reorganization of the old ones. In 1914 Russia had sixty-seven schools of higher education with a total of approximately ninety thousand students. This number included the country's ten universities with a little more than one third of the total enrollment.

Many higher professional schools had no research facilities and were engaged exclusively in training specialists in various technical fields, including medicine. Others were specialized educational institutions that were reorganized to meet both the standards of new education and the growing challenge of research, even though they attached primary importance to teaching. Most prominent among these institutions were various military, agricultural, and engineering schools, each of which published a scholarly journal in the field of its emphasis and also studies of general theoretical significance. The *Bulletin* of the Naval Academy had the honor of publishing the first Russian translation of Newton's *Principia mathematica*, a triumphant event in the history of Russian science.

Most elaborate and promising were the new institutes in which scientific training and research were given equal emphasis. The best representatives of this group were the Electrotechnical Institute and the Polytechnical Institute, both founded in St. Petersburg in the late 1890's, as well as the polytechnical — and technological — in-

[16] "Vysshaia shkola v Rossii," *Ezhegodnik gazety 'Rech' na 1914 godu* (Petrograd, 1914), p. 311.

stitutes founded in Kiev, Warsaw, and Tomsk at approximately the same time. These schools brought science closer to the growing needs of the country, expedited the flow of technological knowledge from abroad, and added modern facilities for research in highly specialized problems. They enriched the science curriculum, added supplementary research facilities and new periodical publications, and made it possible for the universities to concentrate on research of theoretical significance. None of these institutes, however, emerged as a great scientific center comparable with L'Ecole Polytechnique in Paris or with the leading German Technische Hochschulen.

The growing appeal of the universities, as manifested most clearly in the rapidly increasing enrollment, more than counterbalanced the repressive actions of the government. The university appealed both to the careerists who sought a better station in life for themselves and to the idealists who sought a better way of life for Russian society. After the enactment of the Statute of 1884, the enrollment in the universities decreased from 12,939 (in 1885) to 12,495 (in 1890), but then it started a constant upward trend until 1909, when it reached 38,600. During the thirty-year period 1885–1915 the university enrollment tripled. It is important to note that throughout this period a comparatively large number of Russian students attended the leading Western European universities. According to one estimate, in 1912 there were from 7,000 to 8,000 Russian students in Western Europe.[17] Most of these students were kept away from Russian universities on political, national, or religious grounds. Official anti-Semitism was the main reason for the comparatively large enrollment of Russian Jews in Western universities.

Despite the discriminatory policies, the social base of the university enrollment was broadened. As the old estate barriers grew weaker, the lower groups turned to the university as the safest path to a more dignified existence. Whereas in the mid-1860's close to

[17] *Ibid.*, pp. 324–325. According to official German statistics, in 1912–1913 there were 4,658 Russian students in German universities alone. See Botho Brachmann, *Russische Sozialdemokraten in Berlin, mit Berücksichtigung der Studentenbewegung in Preussen und Sachsen* (Berlin: Akademie, 1962), p. 103.

70 per cent of students came from the nobility and other highly placed groups, by 1915 the percentage was reduced to 35.[18]

During the turbulent decades of ideological crisis and political repression, the growth of universities as scientific centers owed much to the work, diversity, and momentum of learned societies formally affiliated with institutions of higher education. These societies depended much more on the enterprising spirit, dedication, and gregariousness of professors and on private donations than on government subsidies. For this reason, most of them became strategic cultural bridges between the universities and the society.

Three types of learned associations operated within the institutional framework of the universities: the old natural history societies, which were functionally and organizationally undifferentiated; the modern general science societies divided into departments, each with a great deal of operational autonomy; and the specialized societies.

The Moscow Society of Naturalists typified the old-fashioned undifferentiated naturalist association in which the encyclopedic scientific interest was matched by irrevocable commitment to "empirical science." Through regular exchanges of publications with numerous foreign learned associations, it possessed one of the major Russian libraries in the natural sciences and assured scholars of access to the newest works in their fields. Since most of its own publications were in foreign languages, mostly German, the Society was popular among foreign scholars accustomed to keeping abreast with scientific developments in Russia. It was not a research organization but a science club, where scholars met in an atmosphere unburdened by formalities to hear and criticize one another. It sponsored research by giving financial aid to scholars engaged in botanical, zoological, and geological fieldwork.

The St. Petersburg Society of Natural Scientists was the most advanced of modern differentiated learned societies organized in every university. Unlike the old naturalist societies, it was divided into specialized departments each with its own membership, tradi-

[18] For details on the social class origin of St. Petersburg and Khar'kov university students during the 1890's, see Miklashevskii, "K voprosu o professorskom gonorare," pp. 14–15.

tion, and interests. Among its most active and productive associates were many members of the St. Petersburg Academy of Sciences. It also benefited from close cooperation with such national learned societies as the Russian Geographical Society, the Russian Mineralogical Society, and the Free Economic Society. Some of the most important papers of the leading Russian mineralogists, crystallographers, physiologists, botanists, and microbiologists were published in the *Proceedings* of the Society. The Society helped organize several complex scientific expeditions to various parts of Russia and was the prime mover in the establishment of a biological station on the White Sea which was engaged in the study of marine life and served as a training laboratory for graduate students and young scientists in the anatomy, embryology, and taxonomy of sea fauna.[19]

No other learned group surpassed the St. Petersburg Society of Natural Scientists in the ambitious endeavor normally labeled "the popularization of science." It organized many natural history excursions led by experts in botany, physical geography, geology, soil science, and agriculture, and membership was open to all interested citizens regardless of their academic qualifications. It conducted an intensive and successful campaign among zemstvo authorities for the establishment of local museums and schools. Private citizens interested in science as an avocation were included in some of its research coordinating committees whose success depended on the organic unity of scientific inquiry and civic spirit. Not the least important contribution of the Society to the popularization of science was its extensive participation in the congresses of Russian naturalists and physicians.

The third category of learned associations affiliated with the universities were specialized societies, typified by the Moscow Mathematical Society and the Russian Physical and Chemical Society at St. Petersburg University.[20] These two societies were truly national

[19] *Otchet deiatel'nosti S.-Peterburgskogo Obshchestva estestvoispytatelei za pervoe dvadtsatipiatiletie ego sushchestvovanii: 1868–1893* (St. Petersburg, 1893), pp. 14–17.

[20] Other leading societies of this type were the Khar'kov Mathematical Society, founded in 1879, the St. Petersburg Mathematical Society, founded in 1890, and the Kazan Physical and Mathematical Society, founded in 1890.

and representative of the highest developments of Russian science. They had no interest in the popularization of scientific knowledge and were dedicated to the widening of the theoretical and methodological horizons of modern science. Their membership included only persons with higher academic degrees and proved scholarly acumen. All papers published by the journals of these societies were in Russian, a novel practice which in a way helped democratize the pursuit of exact sciences and develop distinct national traditions in several sciences, particularly mathematics. The pressure for the use of Russian as the language of science came primarily from scholars of middle-class origin who, unlike their aristocratic colleagues, had not benefited from private tutoring in foreign languages in their childhood. The St. Petersburg Academy of Sciences continued to publish most papers in foreign languages, and most of the leading Russian mathematicians, physicists, and chemists published translations of their important papers in the major Western European journals.

Medical societies of every description added a vital dimension to the intellectual life of each university. In 1911, Moscow University alone had seven such societies, most of them founded during the last decade of the nineteenth century.[21] Most societies published annual symposia in their respective fields, producing unusually rich and representative literature in many branches of medicine. Through these societies the newest scientific ideas reached the medical community with remarkable speed; at the same time, the feedback of practical experience gave new and resourceful challenges to university experts, clinics, and laboratories. Some societies were equally concerned with the ties between medicine and the natural sciences and with the flow of modern medical ideas to practicing physicians. Some paid more attention to the multiple social problems of medicine. None produced startling scientific ideas, and none attracted the attention of Western scholars. But jointly they played an exciting and beneficial role in the growth and diffusion of modern medical knowledge in Russia.

[21] *Otchet o sostoianii i deistviiakh Imperatorskogo Moskovskogo universiteta za 1911 god* (Moscow, 1912), pp. 168–186.

During the reign of Nicholas II, the universities received tangible help from private endowments. Private funds helped maintain a relatively high ratio of students receiving financial grants by offsetting the reduction of government aid. They helped university libraries meet the challenge of the rapidly increasing publication of books in Russia and abroad. In 1911, for example, 80 per cent of the new acquisitions of the library of St. Petersburg University were purchases from private funds. Bequests of entire personal libraries, often the cherished treasures of leading aristocratic and commercial families, were a common phenomenon.[22] Although some learned societies received government assistance, most of them — particularly the naturalist societies — depended primarily on private donations. Many laboratories were also the beneficiaries of private endowments. Moscow University's modern clinics at Devich'e Pole owed their existence to the combined financial aid of the government, municipal authorities, and private donors.[23]

In 1909, the Kh. S. Ledentsov Society for the Advancement of the Exact Sciences and Their Practical Application, a completely new kind of learned society, appeared on the Russian academic scene: it was sustained completely by one private donor.[24] Anchored to Moscow University and the Moscow Higher Technical School, it gave research grants to deserving scholars, maintained extensive exchange of scientific periodical literature with many Western institutions, sponsored many "commissions of experts" in search of scientific projects worthy of financial support, and embarked on an intensive program of exploration in industrial applications of scientific knowledge. Whereas the naturalist societies sponsored scientific work in which professionals met with dedicated amateurs and in which "science" covered the widest possible area of inquiry ranging from the mere cataloguing of observed natural phenomena

[22] N. A. Bulgakov, *Otchet o sostoianii i deiatel'nosti Imperatorskogo S.-Peterburgskogo universiteta za 1911 god* (St. Petersburg, 1912), pp. 51–68.
[23] V. V. Kovanov *et al.*, eds., *Ocherki po istorii I. Moskovskogo ordena Lenina Meditsinskogo instituta imeni I. M. Sechenova* (Moscow, 1959), p. 32.
[24] S. A. Fedorov, "Pamiati Khristofora Semenovicha Ledentsova," *Vremennik Obshchestva sodeistvii uspekham opytnykh nauk i ikh prakticheskikh primenenii imeni Kh. S. Ledentsova*, No. 1 (1911), p. 42.

and collecting museum specimens to the most modern theoretical involvement, the Ledentsov Society had room only for scholars of proved talent and promise.

The temporary closing of Moscow University in 1911 opened a new phase in the history of the Ledentsov Society. It acted quickly and resolutely to help professors who, by resigning from their university posts, lost access to laboratory facilities and were unable to continue research. The plight of Peter Lebedev became a rallying point for forces searching for a new and healthier institutional base for Russian science. He turned down the invitations of Svante Arrhenius to join the research staff of the Nobel Institute in Stockholm and of several of his colleagues to move to St. Petersburg and work in the Office of Weights and Measures, the institution which Mendeleev joined after his resignation from St. Petersburg University. The great physicist — whose laboratory was considered second only to Pavlov's as an internationally recognized center of modern scientific inquiry in Russia — received direct or indirect help from three private institutions: Shaniavskii University provided the space for a temporary laboratory, the Moscow Society for the Physical Institute assumed the task of soliciting private support for a new research center, and the Ledentsov Society advanced sufficient funds to build a modern institute of physics.

The disturbing effects of student unrest and government retaliation since the late 1890's gave birth to the idea of a private sector in higher education, complementing the government sector. There was a strong feeling in some quarters that in private schools, subject to their own administrative regulations, the rate and intensity of student unrest would be drastically reduced. The advocates of private universities also argued that the demand for higher education and scientific research was growing so fast that it could not be met satisfactorily by government resources and institutions alone. Lebedev pointed out that the chronic turmoil in the universities disrupted continuity in scientific research, without which Russia could not build a scientific tradition; he pleaded for the establishment of privately endowed research institutes free of teaching duties.[25]

[25] Peter Lebedev, *Sobranie sochinenii* (Moscow, 1963), p. 357.

The misfortunes of Moscow University showed that the country was in need of a leading learned association independent of government funds and supervision. The organizers of the Moscow Society of the Physical Institute did not hide the fact that they were interested in founding a private academy of sciences, a united forum of "national research institutes." However, the government's negative attitude toward a private domain in education and research, the organizational and financial difficulties engendered by World War I, and the unrealistic assessment of the institutional strength of Russian science by interested scholars combined to prevent the establishment of a private academy.

The Moscow Society of the Physical Institute failed in its aspiration to become a private center of national effort in science, but it was eminently successful in collecting sufficient funds to establish the Physical Institute in Moscow, an elaborate and highly functional system of laboratories and libraries in which a surprisingly large number of young physicists began their careers in research. It opened its doors in 1917. In 1918 the Soviet authorities nationalized it and made it a model for modern and complex workshops in many fields of scientific endeavor.

The universities and other schools of higher education were not the only institutions dedicated to the advancement and diffusion of scientific knowledge. The national learned societies — such as the Russian Geographical Society, the Russian Mineralogical Society, and the Russian Astronomical Society — sponsored collective research projects, interdisciplinary fieldwork, extensive publication activities, and popularization of science as a system of knowledge, a mode of inquiry, and an attitude. They were particularly dedicated to bringing science closer to the current needs of society. These societies were guided by professors and were in a sense a popular extension of the universities.

The St. Petersburg Academy of Sciences, a scientific institution with a longer history than any existing Russian university or learned society, occupied the pre-eminent position in the scientific family. Its membership was made up of the most accomplished scholars — in most cases, distinguished university professors. Although the

Academy had its own laboratories, museums, and libraries, and was engaged in extensive publication activity, it was essentially an exhibit of the best that university scholarship could offer.

At the turn of the century, the Russian scholars achieved numerical supremacy in the Academy, and for the first time the Academy became a truly national institution. Although earlier the strength of this institution depended on unpredictable luck in attracting foreign scholars to Russia, now it depended on the predictable choice of native scientists of widely acknowledged achievement or promise. For the first time, the work of the Academy became a true reflection of the accomplishments and resourcefulness of Russian university science. This, however, did not mean that full harmony prevailed in the relations between the Academy and the universities. Since the Academy represented an aristocratic principle in the organization of the house of science, it was resented by most scholars who by their status and aspirations favored the essentially equalitarian organization of university scholarship.

♟ ♟ ♟

THE Russian universities entered the twentieth century with increased academic depth and a broadened range of scientific interests. Their growing responsiveness to the economic and cultural needs of the country made them true national institutions. The contributions of university professors to the advancement of science came from many lines of endeavor. There were scholars who added more refinement and substance to strong national traditions in individual sciences. Thanks to the mathematical contributions of A. A. Markov and A. M. Liapunov to the probabilistic study of random variables and to the general theory of stochastic processes, the St. Petersburg "school of mathematics" was enriched and consolidated and acquired international reputation.[26]

[26] In the maze of Western literature on the modern elaboration of the mathematical legacy of Markov and Liapunov, the following two works are most comprehensive: Albert T. Bharucha-Reid, *Elements of the Theory of Markov Processes and Their Applications* (New York: McGraw-Hill, 1960), and Wolfgang Hahn, *Theory and Application of Liapunov's Direct*

Several scholars produced challenging taxonomic work. V. V. Dokuchaev and his disciples arrived at a general classification of the types of soil, V. I. Vernadskii classified the elements of the periodic table in terms of their geochemical role in the formation of the earth's crust, and E. S. Fedorov established the existence of two hundred and thirty types of basic geometrical designs of crystals. Fedorov's contributions became a mathematical basis of modern crystallography; according to Felix Klein, he postulated a more complete structural theory in crystallography than any of his predecessors.[27]

Several leading Russian scholars were among the pioneers in the research areas where two or more established disciplines meet. Dokuchaev is a founder of soil science and Mikhail Tsvet is the inventor of chromatography. N. E. Zhukovskii is one of the leading pioneers in aerodynamics and K. E. Tsiolkovskii in rocket dynamics and the theory of interplanetary flight. An intensive study of tobacco mosaic in 1892 led D. I. Ivanovskii to discover the first ultramicroscopic, filterable virus and to show that there are forms of life that are smaller than bacteria. S. N. Vinogradskii discovered nitrifying bacteria in soil and showed the way in which they obtain energy from the oxidation of ammonia and use it to assimilate carbon dioxide. He helped build a rich national tradition in soil science — a discipline treating soil as a complex and dynamic physical, chemical, and biological phenomenon held in balance by mineral salts and humus.[28] According to the American microbiologist Selman A. Waksman, "the name of Vinogradskii has assumed a permanent place in bacteriology through the profound influence of his investigations upon the subsequent development of many important branches of this science."[29] S. Korzhinskii added substantially to the new theory of mutations in biological evolution by adducing a great

Method, trans. from the German by S. H. Leknigk (Englewood Cliffs, N.J.: Prentice-Hall, 1963).

[27] *Vorlesungen über die Entwicklung der Mathematik im 19. Jahrhundert* (Berlin, 1926), Vol. I, p. 344.

[28] Thomas D. Brock, ed. & trans., *Milestones in Microbiology* (Englewood Cliffs, N.J.: Prentice-Hall, 1961), pp. 231–233.

[29] *Sergei N. Winogradsky: His Life and Work* (New Brunswick, N.J.: Rutgers University Press, 1953), p. vii.

many examples of the modifications of species as a result of saltatory, rather than gradual, transformation. In 1901 Peter Lebedev made the first successful measurement of pressure exerted on bodies by light giving experimental proof to Maxwell's theory of radiation pressure, an important idea of modern astrophysics.[30]

There were many other Russian scientists with varied interests and achievements. At the bottom were the old-fashioned empiricists, weak in theory but rich in dedication to the cause of science. At the top were three giants, each unique in his personality and philosophical outlook, but all equally great contributors to modern science.

Dmitrii Mendeleev entered the epoch of Nicholas II as a world-renowned scientist. In 1869 his periodic law of chemical elements was only a hypothesis; by the end of the 1880's it was a verified scientific fact — the keystone in the atomistic theory of the nineteenth century. The periodic law recognizes the diversity and the unity of chemical elements as complementary scientific ideas. The diversity of elements rests on their unique chemical qualities making them immutable and genetically unrelated. The unity of elements is shown by the established fact that each occupies a definite place in an overall natural pattern based on ascending atomic weights and periodic recurrence of similar characteristics. Modern science has been unkind to Mendeleev's notion of the immutability of the chemical characteristics of elements, but it has firmly upheld his idea of the unity of nature. The law of the periodic recurrence of similar qualities of chemical elements is a cornerstone of modern science.

The great diversity of Mendeleev's scientific interests, which covered the entire gamut from metrology to economics, prevented him from forming a special school of followers in chemistry. But his discovery of a structural principle in the natural arrangement of chemical elements influenced many other Russian scientists to search for similar principles in other categories of natural phenomena. Structuralism is an outstanding feature of modern Russian scientific tradition.

No Russian scientist equalled the depth of Mendeleev's investiga-

[30] Max von Laue, *History of Physics*, trans. from the German by R. Oesper (New York: Academic Press, 1950), p. 89.

tions in the social usefulness of science. From the early 1880's, he spoke and wrote extensively on the scientific foundations of industrialization, industrial organization, and industrial economy in Russia. He approached the problem of expanding industry primarily from the vantage point of a scientist, particularly a chemist, but his comments on the economic and sociological correlates of industrialization are equally perceptive and challenging. Using the growing efficiency of industrial technology as the key index of cultural progress, he fought the Slavophile and populist ideologies, which were dedicated to the preservation of Russia as a predominantly agricultural country. According to one of his biographers, he was a *philosopher* in chemistry, physics and other branches of natural science . . . and a *natural scientist* in philosophy, political economy and sociology.[31]

Ilya Mechnikov is also a product of the great cultural upsurge of the 1860's. He and Alexander Kovalevskii belonged to the small group of truly dedicated scholars whose studies of the embryonic growth of numerous marine invertebrates placed the weight of comparative embryology behind Darwin's theory of evolution. After two decades of intensive research in embryology, Mechnikov was attracted to comparative physiology. A study in intracellular digestion among starfish and holothurians set the stage for the formulation of a biological theory of the defensive functions of mesodermal cells — named phagocytes by Mechnikov. By logical steps, and tedious observation, he moved in a continuous sweep from the embryology of the minute marine fauna to human pathology. What appeared at the beginning as a detached academic pursuit without foreseeable practical prospects ended as a cornerstone of modern medicine.

Mechnikov contributed to modern immunology a scientific explanation of organisms' built-in defensive systems against the damaging effects of inflammations caused by destructive cells. He found a natural bridge between Pasteur's disease-carrying bacteria and Virchow's protective white corpuscles. Little wonder, then, that

[31] L. A. Chugaev, *Dmitrii Ivanovich Mendeleev: Zhizn' i deiatel'nost'* (Leningrad, 1924), p. 16.

ALEXANDER VUCINICH

he became one of the most eloquent modern defenders of scientific optimism. At the end of the 1880's he became the director of the Pasteur Institute and in 1908 he received a Nobel Prize.

Ivan Pavlov, the first Russian scholar to receive a Nobel Prize, was the chief protagonist in the very rich and unusually dynamic Russian tradition in physiology. Pavlov's remarkable experimental methods, his pioneering research and discoveries in the physiology of digestive systems and the psychophysiology of conditioned reflexes, and his philosophy of science are closely interrelated and form one of the brightest pages in the annals of Russian science. Pavlov's scientific ideas were the results of a confluence of several rich research currents in Russian physiology. In his youth he was strongly influenced by Ivan Sechenov, "the father of Russian physiology," who dedicated his life to experimental studies of the physiological foundations of psychic phenomena and who introduced "reflex" as the key concept for the understanding of the psychological make-up of man and beast. But he was equally influenced by the Nihilist Dmitrii Pisarev, who, though not a scientist, was an eloquent champion of the natural sciences as the only source of cultural progress. Since the 1860's, physiology appealed to the Russian intelligentsia, who read into its theories a broader sociological significance. Chernyshevskii and Dobroliubov, the critics of autocratic ideology, wrote popular articles about its basic contributions and underlying philosophy. The typical representative of the intelligentsia was inclined to think that an understanding of the higher nervous activity of man was imperative for the discovery of sound guidelines to a more efficient political community.

Pavlovian physiology is dominated by three key principles: the unity of the organism, the dynamic interaction of the organism with the environment, and the limitless power of the experimental method. Structuralism, environmentalism, and objectivism — each freed from sharp edges and explicit categorization — were the guiding lines of Pavlov's scientific orientation. Pavlov made his great scientific contributions not by embarking upon previously unopened paths of inquiry but by bringing the Russian physiological tradition to a culminating point. The work of such great contemporaries as Vvedenskii, Bekhterev, and Ukhtomskii added rich substance and experimental versatility to what became known as the Pavlovian tradition in Russian physiology. The overpowering influence of Pavlov's theories on the development of psychology in Russia — and in the Soviet Union — has been a reason for the exceedingly slow development of the branches of psychology not directly related to neurophysiology.

Underlying the diversity of the scientific interests of Mendeleev, Mechnikov, and Pavlov was a pronounced similarity in the philosophical point of view which they shared with many other Russian scientists. Their philosophy of science was a blend of Comtean positivism and Newtonian mechanistic absolutism. They agreed with Comte that science, as the clearest and most powerful expression of rationality, is the quintessence of modern culture. They fully accepted the idea of a universe governed by strict causality and reducible to simple principles and universal laws. Their thinking was unaffected by the current philosophical crisis which saw the emergence of new critical thought related to relativistic views in science.

They also shared a common philosophy of history. The progress of history was to them the history of the human mind, and the history of the human mind was a general and predictable accumulation of positive knowledge and objective methods of inquiry.

Their social philosophy had two cornerstones: the belief in social evolution, rather than social revolution, and the idea of the full unity of science and morality. They believed that the progress of science was at the same time progress toward higher moral standards. They were firmly convinced about the growing role of positive knowledge as a source of social welfare, intellectual freedom, and true feelings of human dignity and equality. They agreed with Marcellin Berthelot, the French chemist and statesman, that science develops intellect, destroys obsolete institutions, and engenders a feeling of solidarity and justice of global proportions.

[Leo Tolstoi charged that Russia suffered more than any other European country from "the superstitious belief" that the pursuit and knowledge of experimental sciences could satisfy "all the spiritual demands of humanity."[32] Mechnikov was much closer to the sentiments of his colleagues when he asserted that experimental science is much more than laboratory experiments and that true scientists combine supreme intellectual endeavor with a profound dedication to humanity. Tolstoi's criticism was applicable to Nihilism and its views on science as a panacea for all human ills and as the sole expression of humanity; it was prompted by a misconception of the philosophy and aspirations of modern scientists. Vladimir Vernadskii expressed the sentiments of his colleagues when he combined the intellectual grandeur of modern science with an uncompromising attack on scientism — the philosophy underrating the nonscientific sources of wisdom. One cannot appreciate the power of modern science, according to him, before he understands and acknowledges its intrinsic limitations and its symbiotic relationship with religious, moral, philosophical, technical, and aesthetic modes of inquiry.

Vernadskii recognized the great contributions of Nihilism to the development of rationalist thought and science in modern Russia, but he was equally careful to emphasize that most scientists, influenced by the writings of the Nihilists of the 1860's to select the pursuit of science as a vocation, gradually abandoned Nihilist scientism and learned to live with a more modest view of science as a part of modern culture.[33] According to him, "It is difficult to say at the present time which is larger: the field occupied by science in the areas previously dominated by religion and philosophy, or the field acquired by religion and philosophy thanks to the growth of the scientific world view."[34]

[32] *The Works* (New York: Crowell, 1899), Vol. XII, p. 513.
[33] *Ocherki i rechi* (Petrograd, 1922), Vol. II, p. 49.
[34] *Ibid.*, p. 29.

The Cultural Renaissance

♟ ♟ ♟

IN SPEAKING of Russian literature of the first decade and a half of the present century, it has become usual to refer to the Silver Age. I do not know who was the first to use this appellation, on whom the blame for launching it falls, but it came to be used even by some leading representatives of that very literature – for example, by the late Sergei Makovskii, the founder and editor of that important and excellent periodical, *Apollon*,[1] and even by the last great poet of that age, Anna Akhmatova (1889–1966).

I regard this usage as very unfortunate and never tire of pointing this out when I deal with this period of Russian literature in my lectures and writing. I greatly prefer the designation of the late Prince Dmitry Svyatopolk-Mirsky (D. S. Mirsky), who also belonged himself to this period – namely, "the Second Golden Age of Russian Poetry."[2] This description certainly fits the poetry of

[1] One of Makovskii's books about this period is even entitled *Na Parnase Serebrianogo Veka* (*On the Parnassus of the Silver Age*), München, 1962.

[2] Mirsky wrote: "Apart from everything else, in spite of their limitations and mannerism, the Symbolists combined great talent with conscious craftsmanship, and this makes their place so big in Russian literary history. One may dislike their style, but one cannot fail to recognize that they revived Russian poetry from a hopeless state of prostration and that their age was a second golden age of verse inferior only to the first golden age of Russian poetry – the age of Pushkin." (*Contemporary Russian Literature, 1881–1925*, ed. Francis J. Whitfield (London: Routledge, 1926), p. 183; or, *A History of Russian Literature*, ed. Francis J. Whitfield (rev. ed.; New

this period: between the first Golden Age, the age of Pushkin, for which this term is generally accepted, and the beginning of the new century, there were some remarkable individual poets (Tiutchev, Fet, Nekrasov), but there was no such all-round florescence of poetry, no such poetic *épanouissement*, as was to be witnessed in the first decade of this century.[3] One modern Russian literary scholar and critic, Boris Eichenbaum, used the poetic revival at the beginning of the twentieth century in support and illustration of his theory of cyclical development of Russian literature: the Golden Age of Russian poetry gave way to the great age of the Russian novel, and the latter, after a short interval, was followed by a period during which poetry once more came to the fore. The cycle repeated itself after approximately a hundred years.

It is true that at the beginning of this new age in Russian literature the terms *decadence* and *decadentism* (*dekadentstvo*) were frequently applied to the new trends in literature and arts by their detractors, and sometimes accepted by their practitioners; that they are still in common use among Soviet literary scholars and critics; and that some independent Western scholars of modern Russian literature also cling to them when they wish to draw a distinction (a rather arbitrary one) between those whom they designate as "Decadents" (*dekadenty*) and those whom they describe as "Symbolists." But although it is true that there were, in the literature of those days, certain elements and aspects that could be characterized as "decadent," it is quite wrong to use that term as a general description of the period. And though "the Second Golden Age" can be quite legitimately applied to the poetry of this period, for an overall description of it I should prefer such a term as *Renaissance*. It was indeed a Russian cultural renaissance, encompassing all the areas of cultural and spiritual life — arts, letters, philosophy,

York: Knopf, 1959), p. 432. A newly revised edition of *A History of Russian Literature* was published in 1968 (London: Routledge).)

[3] It is also significant that of the three just-named great poets, who came in between, the first two were neglected and largely unrecognized by their contemporaries, and had to be "resurrected" later by the Modernists or by their immediate precursors, such as Vladimir Soloviev, and Nekrasov's fame and popularity rested during his lifetime not on what was best and genuine in his poetry but on its sociopolitical message.

180

religious, social, and political thought; a period of great richness, variety, and vitality.[4]

The beginnings of Russian Modernism in arts and letters are to be sought in the last decade of the nineteenth century. Both Russian and foreign influences were at work in shaping it and determining its course.

As early as 1890, Konstantin Leontiev (1831–1891), a remarkable Russian thinker, who has more than once been described as a Russian Nietzsche and whom some regard — with much less justification, I think — as a precursor of Fascism, wrote a controversial but stimulating essay on Tolstoi and his novels.[5] In this essay he announced the demise of the dominant "realist" school in Russian literature. He saw that school as something "quite intolerable in some respects." One of its great weaknesses appeared to him to be its harping on minute, "superfluous" details, whether they be physical or psychological. He referred to them as "flyspecks" and said that by way of natural reaction one could prefer almost anything, so long as it was different, to this prevalent brand of Russian imaginative literature. He named such disparate works as Byron's *Childe Harold* and Zhukovskii's "Undine," the Lives of Saints and Voltaire's philosophical *contes*, Tiutchev's metaphysical poetry and Barbier's fiery revolutionary iambs, Victor Hugo and Goethe,

[4] The term "Golden Age" was also used without hesitation, in speaking of this period, by a critic who in many ways stood much closer than the Modernists to the nineteenth-century intelligentsia, R. V. Ivanov-Razumnik. He used it in an article signed "Ippolit Udushiev" (a personage mentioned in Griboedov's *Gore ot uma — Woe from Wit*) in the collection of essays *Sovremennaia literatura* (*Contemporary Literature*) (Leningrad, 1925), p. 161. For Ivanov-Razumnik, when he wrote, the Second Golden Age was already over, and the Silver Age, the period of decline, had begun. In general, this pseudonymous article of his is full of interesting thoughts and observations.

[5] This essay, the posthumous separate edition (1911) of which has been out of print for many years, has been reprinted in this country: *Analiz, stil' i veianie. O romanakh gr. L. N. Tolstogo* (*Analysis, Style, and Atmosphere. On the Novels of Count L. N. Tolstoi*), with an essay on Leontiev by Vasilii Rozanov and an introductory piece by Donald Fanger, Brown University Slavic Reprint No. 3 (Providence, R.I.: Brown University Press, 1965). This edition contains a short chapter at the beginning which was cut out from the original publication in *Russkii Vestnik* and was not reproduced in the 1911 edition. It was first published in *Grazhdanin*, Nos. 157 and 158 (1890), and then incorporated in the article in Vol. VIII of Leontiev's *Collected Works* (Moscow, 1912).

Calderón and Corneille, George Sand's novels and Monk Parfentii's *Legends of the Holy Land,* Horace's *Odes* and *Manon Lescaut,* the tragedies of Sophocles and the childlike epic songs of the modern Greeks.[6] Leontiev traced the initial stage of this Russian "flyspeck" realism to Gogol; the Tolstoi of his major novels appeared to Leontiev to be the writer in whom it had reached its point of saturation and who himself, with the instinct of a genius, had turned away from it and sought new paths: hence, the new manner, intentionally bare and simple, of his stories for the people. It speaks very much for Leontiev's fairness and objectivity that, guided by purely artistic considerations, he saw those stories of Tolstoi's as superior to his great novels, as a step forward and away from the dead tradition: for the religious and moral views underlying those stories, Leontiev could not possibly have any use.

Leontiev himself, although he also wrote some fiction, can hardly be regarded as a forerunner of any specific trends in modern Russian literature (and because of his "reactionary" world view, his influence during his lifetime was confined to a narrow circle of admirers), but he did, in that essay, voice a reaction against "realism" that was soon to spread far and wide. What is more, underlying his general outlook, his religious, sociopolitical, and historiosophic ideas, there was a deeply rooted aestheticism, which was to become an important factor in shaping the destinies of modern Russian literature. His aristocratic individualism (as expressed, for instance, in his bitingly satirical essay "The Average European as the Means and End of Universal Progress") was also a sign of the times. There is no doubt that in his essay on Tolstoi he had put his finger on the focal point of the malaise which was then affecting Russian literature. Barely a decade had passed since it had completed a great and brilliant cycle of its development – the great age of the Russian novel, of social and psychological realism, had come to an end with the deaths of Dostoevsky (1881) and of Turgenev (1883), and the voluntary (albeit partial and temporary) withdrawal of Tolstoi from art (1879–1880).

Two years after Leontiev's essay (published in 1891), the general

[6] *Ibid.,* p. 14.

crisis in Russian literature was analyzed in greater detail, and in the light of incipient Modernism, by Dmitrii Merezhkovskii (1865–1941) in his celebrated essay "On the Causes of Decline and the New Trends in Russian Literature" (1893). This essay is sometimes treated as the manifesto of Russian Symbolism. I think this is a mistake.[7] Nevertheless, its symptomatic significance was very great. Merezhkovskii became one of the harbingers of that revolt which was soon to spread to a large section of the Russian intelligentsia. It was, above all, a revolt against the traditional values of that intelligentsia as they had become crystallized in the 1860's and 1870's — against its positivism, against its tendency to subordinate art to social utility and to look upon it as a service to the people. It was a revolt in the name of individualism, of aestheticism, of religious and philosophical idealism. Speaking of the first timid manifestations of these new trends in the last decade of the nineteenth century, D. S. Mirsky wrote: "Aestheticism substituted beauty for duty, and individualism emancipated the individual from all social obligations. The two tendencies, which went hand in hand, proved a great civilizing force and changed the whole face of Russian civilization between 1900 and 1910, bringing about the great renascence of Russian art and poetry, which marked that decade."[8]

What was the background of that renaissance and what were its sources? The last decade of the nineteenth century in Russia — that century which the great modern Russian poet Alexander Blok described in his autobiographical and at the same time historical poem "Vozmezdie" (Retribution) as "iron and truly cruel" — is usually thought of as a period of dark reaction, of stagnation, of *bezvremen'e* (an untranslatable Russian word, particularly associated with the futility and frustration which permeate Chekhov's stories and plays). But this is only one side of the medal. It was at the same time a period of political, social, and artistic fermentation; of great and heated controversies. It saw the birth of

[7] See a discussion of this point in Ralph E. Matlaw, "The Manifesto of Russian Symbolism," *The Slavic and East European Journal*, XV, No. 3 (Fall 1957), 177–191.

[8] *Contemporary Russian Literature*, pp. 151–152.

the organized Social Democratic Party in Russia, the violent debate on a number of general and topical issues between the Marxists and the populists (*narodniki*). The end of the century saw also the first defections from the Marxist camp into that of Neo-Kantian idealism, personified in such men as Peter Struve, Nicholas Berdiaev, Sergei Bulgakov, and Simon Frank, all of whom were later to play a prominent part in the Russian religious-philosophical revival and all of whom also ended their lives as exiles under the Soviet regime.

A significant landmark in this movement was the publication of a collection of essays, entitled *Problems of Idealism* (1902), to which all the above-named men contributed. A much later but direct sequel of it was the volume *Vekhi* (*Landmarks*, or *Signposts*, 1909) in which seven authors (described by some of their critics as "the seven penitents") joined forces and subjected to a critical analysis some of the fundamental premises of the outlook of the Russian intelligentsia: its positivism and utilitarianism, as well as its political maximalism. Simon Frank, for example, opposed the ideal of "religious humanism" to the "nihilistic moralism" of the traditional intelligentsia mentality, and Bulgakov, who was then already a practicing Orthodox believer and was later to be ordained as a priest, contrasted the Christian saintly ideal with the ideal of revolutionary heroism. This volume of highly sophisticated political-philosophical essays rapidly became a bestseller and went within one year through several printings — a success unprecedented in the history of Russian letters. The volume also led to a heated controversy with the champions of the intelligentsia's traditional mentality and values. The volume was attacked both by the extreme Left (some of the most venomous attacks on it were made, and continued to be made for years, by Lenin) and by the tradition-bound Liberals.[9]

An important role in *fin-de-siècle* thought was played by Vladimir Soloviev (1853–1900), who combined the religious-mystical approach (with strong eschatological overtones) with political Lib-

[9] Of the seven authors of *Vekhi*, four (Berdiaev, Bulgakov, Frank, and Struve) had been contributors to *Problems of Idealism*.

GLEB STRUVE

eralism, and to whom Russian religious-philosophical revival of the early twentieth century was very much indebted.

In the same period fall the pioneering efforts of such writers as Vasilii Rozanov (1856–1919), Akim Volynskii (pseudonym of A. L. Flekser, 1863–1926), Sergei Andreevskii (1847–1920), and others, to reappraise the heritage of Russian literature, to re-evaluate the reputations of many a writer to whom the dominant social-utilitarian criticism of the nineteenth century had affixed this or that label, with a plus or a minus sign. Rozanov's penetrating studies of Gogol and Dostoevsky; Volynskii's books on Dostoevsky and Leskov and his outspoken debunking of such idols of the nineteenth-century intelligentsia as Belinskii, Chernyshevskii, and Pisarev, parallel with the emphasis laid on such an unfashionable literary critic as Apollon Grigoriev (all this in Volynskii's volume *Russian Critics*); Andreevskii's rediscovery of such a major poet of the Pushkin period as Baratynskii; Soloviev's famous essays on Tiutchev and Fet — all these were important stages in the rapidly proceeding unfreezing of the Russian minds. This work of re-evaluation of the literary reputations of the past was to be continued later by the leading poets of Russian Symbolism (Briusov, Zinaida Hippius, Blok, and others).

There were parallel developments in visual arts — a reaction against the pedestrian realism of the dominant *peredvizhniki* group,[10] and the programmatic or illustrative art with a social message, went hand in hand with the growing interest in the contemporary movements in Western European art — in particular, the English Pre-Raphaelites and the French Impressionists and their offshoots. At the very end of the century, this desire to renovate Russian art and to put it abreast of Western movements found its vehicle in the magazine *Mir Iskusstva* (*The World of Art*), founded in 1898 by Sergei Diaghilev, of future Ballets Russes fame. Diaghilev gathered round him a group of talented young artists who later formed the World of Art group and did much to revolutionize both Russian art and Russian art criticism — men like Alexander Benois, Konstantin Somov, Eugene Lanceray, Nicholas Roerich,

[10] From *Peredvizhnye vystavki* (*Ambulant Exhibitions*).

185

Mstislav Dobuzhinskii, and others. These men were also responsible for a new approach to the past legacy of Russian art, for "discovering" the hitherto neglected world of the Russian icon (the work done in this respect by the art historian Igor Grabar and by the critic Paul Muratov was particularly important, but much credit also goes to the wealthy collectors from the old merchant families, such as Ostroukhov, Riabushinskii, and others) and for reassessing the little-known art of the Russian eighteenth century. Some of the leading artists of this new school, like Benois and Somov, were clearly influenced by this eighteenth-century art and also drew upon it for their subject matter, whereas others, like Roerich, were to some extent influenced by the Russian icon painting and drew upon Russian folklore and Oriental motifs.

The World of Art combined interest in arts with that in literature and stood in the vanguard of modern literary movement. The close alliance between literature and fine arts became a hallmark of Russian periodicals at this time, and the *World of Art* tradition was carried on by such publications as *Vesy* (*The Scales*, 1904–1909), *Zolotoe Runo* (*The Golden Fleece*, 1906–1909), *Apollon* (*Apollo*, 1909–1917), and the short-lived *Sofia* (1914). It is also characteristic of all these periodicals, devoted to both arts and letters, that they followed closely all the latest trends and movements in Western Europe and were at the same time concerned with propagandizing Russian art, both old and modern, in the West. Both *Vesy* and *Apollon* had regular Western collaborators.

In the drama and the theater new paths were also blazed from the 1890's on. In 1898, the Moscow Art Theatre, founded by Konstantin Stanislavsky, today one of the best-known names in the history of the modern theater, initiated with his *Sea Gull* a series of Chekhov productions, which were to bring it its fame (only three years earlier, *The Sea Gull* had met with complete fiasco on the traditional stage in St. Petersburg). Chekhov, who in his dramatic innovations was to some extent influenced by contemporary European drama (by Ibsen and Maeterlinck, in particular), became in turn important in influencing the drama outside Russia, especially in Anglo-Saxon countries. So did, too, some of

186

the principles that underlay the theatrical work of Stanislavsky's Art Theatre. For its part, the Moscow Art Theatre familiarized Russian audiences with such playwrights as Ibsen, Hamsun, Hauptmann, and Maeterlinck. Soon, however, the Stanislavsky's theater itself came to be looked upon by many people as old-fashioned. Its presentation of Chekhov's "atmospheric" plays in the slice-of-life manner and in a minor key was the last word in the "de-theatralization" and "de-conventionalization" of the theater. A reaction against this trend came from different sides and at different levels: Leonid Andreev's symbolical-romantic melodramas (*The Life of Man, Anathema*, and so forth); Gorky's attempts (as in *Lower Depths*) to infuse a broader social meaning and a breath of optimism into the Chekhovian drama; Fedor Sologub's and Zinaida Hippius's endeavors to combine symbolism and realism; Blok's essays in lyrical drama (*The Puppet Show* and *The Stranger*, with their superb romantic irony) and in verse tragedy (*The Rose and the Cross*); Innokentii Annenskii's and Viacheslav Ivanov's revival of ancient Greek myths (in Annenskii's case, with a strong modern flavor). All this took place in the drama, at the same time as, in the theater, Meyerhold and especially Nicholas Evreinov were turning to experiments that were based on principles diametrically opposed to that of Chekhov's and Stanislavsky's de-conventionalization of the theater — namely, the "theatralization" of life. All this can be seen as an attempt to lead the Russian theater out of the Chekhovian impasse. Two outstanding theatrical directors who were later to play an important part in the early post-Revolutionary period, Vsevolod Meyerhold and Alexander Tairov, came to assert the principle of the primacy of the theatrical director not only over the actors (Stanislavsky had also asserted this, although he combined it with the important role assigned to the actors' ensemble as distinct from individual actors), but also over the author. Hence, the liberties which Meyerhold was to take later with the plays of such classical writers as Gogol and Ostrovskii.

In poetry, the period before 1912 was dominated by Symbolism. Just as French Symbolism had been a reaction against Parnassianism and Naturalism, so its Russian namesake (which owed much of its inspiration to French Symbolism) was a reaction against civic-minded Realism. An anticipation of it will be found in Merezhkovskii's book of poems, significantly entitled *Simvoly* (*Symbols*, 1892). In his previously mentioned essay of 1893, Merezhkovskii referred to the French Symbolists. Somewhat earlier they had been the subject of a special article by Mme Zinaida Vengerov in *Vestnik Evropy*. From this article the average Russian reader (*Vestnik Evropy* was a widely read Liberal monthly) learned about the whole modern movement in French literature. But the beginnings of Russian Symbolism as a literary school in its own right date from 1894–1895 when Valerii Briusov (1873–1924), who was then twenty-one, and his friend A. Miropolskii-Lang published three slender volumes under the title *Russian Symbolists*. They contained some original verse and prose, and translations from Verlaine, Rimbaud, and Maeterlinck. There was very little, if anything, of intrinsic value in these little volumes of avant-garde writings (the only author to make subsequently a name for himself was Briusov), but their appearance was symptomatic. The definitions of Symbolism and its intent, which Briusov gave in the first two issues, were derived directly from Mallarmé: "The object of Symbolism is to hypnotize as it were the reader by a series of juxtaposed images, to evoke in him a certain mood . . ."; "The purpose of poetry is not 'objective description,' but 'suggestion' . . ."; "The poet conveys a series of images . . . [which are] to be looked upon as signposts along an invisible road, open to the imagination of the reader. It follows then that Symbolism can be described as . . . poetry of allusions"; and so forth. Primacy of intuition over reason, a refusal to accept a reality which is but a distortion of the real but unattainable world — these fundamental tenets were accepted by the young Russian disciples of Verlaine and Mallarmé and became the common stock of the new movement. The mission of the poet was seen in the revealing, beyond the realm of senses, of the world of higher reality. *De realibus ad realiora* was the slogan proclaimed later by one of the principal theoreticians of Russian Symbolism, Viacheslav Ivanov (1866–1949).

Another leading representative of early Russian Symbolism, Konstantin Balmont (1867–1942), said that whereas the Realists were tied to concrete reality beyond which they saw nothing, the Symbolists were cut off from it and saw in it only their dream — "They look at life through a window." Balmont also developed his philosophy of the moment, "momentalism": "Moments are always unique. The life I live is too quick, and I know no one who loves moments so much as I do . . . I yield myself to the moment," he wrote in a preface to one of the most characteristic volumes of his verse, *Goryashchie zdaniia* (*Burning Edifices*, 1904). This cult of the moment, this glorification of a fleeting, momentary experience, is the keynote of much of Balmont's prerevolutionary poetry.

Another Symbolist poet, Zinaida Hippius (1869–1945), the wife of Merezhkovskii, who sought inspiration in the poetry of Baratynskii and Tiutchev rather than in the French Symbolists, compared poetry to prayers. Andrei Bely (pseudonym of Boris Bugaev, 1880–1934), who became toward 1910 one of the principal theoretical exponents of Symbolism, wrote: "All art is symbolic, whether recent, old, or future. What is then the significance of modern Symbolism? What new message did it bring us? None. The school of Symbolism merely reduces to a unity the statements of artists and poets to the effect that the meaning of beauty is in the artistic image and not in the emotion which that image arouses in us; and certainly not in the rational interpretation of that image. A symbol cannot be reduced either to emotions or to discursive concepts; it is what it is."

If of French Symbolism it has been said that "Du point de vue technique . . . le symbolisme a tenté et réussi l'affranchissement du vers français — sous toutes ses formes," with regard to Russian Symbolism one should speak not so much of the "emancipation" of the Russian verse as of the simultaneous restoration of pristine standards (those of the Golden Age) and complete renovation. The complexity and richness of the poetic world of Symbolism defy a brief analysis. Such poets as Balmont, Briusov, Sologub, Viacheslav Ivanov, Zinaida Hippius, Innokentii Annenskii (whose full stature as a poet became clear only after his death and who, of all the poets of this period, stood closest to some of their French masters), Baltrushaitis, Blok, and Bely, represented different facets of Symbolism. Not all of them were equally indebted to the French. This debt was particularly obvious in the case of Annenskii and Briusov, both of whom translated Verlaine, Rimbaud, and Mallarmé (Annenskii also translated Laforgue and some lesser poets of that period; Briusov came to be strongly influenced by Verhaeren). It was less so in the case of Sologub, although he also paid tribute to the French Symbolists by translating them. Balmont was much more eclectic — his favorite poets were Shelley and Edgar Allen Poe, and he also did a great deal of translating from Spanish. (Poe and Baudelaire, like Nietzsche's *Birth of Tragedy* and Schopenhauer's ideas on music, meant much to nearly all the Russian Symbolists. Baudelaire's "Correspondances," with its "forest of symbols" and the notion of synesthesia, became a kind of credo for them). Zinaida Hippius owed much more, as has been mentioned before, to her Russian masters, Tiutchev and Baratynskii — the former came to be regarded by all the Symbolists as their forerunner, a kind of Symbolist *avant la lettre*.[11] As for Alexander Blok and Andrei Bely, they owed much more to another Symbolist *avant la lettre* (even though he had headed the chorus of those who derided and parodied Briusov's first experiments in a new manner) — namely, Vladimir Soloviev and his mystical philosophy — as did also Viacheslav Ivanov (but in his case there was also a particularly strong influence of Nietzsche). Blok also had affinities with some earlier Russian poets in the Romantic tradition — in particular with Zhukovskii, Lermontov, Fet, and Polonskii — and both he and Bely, at one stage of their poetic development, were very much inspired by the Russian accents of some of Nekrasov's "civic" poetry. In the case of Blok especially, but also of Bely and Ivanov, German influences played a greater part than the French.

Generally speaking, it soon became possible to distinguish between two main currents in Russian Symbolism: the purely aesthetic, represented by Briusov and Balmont, which depended much

[11] See, for example, V. Ivanov, "Zavety simvolizma," *Apollon*, No. 8 (1910), pp. 5–9.

more on foreign models and was concerned above all with formal, technical, prosodic innovations: and the metaphysical or religious one, represented by Blok, Bely, and Ivanov, and to some extent Zinaida Hippius (Sologub occupied a place apart). Blok, Bely, and Ivanov have come to be described often as the "younger Symbolists" (Blok and Bely were actually younger; Ivanov, who was older than Briusov, made his entry into Russian literature much later).

This metaphysical current in Russian Symbolism aspired to be something more than a literary school. Its principal exponents, Bely and Ivanov (Blok was not much of a theoretician, and in any case soon came to differ with the other two), spoke of "a new consciousness," of "mythmaking," of the "theurgical meaning of poetry." The inner crisis in Russian Symbolism came to a head in 1910 when Blok and Ivanov, on the one hand, and Briusov, on the other, engaged in a controversy in the newly founded "Academy of Verse." For Blok, Symbolism at this point was really a thing of the past, and he was soon to desert it and to wander away in a frantic search for closer ties with real life. Symbolism's aloofness from life, its engrossment in abstract profundities, began to frighten him. "Back to the soul, not only to 'man,' but to 'the whole man' — with his spirit, soul, and body, with the everydayness — three times so," he wrote in his diary in 1911.[12] And again, in 1912, "What we need is reality, there is nothing more terrifying in the world than mysticism."[13] Ivanov also began to speak of "realistic symbolism," though what he meant by it was not the same thing and was not dictated by that craving for real life by which Blok was actuated. Bely alone stuck obstinately to his guns, as may be seen from the numerous articles contributed by him in 1912 to the new periodical, *Trudy i Dni* (*Works and Days*), founded by him and Ivanov and in which Blok took but little part.[14] For Bely, Blok had even become a traitor to the common cause.

[12] *Sobranie sochinenii* (Moscow-Leningrad, 1963), Vol. VII, p. 79 (entry dated October 30).
[13] *Ibid.*, p. 134 (entry dated March 19).
[14] This periodical, founded for the explicit purpose of defending and preaching "true" Symbolism, had a short life. Bely published in it a number of important articles, some under his own name, others under the pseudonym Cunctator.

191

At the same time the stronghold of Symbolism came to be attacked from outside. In 1910, one of the talented poets who had remained on the periphery of the Symbolist movement, Mikhail Kuzmin (1875–1936), published in *Apollon* an article entitled "Prekrasnaia iasnost" ("Beautiful Clarity"). It called upon his fellow writers to come down to earth from the nebulous metaphysical heights of Symbolism. Two years later, two younger poets, Nicholas Gumilev (1886–1921) and Sergei Gorodetskii (b. 1884), launched a new movement to which they gave the name of Acmeism (from the Greek word *akme*, meaning "high point"). Gumilev, who had been a disciple of Briusov and of the French Parnassians, became the theoretician and the *maître d'école* of the new group. The principal tenets of Acmeism were stated by Gumilev and Gorodetskii in two separate articles published in the first issue of *Apollon* for 1913.[15] Gorodetskii's association with the movement was more or less accidental, but Gumilev's article came to be looked upon as the manifesto of the new school. To the Symbolists' emphasis on the hidden, associative, musical elements in poetry (Verlaine's "De la musique avant tout chose"), the Acmeists opposed the elements of sense and logic in the art of words. To Ivanov's and Bely's inclination to view the poet as a prophet, a mythmaker, and to stress his passive, mediumistic nature, Gumilev opposed the conception of the poet as a skilled, conscious craftsman; the literary organization founded by him and his consorts was accordingly named "Poets' Guild" (*Tsekh Poètov*). Up to a point, the movement can be seen as part of the general European trend toward neoclassicism, which in France was associated with Jean Moréas, himself a leading ex-Symbolist, and in England with T. E. Hulme. Although it is highly doubtful whether Gumilev was at that time familiar with the ideas and writings of Hulme, or even knew his name (later he was to display some interest in him), he must have known the name and the work of Moréas; and though we have no direct evidence of it at present, it is quite likely that the two

[15] Gumilev's article was entitled "Nasledie simvolizma i akmeizm" ("Acmeism and the Heritage of Symbolism"). It was published in *Apollon*, No. 1 (1913), and reprinted posthumously in *Pis'ma o russkoi poezii* (Petrograd, 1923), pp. 37–42.

met in 1908, when Gumilev spent about a year in Paris and was a frequent visitor to the Closerie des Lilas. The name of Moréas was not mentioned in Gumilev's "manifesto," and there was no reference in it to the *école romane* or to the neoclassical reaction against Symbolism in France. In fact, the four names of writers invoked by Gumilev as those of the "masters" to look up to were quite different and had nothing to do with modern neoclassicism: François Villon, Rabelais, Shakespeare, and Théophile Gautier, of whom Gumilev was a great admirer and whose *Emaux and Camées* he translated into Russian. One can say perhaps that Acmeism lacked both real unity and firm theoretical foundations (verbal lucidity, craftsmanship, manliness, and zest for life were among the tenets its exponents advocated), but that it had some neoclassical characteristics is beyond doubt. It was later to have a number of camp followers and to exercise considerable influence on the developments in Russian poetry after 1917, but its true adherents before the Revolution were very few. They included, however, two major poets whose poetry, in the opinion of most people, is of greater value than that of Gumilev himself: [16] Gumilev's first wife, Anna Akhmatova (1889–1966), and Osip Mandelstam (1891–1938). Both poets with sharply defined poetic individualities, they could hardly be described as Gumilev's followers, but their poetry certainly represented, in different ways, some essential aspects of Acmeism as understood and formulated by Gumilev. Both grew in stature as poets after the Revolution, despite the extremely unfavorable outward conditions and the vicissitudes of their personal life. Akhmatova survived all her ordeals and continued to write (though there were periods when she could not publish her poetry), but Mandelstam ended his life tragically in a concentration camp.

Another movement that arose in opposition to Symbolism, but was also largely its own offspring, was Futurism. It was a movement parallel to, but in many ways different from, the Italian Futurism

[16] In evaluating Gumilev as a poet it is necessary, however, to take into account the fact that his life was cut short at the age of 35, when he was executed for alleged participation in a counterrevolutionary conspiracy. His last volume of poetry, *Ognennyi stolp* (*Pillar of Fire*), published a month or so after his death, bore witness to his remarkably rapid growth as a poet.

of Marinetti. Its very beginnings in Russia were in 1909. By 1912 it was represented by a number of small groups and coteries, bearing such names as Ego-Futurists, Cubo-Futurists, Centrifuga, and The Mezzanine of Poetry. Of these, the Cubo-Futurists came to play the most important role. As the name implies, they wanted to stress their connection with Cubism in painting — the book of Gleizes and Metzenger on Cubism became one of their bedside books. Some of their experiments with words and verse led some students of Futurism to speak of their "verse Cubism," although the analogy seems rather remote and arbitrary.

The Cubo-Futurists were led by two poets who were also painters — David Burliuk (b. 1882) and Vladimir Maiakovskii (1894–1930). Burliuk made his home after the Revolution in New York and became better known as a painter, even though he continued to write poetry in Russian and to preach Futurism. He is still alive, as is Alexei Kruchenykh (b. 1886), one of the early Russian Futurists still living in Russia. It was Maiakovskii, however, who became the acknowledged leader of Russian avant-garde poetry. Connected with them was also Velimir Khlebnikov (1885–1922), sometimes described as the Russian Rimbaud, the most original of the Futurists, and in the opinion of some people, a true poetic genius.

The Futurists proclaimed the absolute autonomy of art, its complete independence from life. In one of their early publications, they declared that, apart from its starting point which is to be seen in the creative impulse, poetry has nothing to do with the external world and is in no way coordinated with it. They saw their mission in "unshackling" words, in freeing them from subservience to meaning, and thus reaching through to "direct perception." Their slogan was the "word per se" or "self-valuable word" (*samovitoe slovo*). They propounded and tried to practice a new, universal language, which they dubbed *trans-sense* (*zaumny jazyk, zaum'* — Professor Chyzhevskyi has suggested as its best equivalent the word *metalogical*). In a way, this approach had already been anticipated by the Symbolists, among whom Andrei Bely especially had freely indulged in coining words. The influence of Mallarmé is equally apparent. Burliuk spoke of both the Russian and the French Symbolists, as well as the French *poètes maudits*, as the Futurists' masters, naming specifically Baudelaire, Rimbaud, Tristan Corbière, and Jules Laforgue. But the Futurists said that whereas the Symbolists had tried both in theory and in practice to deepen the inner meaning of words, and saw the latter as important not per se, but because they were an expression of a symbol, of the world, of existence, of the "soul of things," or of the mystical other world; they, the Futurists, regarded the form of words, their appearance, their sound as more important than their actual or potential meaning. Or, as Professor Markov put it, the "flesh" of the poetic word was more important than its "spirit." [17] What mattered to them was not some new symbols, but a new organization of words. If words can be seen as tonic or graphic material, then they can be "stretched," or divided, or created anew. Hence the cult of form, the intoxication with words, and all sorts of verbal experiments, particularly in the work of Kruchenykh.

Maiakovskii, however, who was to become the post-Revolutionary leader of Russian Futurism — at least so long as it was tolerated by the Party — was never particularly interested in pure verbal experimentation for its own sake; he never indulged in the extremes of "wordmaking" (*slovotvorchestvo*), contenting himself with all sorts of "shifts" (*sdvigi*) in the language — phonetic, morphological, semantic, rhythmical. His principal innovations were in the realm of prosody: he tended to substitute pure tonic verse for the traditional syllabotonic pattern of Russian classical poetry; in this he had some predecessors among the Symbolist poets (in their use of the so-called *dol'niki*), but he adopted much more revolutionary procedures, went far beyond his predecessors, and in his accentual verse created a truly new instrument. Characteristic for Maiakovskii was also the deliberate "de-poetization" of vocabulary and imagery and the use of vulgarisms and colloquialisms, though alongside these he also used archaisms and Church-Slavonicisms, often for contrasting or satirical effects.

[17] Vladimir Markov, "The Province of Russian Futurism," *The Slavic and East European Journal*, VIII, No. 4 (Winter 1964), 403.

Although the Italian Futurism of Marinetti had a distinctly urbanistic flavor, the same cannot be said of Russian Futurism as a whole. Two of its prominent representatives, Khlebnikov and Vasilii Kamenskii (1884–1961), had even a strong anti-urban bias. In Khlebnikov's poetry and in his historiosophic conception, there were elements of utopian romanticism, and he had very strong anti-Western and pro-Asiatic leanings. His verbal experiments, unlike those of some other Futurists, were closely related to his philological studies and his interest in the history of the Russian language and in linguistics in general. His neologisms were often rooted in the linguistic soil of the Russian language. Maiakovskii, on the other hand, was in this respect closer to Western Futurism. In his poetry urban motifs played an important part even before the Revolution, but his urbanism was of a social rather than a technological character, and even before 1917 his poetry had a clearly revolutionary orientation. For Maiakovskii the art of the future, of which all the Futurists spoke, was closely bound up with the coming sociopolitical upheaval, and in his person the alliance between the Bolshevik Revolution and Futurism came as something quite natural in the first post-Revolutionary years.

If I have spoken so far mainly of poetry, it is because this period was indeed dominated by poetry to quite an unusual extent, and because it was in poetry above all that new paths were blazed, first by the Symbolists and then by their successors.

But the period was also rich in prose fiction. Here, however, the scene was not monopolized, or even completely dominated, by the innovators. Much of the new prose fiction, which was to depart from the earlier tradition, came in fact from the poets who played an important part in the Symbolist movement: the historical-philosophical novels of Merezhkovskii; the novels and stories by Briusov and Sologub (including the latter's *Melkii bes* (*The Petty Demon*, 1907), which Mirsky describes as the best Russian novel since Dostoevsky); and the remarkable novels of Andrei Bely (who is sometimes seen as a predecessor of James Joyce), especially his *Petersburg* (1913), with their close ties with his poetry (this is even more true of his earlier prose works, which he designated "symphonies" and which in their diction and technique of writing stand on the borderline between poetry and prose).

But along with this Symbolist production in prose fiction, a number of writers continued, mostly in the realm of the short story (though there were also some novels), the nineteenth-century "realistic" tradition. It is enough to name Gorky (1868–1936), Bunin (1870–1953), Kuprin (1870–1938), Shmeliev (1873–1950), and Boris Zaitsev (b. 1882). At the same time, some of the younger writers attempted to renovate this tradition, to instill new blood into it, and earned for themselves the name of Neo-Realists. The foremost among them were Alexei Remizov (1877–1957) and Alexei N. Tolstoi (1882–1945), and among the still younger ones Eugene Zamiatin (1884–1937), most of whose work belongs, however, to the early post-Revolutionary period. It was Zamiatin who, speaking of his work and of that of some of his masters, gave a good definition of Neo-Realism as distinct both from old-fashioned Realism and from Symbolism: the Neo-Realists can be seen as the link between the prerevolutionary literature and much of what was best and most original in the Soviet literature of the 1920's. Remizov certainly exercised a great influence on many young Soviet writers, but so did also Andrei Bely. In general, one can say that both Symbolism and Neo-Realism had a great seminal significance for the so-called Soviet literature until the advent (or the imposition) of "Socialist Realism," just as post-Revolutionary poetry before 1930 developed as an extension and an offshoot of the poetic schools of the prerevolutionary Second Golden Age.

Let me repeat: the literary scene in Russia between 1890 and 1914 was characterized by great richness and variety (and this was also true of the other arts). There was an abundance of periodicals of high quality, both literary-artistic and general, in the purely and uniquely Russian tradition of the *tolstye zhurnaly* ("fat" monthly reviews), representing a wide range of viewpoints in politics as well as in arts — from the Liberal (and after 1910, Liberal-Conservative) *Russkaia Mysl'*, edited by my father, P. B. Struve, on the right, carrying on the tradition of *Landmarks* and at the same time opening its pages to all that was best in new literature (Blok, Briu-

197

sov, Sologub, Akhmatova, Gumilev, and Viacheslav Ivanov were all among its regular contributors); through the highly respectable *Vestnik Evropy*, orthodox Liberal in politics and stodgily conservative in artistic matters; through the populist *Russkoe Bogatstvo*, artistically speaking just as conservative; and down to the social-democratically oriented *Sovremennyi Mir*, a little more lively and modern on the literary side. A little later, two new "fat" monthly reviews made their appearance, both of them tending toward the Left in politics and favorable to Modernism in the arts. One was *Zavety*, which stood close to the Socialist-Revolutionary Party and the literary policies of which were inspired by the well-known critic Ivanov-Razumnik (1878–1945); the other was *Severnye Zapiski*, vaguely Radical (but nonparty) from the political point of view and of very high literary quality, competing with *Russkaia Mysl'* in attracting some of the best poets and prose writers of that time.

In speaking of the literary scene during this period, one cannot leave out the high level of much of its literary criticism and literary scholarship. Some younger Soviet scholars owe a great debt of gratitude to some of the surviving representatives of that period. And the relatively high level of Soviet literary criticism in the 1920's and early 1930's is an inheritance of the same period. Unfortunately, much of the literary scholarship and literary criticism of that period remains taboo; little of it is reprinted and is therefore inaccessible to the present-day Soviet reader. The critical tradition of the Second Golden Age had to be carried on by the Russians in exile, but this could be done only on a very reduced scale and was doomed to a speedy end.

It is almost as bad with the imaginative literature of the Symbolist era. True, the prestige of Blok stands very high, and there have been two complete editions of his works, the latest, in eight volumes, published between 1960 and 1964,[18] and a great number of "selected" editions. This is due largely, if not entirely, to the fact that Blok was one of the few major writers to welcome the October

[18] An unnumbered ninth volume was added to this edition in 1965; it contains Blok's "Notebooks."

Revolution of 1917 (his subsequent bitter disillusionment with it is glossed over by his Soviet biographers and students of his work). The same is true of Briusov, though not quite to the same extent even though Briusov's "acceptance" of the Bolshevik Revolution was much more thorough. But the situation is quite different with most of the other writers of the Symbolist and post-Symbolist period. Sologub's novel *The Petty Demon* was reissued, after a long interval, in 1933. It was next published in 1958 somewhere in Siberia, with a cautionary note from the publishers to the effect that the novel, which "shows masterfully the rotting of the bourgeois-gentry society," will be read by Soviet readers as "a document and monument of that capitalist order of things, at which, as V. I. Lenin said, our grandchildren will look as at some oddity." None of his other novels have been reissued since before the Revolution, and none of his poetry since 1936.

Andrei Bely's *Petersburg* was last published in 1935. His other prerevolutionary novel, *The Silver Dove*, was never reissued in Russia after 1917. A small volume of his poetry appeared in the late 1930's and soon went out of print. And it was only in 1966 that Bely was granted the honor of being included in the "large series" of the collection known as "The Poet's Library." Writers like Merezhkovskii, Viacheslav Ivanov, Zinaida Hippius, Remizov, Balmont, Kuzmin, Gumilev, and several others are virtually unknown to the general public in the Soviet Union. It is true that some of their poetry is included in some recent anthologies used as college textbooks, but the selections are onesided, unsatisfactory, and incomplete, as are all the references to them in various histories of literature, encyclopedias, and other reference works.[19]

Even today, in the post-Stalin period, when so much of the old

---

[19] Particularly disgraceful in this respect is the last volume of the ten-volume *History of Russian Literature* (*Istoriia russkoi literatury*), published under the auspices of the Soviet Academy of Sciences. This volume appeared in 1954, a year after Stalin's death, and still reflects all the characteristics of the Stalinist age. It covers the period 1890–1917. The chapter on Symbolism, Acmeism, and Futurism, entitled "Poetry of Bourgeois Decadence" (pp. 764–799) (from which are excluded Briusov, Blok, Maiakovskii, treated separately in earlier chapters), is divided among five authors, all of them known for their other studies in the literature of this period: A. Volkov, V. Orlov, N. Stepanov, A. Fedorov, and I. Eventov.

cultural tradition has been, or is being, restored, the great cultural wealth of the modern Russian Renaissance is neglected or dismissed with hostility and contempt (usually accompanied and supported by "telling" quotations from Lenin), and Russian culture, including literature, is all the poorer for this break in continuity. There is, however, much encouraging evidence that the younger generation in the Soviet Union is taking an ever greater interest in this period, which official Soviet historians have either crossed out of history or are studiously distorting, and particularly in its literature and thought. And one constantly hears of literary works of this period circulating privately and clandestinely.

♟ ♟ ♟

IN OCTOBER 1966, when the text of this lecture was being prepared for the press, the Soviet journal *Voprosy Literatury* (*Problems of Literature*) published an article by the well-known literary scholar Vladimir N. Orlov, author of a book on Alexander Blok and of several others, entitled "On the Threshold of Two Epochs (From the History of Russian Poetry at the Beginning of Our Century)." This article represents an abridged version of Orlov's introduction to the forthcoming volume in the "small series" of the Poet's Library, to be called *Poets of the Early XX Century*. Orlov discusses Russian Symbolism and its significance in general (with numerous references to Gorky's opinions of it) and then devotes separate sections to five individual poets, representing in the main the post-Symbolist period: Maximilian Voloshin (1877–1932), Kuzmin, Gumilev, Mandelstam, and Khodasevich (1886–1939). It is clear from the text that all these poets will be included in the volume for which Orlov has written this introduction. For most of them, this will mean a literary resurrection after a period of long neglect and oblivion. A statement on page 124 of Orlov's article suggests that among other poets to be included in the volume will be Balmont, Sologub, Annenskii, and Viacheslav Ivanov.

The following passage is characteristic of Orlov's approach to the literature of the period under discussion. After quoting some sentences from Blok's introduction to his poem "Retribution," Orlov writes: "The period of reaction, to use Blok's formula, 'devastated the minds.' It left a visible imprint on the work of most of the Symbolists and their immediate successors — Voloshin, Kuzmin, Gumilev, Mandelstam, and Khodasevich, who withdrew from great themes and burning questions into aestheticism, mannerism, exoticism, passéism, bookishness, into the dark recesses of their own minds. All of them bore witness to being astonishingly blind and deaf to the tragic, dreadful, and comforting things that were happening at that decisive moment in Russia and in the whole world. Of course, one should not paint the epoch all with one paint. Speaking of Russian poetry alone, we must not forget that it was precisely in those years, which lie between the two revolutions, that were written the third volume of Blok's lyrical poetry, Andrei Bely's *Ashes*, the best poetry of Bunin, and that in those years Akhmatova, Tsvetaeva, and Pasternak came out with their first books, that Khlebnikov was writing, that Maiakovskii and Esenin made their appearance . . . But those are the high peaks."

Acmeism is dismissed by Orlov as a current that was "not only cachectic but in fact a sham one." Gumilev's manifesto is described as "highfalutin" and "snooty," and is compared to a mountain that gave birth to a mouse, the mouse being poetry that was "thin, petty, extraordinarily pretentious" and "affected by a terrible disease — an atrophy of all sense of time." Since Orlov does not specify what poetry and by what poets he has in mind, the reader has to deduce that he is speaking of the work of such poets as Akhmatova, Gumilev, and Mandelstam (all of them leading Acmeists), although later, despite some reservations, he has some very different things to say even about Gumilev and Mandelstam.[20]

[20] *Voprosy Literatury*, No. 10 (1966), pp. 123–124.

RODERICK E. MC GREW

Some Imperatives of Russian Foreign Policy

⚜ ⚜ ⚜

A NATION'S foreign policy is the product of a shifting complex of historical factors which range from individual personalities to the society's moral or spiritual values; in turn, the development of foreign policy, and the results which flow from it, have the most profound effects on the nation's historical destiny. The preceding essays in this collection have treated several aspects of the reign of Nicholas II, and each of the subjects covered, from modernization and industrialization through cultural development to political radicalism, has significant implications for Russian foreign policy. This is another way of saying that a nation's foreign policy is an expression of its total historical milieu, but it also means that an essay devoted to the imperatives of Russian foreign policy must encompass more than the mechanics of diplomacy and find a larger historical context than that provided by a single reign. Following this conclusion, my purpose will be to present certain continuities or necessities that traditionally have affected Russia's international role, and that helped to shape Russian foreign policy on the eve of World War I. There will be no attempt to review Russian diplomacy from 1894 to 1917, though the period will provide applications of my theses, and I shall focus on a series of analytic categories which I consider fundamental for understanding Russia's place in the wider world.

The imperatives of the title create the framework of decision — or perhaps better, the conceptual milieu within which decisions are made. In this sense, imperatives perform a causal function, for they help to define goals or to limit the range of possibilities for active policy. Implied in this concept, however, is a deeper and less obvious relation. Imperatives are also a part of the unconscious vocabulary of response and action which is the substratum of rational thought. No nation's leaders, regardless of personal ideology, can completely escape the intellectual or moral circumstance which tradition has bequeathed them, and their commitment to that environment, their participation in it, is reflected in their mode of thinking and in the alternatives that they are willing to entertain. This means that an analysis of cultural components is essential for understanding the nation's international posture, but it suggests, furthermore, that the study of foreign policy itself becomes an avenue for understanding the cultural character of a nation.

Our discussion turns on the exposition of four major imperatives which have regularly affected Russian foreign policy — geographical position, the structure of international relations, the level of cultural development, and ideological orientation. Although each category has a special character, no one is dominant, and all should be visualized as overlapping and interacting with one another. Thus, geographical position establishes an inescapable frame for action, for no government, regardless of its other attributes, can avoid the problems and challenges inherent in its location on the earth's surface. But geographical position does more than set the physical limits to action; it becomes an element in human attitudes, a creative force in the political mystique, and a component of ideology. When we speak of the German *Drang nach Osten,* France's "natural frontiers," or Russia's "urge to the sea," we deal with attitudes rooted in positional realities which have become part of the cultural context. The second imperative, the structure of international society, functions similarly. Such concepts as the balance of power or the European community establish limits for political behavior as potent in their own way as positional realities, and conditions within and relations among neighboring states conspire to create opportunities or to pose problems. The decline of Turkey, Poland's failure to develop an effective political system, and the emergence of modern Japan were all crucial for Russia's international position and shaped her environment of decision.

Whereas geographical position and the international situation create external imperatives, cultural development and ideological orientation produce equally influential internal categories. Power is an integral function of cultural development, and a culture which is either unable or unwilling to develop the technology of power can neither realize its interests nor protect its boundaries. Patterns of Russian cultural development posed a continuing problem of insufficiency which reached crisis proportions in the later seventeenth century and again in the nineteenth century; the necessity for modernization, which held revolutionary implications for Russian society, profoundly influenced Russia's international policies. Furthermore, the level of cultural development clearly has ideological implications, because ideology, in its broadest sense, is an unrationalized composite of the views, attitudes, responses, prejudices, and formal ideas that constitute a society's value system. The problem of economic insufficiency and cultural underdevelopment fostered an early commitment to Westernization and the idea of Russia as a European state, while an indigenous Russian messianism was exacerbated and fed by the persistent evidences that Russia competed at a disadvantage with her Western neighbors. Such generalized ideas took specific form, especially in the later nineteenth century, in the Pan-Slav movement, in an intensified and extreme Russian nationalism, and in a concept of manifest destiny which not only identified Russia's civilizing role among the Eastern barbarians, but which purported to find the answers to Russia's problems of wealth and power in the unexploited resources of Central and East Asia. The danger when treating ideology, of course, is to explain too much, and I might suggest as a corrective that it has been ideology in its broadest sense of orientation, rather than in its narrow commitment to any particular system, which has been most important for the formation of Russian foreign policy.

Russia has had a major part in modern international relations, and the goals that she has sought, as well as the methods she has used, have had a crucial and lasting influence on modern history. Russia's Asian and Balkan policies were central to the events which produced World War I, but the rationale for Russian policy at the opening of the twentieth century reflected patterns which were part of long-term historical development. The imperatives outlined above provide a means for relating that development to events as they unfolded, and a tool for exposing the needs that shaped Russia's international posture. Russia as a nation had, and continues to have, interests and necessities that influence her behavior regardless of the political system under which she lives, and these are rooted in the material and cultural realities of Russian existence.

♟ ♟ ♟

IT HAS become a historical truism that the Russian State was born without natural frontiers, but it is equally true that from earliest times Russian history has been shaped by the relation between her main centers of settlement and the civilizations which developed on her periphery. Russian history began in a multitude of trading communities that dotted the complex of rivers lying to the west of the Urals, and the rivers themselves provided regular and easy communication on a north-south axis within the Russian lands as well as access through the Baltic to the Germano-Scandinavian world in the north and through the Black and Caspian seas to the Magian world to the south. The great overland caravan routes from Central and West Asia connected the termini of the river system, and the resulting complex provided the Russian lands with commercial and cultural links with the Middle Eastern and Oriental civilizations. During its formative period, the Russian lands stood at the crossroads of the Eurasian world, and until the thirteenth century interdiction in the wake of the Tatar conquests, displayed a cosmopolitanism which did not return again until modern times.

The very openness of the river system fostered internal as well as external movement and trade, and the existence of a host of more or less independent communities contributed to particularism, competition, and conflict. These characteristics in turn produced two requirements which affected the entire course of Russian development — the need to create order and a measure of unity within the Russian lands, and the necessity for stabilizing and controlling the major access routes to the outside world. The first need was satisfied initially in the loose agglomeration of principalities which became Kiev Rus', and later, under totally different historical circumstances, in the establishment of Moscow's primacy and the subsequent evolution of Imperial Russia. The second necessity regularly shaped the external policies of each successive political system established in the Russian lands, and it is to this aspect that we must give our attention.[1]

Although a great many historical particulars are related to the geographical factor, its role as an imperative in the formation of external policies appears in two fundamental problems — accessibility and security. The rivers and seas, as well as the open overland routes, give the Russian lands the physical requisites for easy communication with the outside world, but the routes are so positioned that they may easily be closed or become a highroad to invasion. In the early period, constant military effort was required to maintain the routes both to Europe and to Asia, and the modern period has been marked by a concerted effort through the Black and Baltic seas, and on the Pacific shore, to establish and retain regular communication with the outside world.

In the modern period, the problem of access has really meant a problem in territorial control. Following the period of the Tatar

[1] For a thoughtful treatment of the positional factor and Russian politics, see Cyril E. Black, "The Pattern of Russian Objectives," in Ivo J. Lederer, ed., *Russian Foreign Policy: Essays in Historical Perspective* (New Haven, Conn.: Yale University Press, 1962), pp. 3–38. Robert J. Kerner's *The Urge to the Sea: The Course of Russian History* (Berkeley: University of California Press, 1942) is a special and compelling treatment of geographical factors in Russian history. For the cosmopolitan and eclectic character of early Russia and the importance of position, see George Vernadsky, *The Origins of Russia* (London: Oxford University Press, 1959).

invasions, the Russian territories in the central and northern regions were, in effect, cut off from their major access routes by a succession of Tatar states to the east and south and by the development of Lithuania-Poland to the west and north; in the sixteenth and seventeenth centuries, the Ottoman establishment to the south and the rise of Sweden in the north deepened the barrier between the Russian lands and the outside world. To re-establish commercial and cultural communication through the Black Sea, the Baltic Sea, or even along the old southern river routes required a policy of aggression and territorial expansion which would not only smash the states which controlled the routes, but which would place possession of the access routes in Russian hands. The wars of the sixteenth and seventeenth centuries, culminating in the Great Northern War against Sweden, and the abortive campaigns against Turkey, were generated out of the need to displace those powers which barred access to the outer world and to establish Russian control. By 1725, the routes to the Caspian had been cleared, Russian primacy in the Ukraine was established, and Russian access to the Baltic was firmly fixed. Between 1725 and 1796 these gains were consolidated by the destruction of Poland, by the extension of Russian control to the northern Black Sea littoral, including the Crimean peninsula, and the incursion of Russian interests into the principalities of Moldavia and Wallachia. By the end of the eighteenth century, Russia's rulers had secured the territorial control necessary to guarantee her access routes, and in the process established the political frontiers in Europe which, with minor changes, lasted to 1917.

Naval power was a latent threat to Russia's Baltic outlet, which she attempted to counter both by international agreement and by developing the Baltic fleet, but the crucial problem was territorial control at the head of the Baltic, which was achieved with the acquisition of the Baltic provinces and the addition of Finland as an appendage to the Empire in 1809. The situation in the Black Sea was different, for despite Russia's success in absorbing the northern littoral, and her influence in the Balkans themselves, Turkey controlled access to the Black Sea through the Dardanelles. In

Catherine's reign, and again in that of Nicholas I, Russian policy aimed at the largest measure of control in the Black Sea area which was consistent with the countervailing interests of the other powers concerned, and for more than a decade, from 1829 to 1841, Nicholas I held a dominant position in Turkish affairs. He lost that position, however, with the return to an international guarantee of the Straits, and the Crimean War resulted when the powers refused to recognize Russia's special interests at the Straits. After two decades of passivity, Russia returned to an active Balkan policy to gain control of the Black Sea access route, for, as the Minister of the Navy, Grigorovich, pointed out in 1913, "the Straits in the hands of another state would mean the complete control of the economic development of southern Russia by a foreign power, and the transfer to that state of the hegemony of the Balkans and the key for an aggressive advance into Asia Minor . . ."[2] The Russian effort failed, and in its failure contributed directly to the outbreak of World War I.

The problem of accessibility was paralleled by the need to maintain security. Russia's open frontiers have been a regular invitation to invasion, and the very centrality of her location in the Eurasian land mass has made her vulnerable to incursions from every side. Since the sixteenth century, the primary threat to Russian security has come from the West, and the need to secure the western frontier has been a regular concern for Russian foreign policy. In the early modern period, the problem of the western frontier was essentially the problem of Poland, but Catherine II's successes raised the problem to a new level. After the partitions of Poland, Russia shared a political boundary with the German states and thus became a part of the Central European complex. French expansion under the Directory and Napoleon brought Catherine, and more effectively Paul and Alexander I, to underwrite the European system; Napoleon's victories dramatized the ultimate danger, and

<hr>

[2] Grigorovich to Sazonov, December 9, 1913, *Krasnyi arkhiv*, No. 7 (1924), p. 34, quoted in Ivo J. Lederer, "Russia and the Balkans," in his *Russian Foreign Policy*, p. 420. Francesco Cognasso, *Storia della questione d'Oriente* (Turin: Società Editrice Internazionale, 1949), provides an excellent survey from the sixteenth century to the end of World War II.

the French campaign in Russia in 1812 drove the lesson home: Russia was exposed in Europe, and diplomacy provided the first line of defense. Russia's association with the conservative monarchies of Austria and Prussia after 1815 offered a substantial measure of security, and the combination of Bismarck's interest in securing the peace and Russia's circumscribed diplomacy extended the diplomatic shield in the West past 1870. As Austria and Germany drew closer together, however, and Russian interests increasingly conflicted with those of the German powers, the problem of security took on a new appearance. Bismarck's fall in 1890 and Caprivi's decision not to renew the Re-Insurance Treaty raised the spectre of Russian diplomatic isolation, and when Russia reluctantly turned to France during the last days of Alexander III, the western political barrier was destroyed. From this point forward Russian territorial security rested on military strength and the French alliance. This, as Barbara Jelavich has pointed out, marked the end of "the great period of Russian diplomacy in the nineteenth century," for from this time "conflicts in Asia and the Balkans could result in a direct invasion of Russia. It was not the Crimea that was now in danger but St. Petersburg and Moscow." [3]

Russia's geographical position established the framework for Russian foreign policy and defined fundamental requirements that shaped the outlines of decision. The geographical imperative created two fundamental issues, the problem of access to the wider world and security against invasion, and these issues in turn regularly focused foreign policy decisions. Beyond this operative or instrumental aspect, positional realities helped to shape the Russian view of the world, to develop attitudes which went beyond specific problems. Russia's earliest and most vital cultural ties lay to the south, and throughout her history there was a sense of necessity for achieving dominance in the south which transcended particular

[3] *A Century of Russian Foreign Policy, 1814–1914* (Philadelphia & New York: Lippincott, 1964), pp. 220–221. Cf. Pierre Renouvin, *Le XIXᵉ siècle*. Pt. II. *De 1871 à 1914. L'apogée de l'Europe*. Vol. VI. *Histoire des relations internationales* (Paris: Hachette, 1955), pp. 116–126; William L. Langer, *The Franco-Russian Alliance, 1890–1894* (Cambridge, Mass.: Harvard University Press, 1929), Chs. I, II.

military or economic issues. This manifested itself in the ideas of Russia the protector of the Orthodox, the ideal of the Third Rome, and the modern equivalent of Russia's leading role among the Slavic peoples. Such responses became part of the political vocabulary, but they were related to positional realities, and they added a dimension of cultural significance to geopolitical fact. All of these elements underline the importance of geography as an imperative in foreign policy and establish geography as a primary category for the study of Russia's foreign relations.

♟ ♟ ♟

IN THE modern period Russian foreign policy has developed within the context of the European state system, and the formal structure of the balance of power, as well as domestic developments within the European states, have affected the direction of Russian diplomacy.[4] Communication between Russia and the European world was infrequent and sporadic in the fifteenth and sixteenth centuries, but by the seventeenth century Russia had become involved with the Hapsburgs as well as with Poland and Sweden, and by the latter part of the seventeenth century the Regent Sophia could contemplate participation in a grand European alliance to drive the Turks out of Europe. It was Peter the Great, however, who introduced Russia to the European system, and under Peter's successors, Russia became more and more deeply involved in the complexities of European politics. By the time Catherine II took the throne in 1762, Russia had become a significant component in the European balance of power, Russian statesmen viewed her interests in the context of European dynastic rivalries and power relations, and during Catherine's reign St.

---

[4] See Hajo Holborn, "Russia and the European Political System," in Lederer, ed., *Russian Foreign Policy*, pp. 377–409. An immense literature treats European diplomacy and Russia's role in it. See, for example, Alan J. P. Taylor, *Struggle for Mastery in Europe, 1848–1914* (Oxford: Clarendon Press, 1956); Lewis C. B. Seaman, *From Vienna to Versailles* (London: Methuen, 1956); William L. Langer, *European Alliances and Alignments, 1871–1890* (2nd ed.; New York: Knopf, 1950); Sidney B. Fay, *The Origins of the World War*, 2 vols. (New York: Macmillan, 1928).

Petersburg became one of the most important diplomatic posts in Europe.

Although it is beyond the scope of this paper to rehearse the complexities of European politics before World War I, certain developments demonstrate the operation of the political milieu as an imperative for Russian foreign policy. The European world in the second half of the nineteenth century was dynamic, and though such basic political concepts as the balance of power functioned, the components were changing. Central to the whole period was the emergence of a powerful and united Germany, whose very strength and dynamism created a whole series of new challenges for Russia and for Europe at large. The unification of Italy worked more modest changes, but the development of the new imperialism added a vital dimension to European politics. The hesitant steps of the United States toward a more positive role, especially in Asia, contributed to the complexities of the world situation, and Chinese decadence and the emergence of modern Japan were particularly significant for Russia. Turkey's continued declining course, combined with the growth of the new Balkan states and the internal weakness of the Hapsburg monarchy, were central to Russia's interests and framed her efforts to revitalize her Balkan policies. Important as these developments were, however — and any one of them could serve as an example of my second imperative — there was another factor which bore directly on the formation and pursuit of Russian policy. This factor might be called the 'negative correspondence of interest' between Russia and her allies, and may be explored as a specific example of the impact of the international circumstance on policy formation.

A striking comparison can be made between Russian policy in the eighteenth and in the nineteenth centuries. Catherine II was aided in her dealing with the Polish problem by a 'positive correspondence of interest' with Prussia, and her efforts to advance Russian interests in the Black Sea were seconded by Austria's Joseph II. The reasons for these associations need not concern us, but the fact is that Russian policy in two crucial areas was strengthened and its goals advanced by other major powers who could find advantage for themselves in concerting their actions with those of Russia. Between 1856 and 1914, however, a different situation emerged. Russia found a common footing with Prussia on the question of controlling the Polish revolt in 1863, and her passive neutrality in the Danish War, the Seven Weeks War, and the Franco-Prussian War aided Bismarck's program for unifying Germany, but there was no corresponding support for Russian interests in the Balkans. Indeed, Bismarck's political system was built in part on the assumption that Austria and Russia had conflicting interests in the Balkans which held the potentiality of generating a European war. To avert such a clash, and to prevent Russia from seeking an agreement with France which would threaten Germany and the European peace, Bismarck went to considerable lengths first in the Three Emperors Leagues, later in the Re-Insurance Treaty, to maintain relations with Russia. In order to achieve either significant influence in the Balkans, or, more remotely, dominance at the Straits, Russia required the positive support of another major power to offset England's tenacious opposition and Austria's resistance. In the 1870's Germany seemed to offer the best hope of such support, but such a hope ran against Bismarck's interpretation of the political situation, and when Austria and England protested the Bulgarian settlement after the Russo-Turkish War of 1877–1878, Bismarck's compromise at the Berlin Congress was taken in St. Petersburg as a diplomatic defeat. As the Dual Alliance testified, Austria was more important to Germany than Russia was, and though Bismarck stressed the importance of the line to St. Petersburg, he did so in the context of maintaining stability, easing the potential tension between Austria and Russia, and in effect, restraining Russian policy in the sensitive Balkan complex. The advantages which accrued to Russia in this arrangement were primarily defensive. Her frontiers were secure, and she did not face England alone. On the other side of the coin, she lacked positive support for her policies, and the Bismarckian system had a restrictive influence on her Balkan interests.[5]

[5] This did not mean that Russia withdrew from Balkan issues, but her policy turned toward manipulation and intrigue. For a detailed and enlighten-

The "second diplomatic revolution," which was symbolized by Bismarck's retirement and the construction of the entente system, made no essential change in this situation. The Franco-Russian alliance was built on the twin foundations of mutual economic advantage and military security, and the Anglo-Russian understanding which came thirteen years later demarcated the colonial conflict and served as the basis for strengthening mutual political and military commitments among the entente powers against the possibility of war with Germany. Both France and England remained aloof from the Russo-Japanese War, and following the Portsmouth Conference France worked toward the colonial accommodation which produced the Anglo-Russian Agreement of 1907 and the establishment of the Asian balance of power with defined spheres of influence for the European states and Japan. When Izvolskii returned to the Balkan question, that "graveyard of Russian diplomacy," he did so without the positive support of Russia's allies and in the face of active Austrian and German interest. France, like Bismarck before her, was interested in Russia for reasons other than forwarding her Balkan ambitions, and though the French were less inclined to restrain Russian policy than Bismarck had been, she offered Russia no active support; Britain remained steadfastly opposed to Russian dominance at the Straits. As a consequence, Russia's efforts to intervene in the Balkan crises of 1908 and 1911 were undertaken almost unilaterally, and in neither case was Russia able to extend her influence or protect her protégés. The diplomatic defeats which resulted undoubtedly hardened Russia's resolution when faced with the crisis in 1914 and the Austrian ultimatum to the Serbian government. Even in this case, however, French support for Russia turned on Germany's decision to back Austria, and it was only as the crisis expanded beyond the Balkan locale that the Russian alliances came into play.

Foreign policy may be carried on on many levels and for many different purposes, but it cannot be pursued in a vacuum, and

ing analysis of methods and results, see Charles Jelavich, *Tsarist Russia and Balkan Nationalism: Russian Influence in the Internal Affairs of Bulgaria and Serbia, 1879–1886* (Berkeley: University of California Press, 1958).

213

there must be common interests to be served for agreements to be effective. The necessities which underlay Russia's agreements first with the German powers, later with the entente powers, were real and meaningful, and since they contributed to Russia's internal growth and the establishment of the requisite conditions for political and military security, they were effective. The area of agreement was also fundamentally restrictive, defensive, and passive. Though Russia was defeated in the Crimean War, her determination to establish a position of power in the Balkans and to gain at the least a favorable Straits settlement returned regularly, but the interests of the other powers frustrated this drive. Between 1856 and 1914, no power was willing to unite its interests with Russia's as Prussia did on the Polish question in the eighteenth century. Lacking such support in a vital interest area, Russian Balkan policy was doomed to be merely disruptive or ineffectual, and in the twentieth century it was usually both. Russia fared somewhat better in the colonial field, though the agreements which followed the Russo-Japanese War sharply reduced Russian influence in China and Manchuria and excluded Russia from Korea, and the agreement with England concerning Central Asia and the border-lands imposed a restraint on Russian expansion which was regularly violated between 1907 and 1914. Though restricted, however, Russian interests were recognized, and if the fanatic expansionists who thrust Russia into war with Japan were disenchanted as well as discredited, more moderate men were willing to accept the Asian balance of power and the spheres of influence it defined. The truth was, however, that colonial expansion — particularly, the Russian position in Asia — was lower in the scale of priorities than Europe and, particularly, the Balkan problem; it was in Europe and the Balkans that the realities of the international situation were an especially effective influence and the principle of "negative correspondence of interest" was especially meaningful.

Political developments in the world outside Russia provided a second imperative for Russian foreign policy, and on the eve of World War I, this was essentially a restricting influence. The structure of international politics defined what it was possible for Russia to undertake, and thus impinged directly on policy formation. The existence of the international aspect exerted a controlling, rationalizing influence on Russia's policy makers, since no matter how dynamic the ideals of manifest destiny or national patriotism, the political realities imposed order and form on policy decisions. Positional factors have been of the first importance in determining the thrust of Russian policy, with the international situation providing the political framework within which to deal with positional realities. The second imperative has been primarily a restricting factor, and it has been particularly effective in determining the limits of Russian foreign policy in the modern period.

♟ ♟ ♟

A SOCIETY'S level of cultural development provides the third imperative for foreign policy, because the stage that a nation has reached in technological development, economic growth, social organization, administrative efficiency, and intellectual sophistication determines its power potential and its competitive position in the community of nations. Like geography and the structure of international politics, cultural development plays a double role. On the one side it defines the capacity to act, the ability to realize particular goals, and on the other it creates specific needs which affect policy decisions. Military efficiency and success in war are the most obvious examples of the first function; economic requirements that justify colonial expansion typify the second. In early Russian history, the Kievan principalities could compete on equal terms in the world in which they lived, but in the modern era not only have cultural deficiencies regularly inhibited Russia's capacity to act, but also the necessity for competing with more highly developed societies has profoundly affected the development of Russian social and political institutions. The creation and maintenance of a major power's military establishment were a primary factor in Peter the Great's revolutionary program, and Russia's active international role under Catherine II, Paul, Alexander I, and Nicholas I created immense fiscal and social burdens with no comparable increase in productivity or administrative efficiency. Russia's defeat in the Crimean War reflected massive cultural deficiences and the cumulative result of over-exploiting inadequate resources at the expense of social and economic progress. The cautious policies which Russia followed for more than two decades after the Peace of Paris reflected her leaders' determination to build the bases of power before again committing Russia to another, possibly disastrous, military confrontation. The policy of caution so engendered remained effective despite the rising tide of aggressive nationalism, of militant Pan-Slavism, and the demand for imperial conquest with only two exceptions, the Russo-Japanese War and the mobilization against Germany in 1914. And the exceptions justified caution, for the war against Japan was a debacle, and World War I ended for Russia in the Revolution which swept away the old order.

The reforms initiated after the Crimean War marked the beginning of a period of rapid modernization and industrialization, which, by the twentieth century had transformed Russia's face.[6] The components of an industrial society came into being as basic industries developed, transport improved, and both labor and business organizations made their appearance. Political activism increased, the creative spirit burgeoned, and an immense vitality stirred new forces beneath the covering shell of autocratic control. Significant as these developments were for Russia's history, their immediate effect on foreign policy was slight — despite Russia's immense progress in the later nineteenth century, she remained inferior to the leading Western nations both in the quantity and the quality of her technology and production. The indices of deficiency were legion. Although Russian education expanded greatly in the second half of the nineteenth century, there remained an immense shortage of professional personnel to serve the society as a whole. In public health, for example, despite the expansion of professional

---

[6] See Theodore Von Laue, "Problems of Modernization," in Lederer, ed., *Russian Foreign Policy*, pp. 69ff., and the same author's *Sergei Witte and the Industrialization of Russia* (New York: Columbia University Press, 1963). Von Laue stresses the gap between accomplishment and need, but he also warns against too heavy a stress on "poverty pacificism" as a factor in Russian foreign policy ("Problems of Modernization," p. 87).

training, available medical personnel and facilities were far in arrears of Germany, France, or Austria, and were totally inadequate for the needs of the Russian population. Epidemic disease could rage unchecked, and neither the social nor the sanitary engineering to control it were available. Despite the rapidly ascending production curve, the Russian economy remained heavily dependent on foreign capital, state finances were barely adequate to maintain government services, and business depressions combined with crop failures produced a succession of crises. Emancipation of the serfs had created a whole new range of problems which the government faced reluctantly, and agricultural production increased but slowly. The state administration was sterile and unresponsive; bureaucratic formalism, inefficiency, and corruption continued to waste national resources. The Russian army revealed serious administrative and logistical weaknesses in the war against Turkey in 1877–1878, and in the Russo-Japanese War, and the physical condition of the Russian fleet in 1904 revealed how little actual progress had been made. The first-line Russian armies in 1914 were well equipped, trained, and organized, but the reserves of men and material were distinctly inferior, and neither the economy nor the administration were equal to supplying the vast needs created by the initial disasters on the eastern front or by the attrition which followed. Each of these particulars indicated the deficiency which inhibited Russia's capacity to act, and when World War I began, Russia still required another generation of development to be competitive with the leading European powers.

During the eighteenth and early nineteenth centuries, cultural deficiencies were overcome by extraordinary measures, and though the Russian people suffered as a consequence, eighteenth-century Russia was able to compete effectively with preindustrial Europe. Industrialization, however, vastly accelerated cultural growth, and the nonindustrial society found itself laboring under the double disadvantage of backward technology and the lack of productive capacity necessary for a sustained effort. Russia clearly suffered from both disadvantages during the nineteenth century, and her most sensitive leaders recognized the fact. I commented earlier that when Russian policy ran into the opposition of other major powers in the Balkans, in Central Asia, or in the Far East, it turned aside rather than risking war. Russia fought Turkey in 1877 with a European mandate, and Turkey was clearly in a state of military decline and political disintegration. Russian expansion in Asia was carried out against vastly inferior tribal cultures — the Chinese Empire itself was inept militarily and on the verge of collapse, and Russia's intervention against Japan to revise the Treaty of Shimonoseki was undertaken in company with France and Germany. The decision to fight Japan was taken over Witte's objections on the utterly false premise of Russian military superiority, and the defeat which followed eclipsed the Asian warhawks and returned Russian policy to a more cautious line. The Eastern mistake was not repeated in the Balkan crises of 1908 and 1911, even though the provocation was greater and Russia's emotional commitment was far deeper and more widely held. Indeed, Russia's Balkan policies in the nineteenth century were more a matter of intrigue and maneuver than military aggression, and from the Congress of Berlin through the Second Balkan War, Russia avoided any serious military confrontation, employing instead a series of cultural offensives using special agents and benevolent societies throughout the Near East.[7] The Russian decision to mobilize in 1914 was a direct response to Austria's military action against Serbia and to the threat to Russian territory which Germany's support of Austria posed. Political and military considerations outweighed economic deficiencies, and the policy of caution was put aside. This, however, marked a departure from the normal pattern, and it reflected the unusual circumstances which conspired to produce World War I.

Apart from defining the capacity to act, cultural development itself generates needs and goals that affect the formation of foreign policy. The commercial character of Kievan cities influenced their relations with the Byzantine Empire; Ivan IV was moved to propose

[7] For this aspect of Russian foreign policy, see Theofanis G. Stavrou, *Russian Interests in Palestine, 1882–1914: A Study of Religious and Educational Enterprise* (Thessaloniki: Institute for Balkan Studies, 1963).

diplomatic connections to the Emperor, Charles V, in part to gain the services of artisans and technical innovators necessary to the Muscovite economy; and Russia's eighteenth-century relations with England were regularly influenced both by the English merchant community, which was an essential part of Russia's economy, and by the need for English and Dutch capital to prosecute Russia's wars. Alexander's final break with Napoleon was intimately connected with Franco-Russian economic relations, and Russian tariff policy under Nicholas I strained Russo-Prussian relations. The problem of cultural deficiency itself gave rise to two related developments which affected Russian policy on the eve of World War I: the first was the need for capital to promote both internal growth and external expansion, and the second was the idea that expansion was a function of internal development and would lead to economic progress. Both ideas were generated out of recognized deficiencies in Russian cultural, particularly economic, development, and both directly affected the formation of specific policies.

The need for foreign capital was consistent through both the preindustrial and industrial phases of modern Russian development, but the process of industrialization made the need particularly pressing. Russian loans were regularly subscribed by foreign bankers, and though the Ministry of Finance periodically attempted to reduce Russian dependence on external financial resources, no permanent resolution for the problem was found. When Bismarck wished to apply sanctions to Russia, he struck at Russian credit in Germany, and though he intended no more than a threatening gesture, his action sharpened the demand for other and independent sources of foreign loans. Between 1888 and 1894 a series of Russian loans were negotiated and subscribed in Paris, and the financial bond was cemented in the Franco-Russian alliance. Between 1894 and 1910 millions of francs were exported to Russia, and though the Russian government used these funds partly to finance railroad construction in the Far East and to underwrite the Russo-Chinese Bank, they filled an enormous gap in the Russian economy. Financial necessity affected political decision, and France used her growing influence in Russian political circles to advance the colonial settlement between England and Russia in 1907 and the agreements with Japan which were completed by 1910. At the same time Russian military commitments to France were more clearly defined, and the financial bond helped to solidify Russian support for the entente system.[8]

The second idea was broader and was related to the whole conception of economic and social progress. The new lands of Central Asia and the Far East held forth the promise of riches yet untapped, and the idea grew that the forward thrust which Russia needed could come from exploitation of the new territories. While pressing for railroad construction in the East, the judicious Witte espoused a cautiously expansionist view, though he retreated when it became apparent that the imperialist cabal led first by General Kuropatkin, and later by von Plehve and Alexander Bezobrazov, was pushing Russia into war. These men, infected with the Asian dream, as well as national glory, carried Nicholas II with them in pursuit of Russia's civilizing mission in Asia with its promise of an ultimate, though ill-defined, economic reward. Russian expansion ran against Japanese interests, and in the wake of defeat, the Russian position in the Orient stabilized, but the dream continued. Russia accepted the Asian balance of power with the demarcation of spheres of influence, and after 1910 restricted her expansion to the penetration of Mongolia and shifted the focus of her attention to the growing tension in Europe. During nearly a half century of internal growth, however, Asian expansion was related to progress and modernization, the development of national power, economic self-sufficiency, and the civilizing mission. As Dostoevsky argued, in Europe Russians "were hangers-on and slaves, whereas we shall go to Asia as masters," for ultimately Asia was a new world in which to regenerate the old.[9]

[8] A recent Soviet study has developed this point in detail. See E. M. Rozental, *Diplomaticheskaia istoriia russko-frantsuzkogo soiuza v nachale xx veka* (Moscow, 1960).

[9] *The Diary of a Writer*, 2 vols., trans. by Boris Brasol (New York: Scribners, 1949), Vol. II, p. 1048. It is worth quoting Dostoevsky at length on Asia's potential regenerative impact on Russia: "You see . . . when we turn to Asia . . . in Russia there may occur something akin to what happened in Europe when America was discovered . . . With an aspiration

Cultural development, as the third imperative in modern Russian foreign policy, exerted a limiting effect on Russian action because Russia lacked the material tools with which to compete with her contemporaries. In this sense, it fostered a sense of caution, a true conservatism where there was a possibility of conflict with other major European states. In another sense, the fact of cultural deficiencies led to specific attempts to resolve them, and drew Russia toward new sources of finance capital and into an expansionist policy in Asia. In the last analysis, however, the largest importance which may be attached to cultural development as a foreign policy imperative lies in its role in defining the capacity of the nation to compete.

⚜ ⚜ ⚜

THE fourth imperative for Russian foreign policy is the ideological. In one sense, this imperative has been the most important of all, for it contains elements of all the others combined with broad value judgments that establish moral priorities. Though important, ideology is difficult to evaluate, for its very pervasiveness is a temptation to make it the explanation of everything, and its character as a quasi-system of ideas opens a deceptively simple road to analyzing motivation through expressed moral or cultural principles. Without attacking the problem exhaustively, there are two levels on which ideology is significant historically. First, ideology expresses a society's view of itself in relation to other societies and to the values which it considers important. Second, in a more limited sense, ideology becomes a specific commitment to a particular idea and the effort to realize that idea in the real world. On

for Asia, our spirit and forces will be regenerated . . . Our civilizing mission in Asia will bribe our spirit and drive us thither . . . Build only two railroads; begin with the one to Siberia, and then — to Central Asia . . . Do you know that in Asia there are lands which are less explored than the interior of Africa? And do we know what riches are concealed in the bosom of these boundless lands? [If Englishmen or Americans lived in Russia] they would get at everything — metals and minerals, innumerable coal fields; they would find and discover everything . . . Let it be only slightly fathomed (but fathomed) that Asia is our future outlet, that our riches are these, that there is our ocean . . ." (*ibid.*, pp. 1048–1049).

this level, ideology may be identified with movements, the so-called isms of a generation, but in turn the isms are a manifestation of the cultural milieu.[10]

Taking the broader approach first, two orientations have characterized Russian ideology — cosmopolitanism and an inward-turning sense of cultural uniqueness which approaches xenophobia and which exhibits a messianic complex as one of its most important dimensions. The dialectical interplay between these concepts has given a creative tension to Russian historical development, and both elements have been crucial in Russian cultural life in the modern era. The Westernizing movement from the seventeenth century to the Revolution of 1917 interpreted Russian culture in a comparative and cosmopolitan frame of reference, considered Russia a member of the European family of nations, and looked to Europe for the instruments with which to advance Russian creativity. Traditional Russia soon lost its hold among the influential and the educated, but it lived on in popular culture — the Old Believers clung tenaciously to their faith in unreformed Russian Orthodoxy as the last true Christian community and in Old Russian culture as the embodiment of God's will. The doctrine of the Third Rome gave Russia a unique role among the nations, and the exclusivist and messianic implications of that doctrine remained latent in the Russian cultural vocabulary to reawaken in more recent times. The ideas of cultural and spiritual uniqueness took root among the educated classes under the influence of the later Enlightenment and organic historicism, appearing in the more extreme nationalist ideals of the Decembrists, in the Slavophil and later the Pan-Slav movement, and above all in Dostoevsky's affirmation of intuition, spirituality, and love against Western rationalism. By the latter part of the nineteenth century Russia's unique spirit had become a dominant theme, and though Russian Marxism began as a materialist and cosmopolitan ideology, its development

[10] For a stimulating discussion of ideology and its significance which defines the concept differently, see Daniel Bell, "Ideology and Soviet Politics," with comments by George Lichtheim and Carl J. Friedrich, *Slavic Review*, XXIV, No. 4 (December 1965), 591–621. Cf. Adam B. Ulam, "Nationalism, Panslavism, Communism," in Lederer, ed., *Russian Foreign Policy*, pp. 39–67.

RODERICK E. MC GREW

after the Revolution of 1917 contained both nationalist and messianic implications.

The broad ideological orientations I have described are applicable in different ways on different levels of Russian society, and it would be tempting at this point simply to associate Russian expansion with messianism, or to explain the drive toward Constantinople as a reaffirmation of revived Orthodoxy. Two problems stand in the way of such an approach: First, Russian society from the seventeenth century on divided along at least three major lines of cleavage, and each assumed a somewhat different ideological posture. Second, the power of decision remained concentrated in the hands of the tsar and his immediate advisers, and as a consequence the conduct of foreign policy was largely insulated against both the cultural dynamism of the nineteenth century and the impact of particular ideological conceptions. Indeed, it might be argued that some of the most characteristic features of Russian intellectual development were irrelevant in any direct sense to the formation of foreign policy, and that this very sense of irrelevance deepened the division in Russian society between the rulers and the educated classes.[11]

In the modern period the largest part of Russian society was sunk in ignorance, unaware of the real nature of the outside world, and restricted in its political behavior to a kind of responsive reflex. Among these reflexes was fear and hatred of the foreigner, and in times of stress or crisis, the peasants made foreigners their scapegoats, venting their fear and frustration in violence. This attitude could be a powerful weapon when Russia was invaded, as in 1812, and it may have contributed to the fighting qualities of the Russian soldier, but it also served to emphasize how far the ordinary person was removed from the Russian political world and how essentially meaningless its complexities were for the common people. Until 1825, on the other hand, there was a common ideological footing among the educated classes, and the cosmopoli-

[11] See Richard E. Pipes, "Domestic Politics and Foreign Affairs," in Lederer, ed., *Russian Foreign Policy*, pp. 147–150, for a comment on the separation of decision centers from the developments in society. Cf. Robert M. Slusser, "The Role of the Foreign Ministry," in *ibid.*, pp. 197–211.

223

tanism which Peter the Great fostered became characteristic of enlightened society. The cultural heirs of Muscovy were unable to challenge the Europeanism which formed the core of the official viewpoint, and the newly aware cultural nationalists of the later eighteenth century had not developed exclusivist tendencies. In the wake of the Decembrist Revolution, however, during the reign of Nicholas I, a widening rift between the new intelligentsia and the official world developed, and as sterile official nationalism hardened into ideology, educated Russians turned away in disgust. The conservative doctrines which shaped official views from Karamzin through Pogodin and Shevyrev to Pobedonostsev shared intellectual roots with many aspects of the intelligentsia's thought, but the identification of Russia's historical culture with the autocratic principle created an insuperable barrier. The intellectual flux generated in Russia's new cultural life thus ran in other channels; the milieu of political decision remained the traditional one in which Russia's interests were placidly pursued within a cosmopolitan European context, and Russia remained committed to stability, order, and the European system.

The sense of historical uniqueness, and the messianic impulses which flowed from it, sharpened the sense of competition between Russia and the West, but as regularly as Russian intellectuals argued for her cultural superiority, Russia suffered defeat after defeat, and a violent reaction against the government and its policies resulted. Again and again Russia's reach was longer than her grasp was strong: the imperial regime failed to gain preponderance in the Balkans or dominance at the Straits, and in the Far East what should have been an obviously inferior Oriental state administered a succession of crushing military and naval defeats. The complex reactions which these failures engendered further alienated society from the government, fed the patriotic hysteria which greeted the outbreak of World War I, and turned upon the government when it failed once more in the military campaigns of 1914–1917. Nationalism, which had been a regular component of the official ideology, justified and motivated the revived assault on the Balkan problem, and even after the event Sazonov could argue that public opinion supported the government's position, implying an ideological unity which simply did not exist. Nationalism as an expression of a unified society did not apply in Nicholas II's Russia, and the result of military defeat was political disintegration. The ideological milieu of foreign policy decision was abstracted from the stream of Russian life, and while the imperial regime weighed its decisions on the traditional scales of Russian polity, Russian society demanded new standards in a new world.

Before the reign of Nicholas II, particular ideologies had relatively little influence on foreign policies. Pan-Slavism, one of the most vociferous of the nineteenth-century movements, had a greater impact on Paris and Berlin than it did on St. Petersburg, and neither Ignatiev at Constantinople nor General Skobelev did more than complicate the political situation. The men who directed Russia's foreign policy from Prince Gorchakov to Giers, including Sergei Witte, were statesmen in the European mode who worked within the limited and rationalist framework of the European state system, avoiding the feverish or the fanatic, manipulating particular issues as they arose and eschewing extremist views, whether nationalist or imperialist. This mode of operations suited both Alexander II and Alexander III, and it closely followed the traditional outlook on Russian diplomacy. During Nicholas II's reign a succession of weak ministers together with the diffusion of responsibility for decisions bearing on foreign policy, a condition endemic in Russian administration, and the vacillating character of the Tsar himself allowed special interests to influence policy formation. The most striking instance was the success of the imperialist cabal in pushing Russia toward war with Japan, and to the extent that imperialism was an ideological formation, it played a role in policy formation.[12] The new emphasis on the Balkans which came after 1905 marked a return to a well-established political goal, and one by no means incompatible with the traditional interpretations of Russia's interests. Both Izvolskii and Sazonov

[12] See Andrew Malozemoff, *Russian Far Eastern Policy, 1881–1904; with Special Emphasis on the Causes of the Russo-Japanese War* (Berkeley: University of California Press, 1958); David J. Dallin, *The Rise of Russia in Asia* (New Haven, Conn.: Yale University Press, 1949).

expressed the national and conservative outlook consistent with the official world, and if the Russian government overplayed its hand in 1914, it did so on the basis of error and miscalculation rather than ideological fervor. In sum, particular ideologies at the most provided emphases, a special flavor in the political cuisine, and at no time were a major formative influence on Russian foreign policy.

It is in the first, or more generalized sense of ideology that we find a meaningful relation with foreign policy, for the traditional milieu of the official world was the environment of decision. The official world was oriented toward Russia as a Great Power and a member of the European family, toward political conservatism and the pursuit of national interest within the balance of power. Policy goals reflected political interests that a complex of external realities imposed upon the monarchy, and those interests became a part of the ideological orientation — among these, the most important were the maintenance of secure frontiers, the establishment of a position on the Black Sea and the control of the Straits, security in the Baltic, and the exploitation of contiguous borderlands to attain economic rewards and political stability. The official outlook also displayed national pride, sensitivity on questions of prestige, and the ambition to realize Russia's national interests. The official viewpoint, by my first definition, represented an ideological commitment, and in that sense ideology shaped foreign policy decisions. This was not, however, the world view of the creative intelligentsia, nor did it represent a unified pattern of motives and values which could be generalized for educated society or for society as a whole. Russia was a multiplicity of worlds exhibiting contradictory values and only incidentally or sporadically achieving unity on occasional means. The power to formulate policy lay with only one of these worlds, and it was the outlook of moribund officialism which defined the main outlines of Russian foreign policy.

♟ ♟ ♟

ON JULY 31, 1914, Germany declared war on Russia, and by August 4 all the major European powers, with the exception of Italy, were committed. The cataclysm which resulted ended the European world as it had been and spawned a new age of search and struggle, a revolutionary era whose successive climaxes twisted the world's cultural topography into a bizarre wasteland where well-known landmarks were obliterated and new paths ended in precipices. The terrible and utterly unforeseen consequences of that first holocaust have given the issue of responsibility for the war's coming a moral significance which attaches to a few historical events, yet neither a comfortable syncretism nor the strident prosecutors of Germany, Austria, or Russia seem to reach the heart of the problem. The reason lies in the peculiar complexity of political decision itself. No nation, as no individual, acts according to a single pattern of motivation, and the imperatives which shape policy decision are the product of each nation's historical circumstance. Men must take responsibility for the way they interpret and treat that environment, but the possibilities for decision, the alternatives among which they choose, are the product of a complex historical process.

Russian policy from 1894 to 1914 was neither single-mindedly aggressive nor blindly fanatic. Rather, it reflected the constant interaction of historical conditions which tempered and qualified the most extreme positions while establishing specific minima which had to be realized to maintain political security and the potentiality for internal development. Russia expanded territorially in the second half of the nineteenth century, and further, in common with other European states, she extended her political and economic influence toward China, Korea, Persia, and the Balkans. There was no possibility for unilateral action in the Balkans, and without the firm support of other European powers Russia was reduced to the expedients of maneuver and intrigue. The Russian commitment to dominate the eastern Balkans and the Straits was a consistent theme in the nineteenth century, but the interests of other powers, combined with Russia's inability to generate the force necessary to achieve her ends by war, made caution her watchword. During the first decade of the twentieth century Russia was forced to accept a similar limitation on her activities in Central

Asia and the Far East, and by 1910 the territorial limits to expansion had been defined and the edge of Russian aggression had been blunted.

A combination of domestic economic issues and imperial problems dictated the reorientation of Russian policy from its traditional German focus to one of alliance with France and England. This turn afforded little territorial advantage for Russia, whereas the immediate problem of military security was actually enlarged. During the century from the reign of Catherine II through that of Alexander III, Russia, with the exception of the Napoleonic period and briefly at the time of the Crimean War, had been able to maneuver diplomatically behind the screen afforded by friendly relations with Austria and Prussia, but the emergence of a united Germany pushed Russia toward a Western alliance which put the security of her Western frontiers on a military rather than a political footing. The potential danger in such a situation had appeared briefly when Austria threatened Russian territory in the Crimean War, but the threat became actual when Germany gave Austria her military backing in the confrontation with Serbia. Yet the road which led to war was marked out in a succession of decisions necessitated by other, if related, issues. The positional imperative, and the question of security which it raised, was immediately significant, but the orientation of Russian policy which finally led to conflict developed out of a complex of responses and needs. The imperatives for Russian foreign policy which operated throughout the modern era defined the alternatives, the choice among which produced the tragic dilemma of 1914.

The four imperatives defined here represented broad streams of continuity in the development of Russian history. Particular historical circumstances change, and each period, or each problem, must be considered in terms of its own shape and consistency; but the particular, in turn, always exists in a context, and the men who must deal with it form their ideas out of a complex of attitudes, values, or priorities that composes the cultural milieu. Russia's geographical orientation and position provided a series of fixed points, of established issues, which needed to be resolved. That position in turn shaped the way in which external influences bore upon her and the kind of relations which she had with the outside world. The relations among and within the states surrounding Russia regularly defined the limits of the possible and gave a political form to the particular problems which her position created. The cultural development of Russia herself responded to external influences, but it provided as well the tools with which Russian leaders worked, just as insufficiency and technological backwardness regularly limited Russia's external goals. Finally, the ideological milieu defined the image of Russia's role among the nations and the values by which political priorities were established. This is not to argue that any particular foreign policy decision was the irrevocable product of historical necessity, but it is to suggest that the roots of Russian policy were firmly embedded in the soil of her historical culture. This lesson applies to our own time as it did in the recent, or the distant, past.

ADDITIONAL READING

Additional Reading

With few exceptions, the following selective bibliography consists almost entirely of works in English and is intended primarily for the use of undergraduate and beginning graduate students. Interested scholars and advanced graduate students may consult the detailed references to sources in Russian and Western European languages which appear in the footnotes of the essays.

On Interpreting the Fate of Imperial Russia

Abramovitch, Raphael R., *The Soviet Revolution 1917–1939*. New York: International Universities Press, 1962.

Alexander, Grand Duke of Russia, *Once a Grand Duke*. New York: Cassell, 1932.

Alexandra, Empress Consort of Nicholas II, Emperor of Russia, *The Letters of the Tsaritsa to the Tsar, 1914–1916*, ed. Bernard Pares. London: Duckworth, 1923.

Antsiferov, Aleksei N., *et al.*, *Russian Agriculture during the War*. New Haven, Conn.: Yale University Press, 1930.

Black, Cyril E., ed., *The Transformation of Russian Society: Aspects of Social Change since 1861*. Cambridge, Mass.: Harvard University Press, 1960.

Charques, Richard, *The Twilight of Imperial Russia*. London: Phoenix House, 1958.

Curtiss, John Shelton, ed., *Essays in Russian and Soviet History*. Leiden: E. J. Brill, 1963.

Dillon, E. J., *The Eclipse of Russia*. New York: Doran, 1918.

Florinsky, Michael T., *The End of the Russian Empire*. New Haven, Conn.: Yale University Press, 1931.

Florinsky, Michael T., *Russia: A History and an Interpretation*, Vol. II. New York: Macmillan, 1955.

Gerschenkron, Alexander, *Economic Backwardness in Historical Perspective*. Cambridge, Mass.: Harvard University Press, 1962.

ADDITIONAL READING

Golder, F. A., ed., *Documents of Russian History, 1914–1917*. New York & London: Century, 1927.

Gurko, Vladimir I., *Features and Figures of the Past: Government and Opinion in the Reign of Nicholas II*. Stanford: Stanford University Press, 1939.

Haimson, Leopold H., "The Problem of Social Stability in Urban Russia, 1905–1917," *Slavic Review*, XXIII (December 1964), 619–642; XXIV (March 1965), 1–22.

Haimson, Leopold H., "Reply," *Slavic Review*, XXIV (March 1965), 47–56.

Hoetzsch, Otto, *Russland: eine Einfuhrung auf Grund seiner Geschichte von 1904 bis 1912*. Berlin: G. Reimer, 1913.

Karpovich, Michael, *Imperial Russia 1801–1917*. New York: Holt, 1932.

Kerensky, Alexander, *Russia and History's Turning Point*. New York: Duell, 1965.

Kochan, Lionel, *Russia in Revolution, 1890–1918*. New York: New American Library, 1966.

Leroy-Beaulieu, Anatole, *The Empire of the Tsars and the Russians*, 3 vols., trans. from 3rd French ed. by Zenaide A. Ragozin. New York, London: Putnam, 1893–1896.

Massie, Robert K., *Nicholas and Alexandra*. New York: Atheneum, 1967.

Maynard, Sir John, *Russia in Flux*. New York: Macmillan, 1948.

Mendel, Arthur P., *Dilemmas of Progress in Tsarist Russia: Legal Marxism and Legal Populism*. Cambridge, Mass.: Harvard University Press, 1961.

Mendel, Arthur P., "Peasant and Worker on the Eve of the First World War," *Slavic Review*, XXIV (March 1965), 23–33.

Miliukov, Paul N., *Russia and Its Crisis*. Chicago: University of Chicago Press, 1905.

Nicholas II, Emperor of Russia, *The Letters of the Tsar to the Tsaritsa, 1914–1917*, trans. A. L. Hynes, ed. C. E. Vulliamy. New York: Dodd, 1929.

Pares, Bernard, *The Fall of the Russian Monarchy*. New York: Knopf, 1939; Vintage, 1961.

Pares, Bernard, *Russia and Reform*. London: Constable, 1907.

Pethyridge, Roger, ed., *Witnesses to the Russian Revolution*. New York: Citadel Press, 1964.

Pipes, Richard, ed., *Revolutionary Russia*. Cambridge, Mass.: Harvard University Press, 1967.

Pipes, Richard, ed., *The Russian Intelligentsia*. New York: Columbia University Press, 1961.

Pushkarev, Sergei, *The Emergence of Modern Russia, 1801–1917*. New York: Holt, 1963.

Rodzianko, Mikhail V., *The Reign of Rasputin: An Empire's Collapse, Memoirs of M. V. Rodzianko*, trans. Catherine Zvegintzoff. New York: A. K. Philpot, 1927.

Seton-Watson, Hugh, *The Decline of Imperial Russia, 1855–1914*. London, New York: Praeger, 1952.

Seton-Watson, Hugh, *The Russian Empire, 1801–1917*. Oxford: Clarendon Press, 1967.

Shukman, Harold, *Lenin and the Russian Revolution*. New York: Putnam, 1967.

Simmons, Ernest J., ed., *Continuity and Change in Russian and Soviet Thought*. Cambridge, Mass.: Harvard University Press, 1955.

234

Tompkins, Stuart Ramsey, *The Triumph of Bolshevism: Revolution or Reaction.* Norman: University of Oklahoma Press, 1967.

Treadgold, Donald W., ed., *The Development of the U.S.S.R.: An Exchange of Views.* Seattle: University of Washington Press, 1964.

Treadgold, Donald W., *Twentieth Century Russia.* Chicago: Rand McNally, 1959.

Troyat, Henry, *Daily Life in Russia under the Last Tsar.* London: Allen & Unwin, 1961.

Von Laue, Theodore H., "The Chances for Liberal Constitutionalism," *Slavic Review*, XXIV (March 1965), 34–46.

Von Laue, Theodore H., *Sergei Witte and the Industrialization of Russia.* New York: Columbia University Press, 1963.

Von Laue, Theodore H., *Why Lenin? Why Stalin?* Philadelphia & New York: Lippincott, 1964.

Vucinich, Wayne S., ed., *The Peasant in Nineteenth-Century Russia.* Stanford, Calif.: Stanford University Press, 1968.

Walkin, Jacob, *The Rise of Democracy in Pre-Revolutionary Russia: Political and Social Institutions under the Last Three Czars.* New York: Praeger, 1962.

Wallace, Sir Donald M., *Russia*, rev. ed. London: Cassell, 1912.

Weidlé, Wladimir, *Russia: Absent and Present*, trans. A. Gordon Smith. New York & London: Hollis & Carter, 1953, 1961.

Williams, Harold W., *Russia of the Russians.* New York: Scribners, 1914.

Witte, Count Sergei, *The Memoirs of Count Witte*, trans. & ed. Abraham Yarmolinsky. New York: Doubleday, 1921.

Youssoupoff, Feliks, *Lost Splendor*, trans. from the French by Ann Green & Nicholas Katkoff. New York: Putnam, 1954.

Russian Conservative Thought before the Revolution

Adams, Arthur E., "Pobedonostsev and the Rule of Firmness," *Slavic and East European Review*, XXXII, No. 78 (1953), 132–139.

Adams, Arthur E., "Pobedonostsev's Thought Control," *Russian Review* (New Haven), XV, No. 4 (1952), 241–246.

Berdiaev, Nikolai A., *Leontiev*, trans. George Reavey. London: Centenary Press, 1940.

Bryant, Arthur, *The Spirit of Conservatism.* London: Methuen, 1929.

Byrnes, Robert F., *Pobedonostsev: His Life and Thought.* Bloomington: Indiana University Press, 1968.

Byrnes, Robert F., "Pobedonostsev on the Instruments of Russian Government," *Continuity and Change in Russian and Soviet Thought*, in Ernest J. Simmons, ed. Cambridge, Mass.: Harvard University Press, 1955, pp. 113–129.

Byrnes, Robert F., "Pobedonostsev's Conception of the Good Society: An Analysis of His Thought after 1880," *Review of Politics*, XIII (1951), 169–190.

Christoff, Peter K., *An Introduction to Nineteenth-Century Russian Slavophilism: A Study in Ideas*, Vol. I, *A. S. Xomjakov.* The Hague: Mouton, 1961.

Curtiss, John S., *Church and State in Russia: The Last Years of the Empire, 1900–1917.* New York: Columbia University Press, 1940.

Dillon, Emile J., *The Eclipse of Russia.* New York: Doran, 1918.

ADDITIONAL READING

Epstein, Klaus, *The Genesis of German Conservatism*. Princeton, N.J.: Princeton University Press, 1966.

Gratieux, Albert, *A. S. Khomiakov et le mouvement slavophile*. Paris: Les Editions du Cerf, 1939.

Katz, Martin, *Mikhail Katkov: A Political Biography 1818–1887*. The Hague: Mouton, 1966.

Lossky, Nikolai O., *History of Russian Philosophy*. New York: International Universities Press, 1951.

Lukashevich, Stephen, *Ivan Aksakov 1823–1886. A Study in Russian Thought and Politics*. Cambridge, Mass.: Harvard University Press, 1965.

Lukashevich, Stephen, *Konstantin Leontev 1831–1891. A Study in Russian "Heroic Vitalism."* New York: Pageant Press, 1967.

MacMaster, Robert F., *Danilevsky, A Russian Totalitarian Philosopher*. Cambridge, Mass.: Harvard University Press, 1967.

Masaryk, Thomas Garrigue, *The Spirit of Russia: Studies in History, Literature and Philosophy*, Vols. I & II trans. Eden and Cedar Paul; Vol. III ed. George Gibian with Robert Bass & trans. Robert Bass. New York: Barnes & Noble, 1961, 1967.

Mosolov, Aleksandr A., *At the Court of the Last Tsar: Being the Memoirs of A. A. Mosolov, Head of the Court Chancellery, 1900–1916*, trans. E. W. Dickes, ed. A. A. Pilenko. London: Methuen, 1935.

Pobedonostsev, Konstantine P., *Reflections of a Russian Statesman*, trans. Robert C. Long. London: Grant Richards, 1898; Ann Arbor: University of Michigan Press, 1965.

Riasanovsky, Nicholas, *Russia and the West in the Teaching of the Slavophiles*. Cambridge, Mass.: Harvard University Press, 1952.

Rossiter, Clinton L., *Conservatism in America*. New York: Knopf, 1955.

Samuel, Maurice, *Blood Accusation, The Strange History of the Beiliss Case*. New York: Knopf, 1966.

Steinmann, Friedrich, & Elias Hurwicz, *Konstantin Petrowitsch Pobjedonoszew, der Staatsmann der Reaktion unter Alexander III*. Konigsberg Pr. & Berlin: Ost-Europa Verlag, 1933.

Thaden, Edward, *Conservative Nationalism in Nineteenth Century Russia*, Seattle: University of Washington Press, 1964.

Vucinich, Wayne S., ed., *The Peasant in Nineteenth-Century Russia*. Stanford, Calif.: Stanford University Press, 1968.

Winter, Eduard, *Russland und die slawischen Völker in der Diplomatie des Vatikans, 1878–1903*. Berlin: Akademie, 1950.

Yaney, George L., "The Concept of the Stolypin Land Reform," *Slavic Review*, XXIII (1964), 275–293.

Zenkovsky, V. V., *A History of Russian Philosophy*, trans. George L. Kline. New York: Columbia University Press, 1953.

Russian Radical Thought, 1894–1917

Avrich, Paul, *The Russian Anarchists*. Princeton, N.J.: Princeton University Press, 1967.

Baron, Samuel H., *Plekhanov: The Father of Russian Marxism*. Stanford: Stanford University Press, 1963.

Billington, James H., *The Icon and the Axe: An Interpretive History of Russian Culture*. New York: Knopf, 1966.

236

ADDITIONAL READING

Broido, Eva, *Memoirs of a Revolutionary*, trans. & ed. Vera Broido. New York: Oxford University Press, 1967.

Cole, G. D. H., *A History of Socialist Thought: The Second International, 1889–1914*. London: Macmillan, 1956.

Dan, Theodore I., *The Origins of Bolshevism*, trans. & ed. Joel Carmichel. New York: Harper, 1964.

Daniels, Robert V., "Lenin and the Russian Revolutionary Traditions," in *Harvard Slavic Studies*, Vol. IV. Cambridge, Mass.: Harvard University Press, 1957, pp. 339–353.

Deutscher, Isaac, *The Prophet Armed. Trotsky: 1879–1921*. London & New York: Oxford University Press, 1954.

Elkin, Boris, "The Russian Intelligentsia on the Eve of the Revolution," in Richard Pipes, ed., *The Russian Intelligentsia*. New York: Columbia University Press, 1961.

Fischer, George, *Russian Liberalism: From Gentry to Intelligentsia*. Cambridge, Mass.: Harvard University Press, 1958.

Fischer, Louis, *The Life of Lenin*. New York: Harper, 1964.

Gankin, Olga H., *The Bolsheviks and the World War: The Origin of the Third International*. Stanford: Stanford University Press, 1940.

Getzler, Israel, *Martov, A Political Biography of a Russian Social Democrat*. Melbourne: Cambridge University Press, 1967.

Haimson, Leopold H., "The Problem of Social Stability in Urban Russia, 1905–1917," *Slavic Review*, XXIII (December 1964), 619–642; XXIV (March 1965), 1–22.

Haimson, Leopold H., *The Russian Marxists and the Origins of Bolshevism*. Cambridge, Mass.: Harvard University Press, 1955.

Harcave, Sidney, *First Blood: The Russian Revolution of 1905*. New York: Macmillan, 1964.

Hare, Richard, *Portraits of Russian Personalities between Reform and Revolution*. New York: Oxford University Press, 1959.

Joll, James, *The Second International 1889–1914*. London: Weidenfeld & Nicolson, 1955.

Karpovich, Michael, "Two Types of Russian Liberalism: Maklakov and Miliukov," in Ernest J. Simmons, ed., *Continuity and Change in Russian and Soviet Thought*. Cambridge, Mass.: Harvard University Press, 1955, pp. 129–143.

Keep, J. L. H., *The Rise of Social Democracy in Russia*. London: Oxford University Press, 1963.

Kennan, George, *Siberia and the Exile System*. New York: Century, 1891.

Kindersley, Richard, *The First Russian Revisionists: A Study of "Legal Marxism" in Russia*. New York: Oxford University Press, 1962.

Krupskaia, Nadezhda K., *Reminiscences of Lenin*, trans. E. Verney. New York: International Publishers, 1967. Also, Moscow: Foreign Languages Publishing House, 1959.

Lane, D. S., *Social and Organizational Differences Between Bolsheviks and Mensheviks, 1903–1907*. London: University of Birmingham Press, 1964.

Leontovitsch, Victor, *Geschichte des Liberalismus in Russland*. Frankfurt: Klostermann, 157.

Mendel, Arthur P., *Dilemmas of Progress in Tsarist Russia: Legal Marxism and Legal Populism*. Cambridge, Mass.: Harvard University Press, 1961.

Meyer, Alfred G., *Leninism*. Cambridge, Mass.: Harvard University Press, 1957.

Pipes, Richard, "Communism and Russian History," in Donald W. Treadgold, ed., *Soviet and Chinese Communism: Similarities and Differences*. Seattle: University of Washington Press, 1966.

Pipes, Richard, *Social Democracy and the St. Petersburg Labor Movement, 1885–1897*. Cambridge, Mass.: Harvard University Press, 1963.

Pipes, Richard, ed., *Revolutionary Russia*. Cambridge, Mass.: Harvard University Press, 1967.

Poggioli, Renato, *The Poets of Russia, 1890–1930*. Cambridge, Mass.: Harvard University Press, 1960.

Possony, Stefan T., *Lenin: The Compulsive Revolutionary*. Chicago: Regnery, 1964.

Radkey, Oliver H., *The Agrarian Foes of Bolshevism: Promise and Default of the Socialist Revolutionaries, March to October, 1917*. New York: Columbia University Press, 1958.

Rosenberg, Arthur, *A History of Bolshevism from Marx to the First Five Years' Plan*. New York: Doubleday, 1967.

Schapiro, Leonard, *The Communist Party of the Soviet Union*. New York: Random House, 1960.

Schapiro, Leonard, "The *Vekhi* Group and the Mystique of Revolution," *Slavic and East European Review*, XXXIV (1955), 56–76.

Schapiro, Leonard, & Peter Reddaway, eds., *Lenin: The Man, the Theorist, the Leader, a Reappraisal*. New York: Praeger, 1967.

Schwarz, Solomon M., *The Russian Revolution of 1905: The Workers' Movement and the Formation of Bolshevism and Menshevism*, trans. Gertrude Vakar. Chicago: University of Chicago Press, 1967.

Seth, Ronald, *The Russian Terrorists: The Story of the Narodniki*. London: Barrie & Rockliff, 1966.

Shub, David, *Lenin: A Biography*. New York: Doubleday, 1948.

Shukman, Harold, *Lenin and the Russian Revolution*. New York: Putnam, 1966.

Tompkins, Stuart Ramsay, *The Triumph of Bolshevism. Revolution or Reaction*. Norman: University of Oklahoma Press, 1967.

Treadgold, Donald W., *Lenin and His Rivals: The Struggle for Russia's Future, 1898–1906*. New York: Praeger, 1955.

Ulam, Adam B., *The Bolsheviks*. New York: Macmillan, 1965.

Venturi, Franco, *Roots of Revolution: A History of the Populist and Socialist Movements in Nineteenth-Century Russia*, with an introduction by Isaiah Berlin, trans. from the Italian by Francis Haskell. London: Weidenfeld & Nicolson, 1960.

Wildman, Allan K., *The Making of the Workers' Revolution: Russian Social Democracy, 1891–1903*. Chicago: University of Chicago Press, 1967.

Wittfogel, Karl A., *Oriental Despotism: A Comparative Study of Total Power*. New Haven, Conn.: Yale University Press, 1957, 1963.

Wolfe, Bertram D., *Three Who Made a Revolution: A Biographical History*. New York: Dial Press, 1948.

Russian Constitutional Developments

Amburger, Erik, *Geschichte der Behördenorganisation Russlands von Peter dem Grossen bis 1917*. Studien zur Geschichte Osteuropas, X. Leiden: E. J. Brill, 1966.

ADDITIONAL READING

Astrov, N. I., & Gronsky, P. P., *The War and the Russian Government.* New Haven, Conn.: Yale University Press, 1929.

Badayev, Aleksei E., *The Bolsheviks in the Tsarist Duma, with an Article by Lenin on the Work and Trial of the Bolshevik Group in the Duma and an Introduction by Em. Yaroslavsky.* New York: International Publishers, 1932.

Baring, Maurice, *A Year in Russia.* London: Methuen, 1907.

Bing, E., *The Secret Letters of the Last Tsar; Being the Confidential Correspondence between Nicholas II and His Mother, Dowager Empress Marìa Feodorovna.* New York: Longmans, 1938.

Charles, Pierre, *Le parlement Russe: Son organisation, ses rapports avec l'Empereur.* Paris: A. Rousseau, 1910.

Daniels, Robert V., ed., *A Documentary History of Communism.* New York: Random House, 1960.

Duff, J. D., ed., *Russian Realities and Problems.* Cambridge: Cambridge University Press, 1917.

Fischer, George, *Russian Liberalism: from Gentry to Intelligentsia.* Cambridge, Mass.: Harvard University Press, 1958.

Golder, Frank A., ed., *Documents of Russian History, 1914–1917.* New York, London: Century, 1927.

Guchkov, Alexander I., "Types of Russian Parliamentary Oratory, Speeches on the Naval and Military Estimate of 1908 by Alexander Guchkov," *Russian Review* (London), II, No. 1 (1913), 111–121.

Guchkov, Alexander I., "Types of Russian Political Oratory. The General Political Situation and the Octobrist Party. Speech Delivered by Mr. A. I. Guchkov on November 21, 1913, at the Conference of the Octobrist Party in St. Petersburg," *Russian Review* (London), III, No. 1 (1914), 141–158.

Gurko, Vladimir I., *Features and Figures of the Past: Government and Opinion in the Reign of Nicholas II,* ed. J. E. Wallace Sterling, Stanford: Stanford University Press, 1939.

Hans, Nicholas A., *History of Russian Educational Policy.* London: P. S. King, 1931.

Hare, Richard, *Portraits of Russian Personalities between Reform and Revolution.* New York, London: Oxford University Press, 1959.

Harper, Samuel N., "The Budget Rights of the Russian Duma," *Journal of Political Economy* (Chicago), XVI (1908), 152–156.

Harper, Samuel N., *The New Electoral Law for the Russian Duma.* Chicago: University of Chicago Press, 1908.

Hodgson, John H., "Finland's Position in the Russian Empire, 1905–1910," *Journal of Central European Affairs* (Boulder, Colo.), XX (1960), 158–173.

Kokovtsov, Vladimir N., *Out of My Past: The Memoirs of Count Kokovtsov, Russian Minister of Finance, 1904–1914.* Stanford: Stanford University Press, 1935.

Kovalevsky, Maxim, "The Upper House in Russia," *Russian Review* (London), I, No. 2 (1912), 60–70.

Kovalevsky, Evgrav, "The Duma and Public Instructions," *Russian Review* (London), I, No. 3 (1912), 64–79.

Kucherov, Samuel, *Courts, Lawyers and Trials under the Last Three Tsars.* New York: Praeger, 1953.

Levin, Alfred, *The Second Duma: A Study of the Social-Democratic*

ADDITIONAL READING

Party and the Russian Constitutional Experiment. New Haven, Conn.: Yale University Press, 1940.

Levitskii, Sergei, "Interpellations According to the Russian Constitution of 1906," *Etudes Slaves et Est-Européennes*, I (1957), 220–231.

Levitsky, Serge L., *The Russian Duma: Studies in Parliamentary Procedure, 1906–1917.* New York: Fordham University Press, 1958.

Maklakov, Vasilii A., *The First State Duma: Contemporary Reminiscences*, trans. Mary Belkin. Bloomington: Indiana University Press, 1964.

Miliukov, Paul N., *Political Memoirs 1905–1917*, ed. Arthur P. Mendel. Ann Arbor: University of Michigan Press, 1967.

Miliukov, Paul N., *Russia and Its Crisis.* Chicago: University of Chicago Press, 1905.

Miliukov, Paul N., *Russia Today and Tomorrow.* New York: Macmillan, 1922.

Pares, Bernard, "Conversations with Mr. Stolypin," *Russian Review* (London), II, No. 1 (1913), 101–110.

Pares, Bernard, *Russia and Reform.* London: Constable, 1907.

Polner, Tikhon I., *Russian Local Government during the War and the Union of Zemstvos.* New Haven, Conn.: Yale University Press, 1930.

Riha, Thomas, "Miliukov and the Progressive Bloc in 1915: A Study in Last Chance Politics," *Journal of Modern History*, XXXII (1960), 16–24.

Riha, Thomas, "*Riech'*: A Portrait of a Russian Newspaper," *Slavic Review*, XXII (1963), 663–682.

Riha, Thomas, *A Russian European: Paul Miliukov in Russian Politics.* Notre Dame, Ind.: University of Notre Dame Press, 1968.

Vinogradov, Sir Paul, *Self-Government in Russia.* London: Constable, 1915.

Von Laue, Theodore H. "The Chances for Liberal Constitutionalism," *Slavic Review*, XXIV (1965), 34–46.

Vucinich, Alexander, "The State and the Local Community," in Cyril Black, ed., *Transformation of Russian Society.* Cambridge, Mass.: Harvard University Press, 1960.

Walkin, Jacob, "Government Controls over the Press in Russia, 1905–1914," *Russian Review* (New Haven), XIII (1954), 203–209.

Walkin, Jacob, *The Rise of Democracy in Pre-Revolutionary Russia: Political and Social Institutions under the Last Three Czars.* New York: Praeger, 1962.

Wallace, Sir Donald M., "Looking Back over Forty Years," *Russian Review* (London), I, No. 1 (1912), 9–17.

Walsh, Warren B., "The Composition of the Dumas," *Russian Review* (New Haven), VIII (1949), 111–116.

Zvegintsev, Alexander, "The Duma and Imperial Defence," *Russian Review* (London), I, No. 3 (1912), 49–63.

Problems of Industrialization in Russia

Beveridge, Albert J., *The Russian Advance.* New York, London: Harper, 1904.

Bill, Valentine T., *The Forgotten Class; the Russian Bourgeoisie from the Earliest Beginnings to 1900.* New York: Praeger, 1959.

Bruford, Walter H., *Chekhov and His Russia; a Sociological Study.* London: Kegan Paul, 1947.

ADDITIONAL READING

Carson, George B., Jr., "The State and Economic Development: Russia, 1890–1939," in *The State and Economic Growth: Papers of a Conference Held on October 11–13, 1956, under the Auspices of the Committee on Economic Growth, New York, 1956.* New York: Social Science Research Council, 1959, pp. 115–146.

Dillon, Emile J., *The Eclipse of Russia.* New York: Doran, 1918.

Feis, Herbert, *Europe the World's Banker, 1870–1914: An Account of European Foreign Investment and the Connection of World Finance with Diplomacy before the War.* New Haven, Conn.: Yale University Press, 1930.

Florinsky, Michael T., *The End of the Russian Empire.* New Haven, Conn.: Yale University Press, 1931.

Gerschenkron, Alexander, "Agrarian Policies and Industrialization: Russia 1861–1917," *The Cambridge Economic History of Europe.* Cambridge: Cambridge University Press, 1966, Vol. VI, Pt. II, pp. 706–800.

Gerschenkron, Alexander, *Economic Backwardness in Historical Perspective.* Cambridge, Mass.: Harvard University Press, 1962.

Ignatiev, Paul N., *et al., Russian Schools and Universities in the World War.* New Haven, Conn.: Yale University Press, 1929.

Kahan, Arcadius, "Government Policies and the Industrialization of Russia," *Journal of Economic History,* XXVII (1967), 460–477.

Kokovtsov, Vladimir N., *Out of My Past: The Memoirs of Count Kokovtsov, Russian Minister of Finance, 1904–1914.* Stanford: Stanford University Press, 1935.

Kovalevskii, Vladimir I., *La Russie à la fin du XIXᵉ siècle; ouvrage publié sous la direction de M. W. de Kovalevsky.* Paris: P. Dupont, 1900.

Lenin, V. I., *The Development of Capitalism in Russia.* Moscow: Foreign Languages Publishing House, 1956.

Lewery, Leonard J. *Foreign Capital Investments in Russian Industries and Commerce.* Washington, D.C.: U.S. Government Printing Office, 1923.

Liashchenko, Peter I., *History of the National Economy of Russia to the 1917 Revolution,* trans. L. M. Herman. New York: Macmillan, 1949.

Mavor, James, *An Economic History of Russia,* 2 vols. New York: Dutton, 1914.

Miliukov, Paul N., *Russia and Its Crisis.* Chicago: University of Chicago Press, 1905.

Miller, Margaret S., *The Economic Development of Russia, 1905–1914.* London: P. S. King, 1926.

Owen, Launcelot A., *The Russian Peasant Movement, 1906–1917.* London, New York: Russell, 1937, 1963.

Pasvolsky, Leo, & Harold G. Moulton, *Russian Debts and Russian Reconstruction: A Study of the Relations of Russia's Foreign Debts to Her Economic Recovery.* New York: McGraw-Hill, 1924.

Pavlovsky, George A., *Agricultural Russia on the Eve of the Revolution.* London: Routledge, 1930.

Portal, Roger, "The Industrialization of Russia," *The Cambridge Economic History of Europe.* Cambridge: Cambridge University Press, 1966, Vol. VI, Pt. II, pp. 801–872.

Portal, Roger, *La Russie industrielle de 1881 à 1927.* Paris: Centre de Documentation Universitaire, 1956.

Prokopowitsch, Sergej N., *Uber die Bedingungen der industriellen Entwicklung Russlands.* Tübingen: J. C. B. Mohr (P. Subeck), 1913.

ADDITIONAL READING

Robinson, Geroid T., *Rural Russia under the Old Regime*. New York: Longmans, 1932.

Treadgold, Donald W., *The Great Siberian Migration: Government and Peasant in Resettlement from Emancipation to the First World War*. Princeton, N.J.: Princeton University Press, 1959.

Turin, Sergei P., *From Peter the Great to Lenin: A History of the Russian Labour Movement with Special Reference to Trade Unionism*. London: P. S. King, 1935; Frank Cass, 1968; New York: Kelley, 1968.

Von Laue, Theodore H., "Russian Labour between Field and Factory," *California Slavic Studies*, III (1964), 33–65.

Von Laue, Theodore H., *Sergei Witte and the Industrialization of Russia*. New York: Columbia University Press, 1963.

Vucinich, Wayne S., ed., *The Peasant in Nineteenth-Century Russia*. Stanford: Stanford University Press, 1968.

Witte, Count Sergei, *The Memoirs of Count Witte*, trans. & ed. Abraham Yarmolinsky. New York: Doubleday, 1921.

Wittschewsky, Valentin, *Russlands Handels-, Zoll- und Industriepolitik von Peter dem Grossen bis auf die Gegenwart*. Berlin: E. S. Mittler, 1905.

Zagorsky, Seman O., *State Control of Industry in Russia during the War*. New Haven, Conn.: Yale University Press; London: Oxford University Press, 1928.

Politics, Universities, and Science

Alston, Patrick L., *Education and the State in Tsarist Russia*. Stanford, Calif.: Stanford University Press, 1969.

Ames, Edward, "A Century of Russian Railroad Construction, 1837–1936," *American Slavic and East European Review*, VI, Nos. 18–19 (1947), 57–74.

Bharucha-Reid, Albert T., *Elements of the Theory of Markov Processes and Their Applications*. New York: McGraw-Hill, 1960.

Billington, James H., *The Icon and the Axe: An Interpretive History of Russian Culture*. New York: Knopf, 1966.

Brachmann, Botho, *Russische Sozialdemokraten in Berlin, mit Berücksichtigung der Studentenbewegung in Preussen und Sachsen*. Berlin: Akademie, 1962.

Brock, Thomas D., ed. & trans., *Milestones in Microbiology*. Englewood Cliffs, N.J.: Prentice-Hall, 1961.

Crisp, Olga, "Russian Financial Policy and the Gold Standard at the End of the Nineteenth Century," *Economic History Review*, 2nd series, VI, No. 2 (December 1953), 156–172.

Crisp, Olga, "Some Problems of French Investment in Russian Joint Stock Companies 1894–1914," *Slavonic and East European Review*, XXXV, No. 84 (December 1956), 223–240.

Gerschenkron, Alexander, "The Rate of Industrial Growth in Russia since 1885," *The Tasks of Economic History: A Supplemental Issue*, VII (1947), 114–174.

Goldsmith, Raymond W., "Economic Growth of Tsarist Russia, 1860–1913," *Economic Development and Cultural Change*, IX, No. 35 (1960–1961), 441–475.

Hahn, Wolfgang, *Theory and Application of Liapunov's Direct Method*, trans. S. H. Lehnigh. Englewood Cliffs, N.J.: Prentice-Hall, 1963.

Hans, Nicholas A., *History of Russian Educational Policy*. London: P. S. King, 1951.

Ignatiev, Paul N., *et al.*, *Russian Schools and Universities in the World War*. New Haven, Conn.: Yale University Press, 1929.

Johnson, William H. E., *Russia's Educational Heritage*. Pittsburgh: Carnegie Institute of Technology, 1950.

Klein, Felix, *Vorlesungen über die Entwicklung der Mathematik im 19. Jahrhundert*. Berlin: J. Springer, 1926–1927.

Kovalevsky, Evgrav, "The Duma and Public Instruction," *Russian Review* (London), I, No. 3 (1912), 64–79.

Laue, Max Theodor F. von, *History of Physics*, trans. R. Oesper. New York: Academic Press, 1950.

Leary, Daniel B., *Education and Autocracy in Russia: From the Origins to the Bolsheviki*. Buffalo, N.Y.: College of Arts & Sciences, 1919.

Lebedev, Peter N., "An Experimental Investigation of the Pressure of Light," *Smithsonian Institution: Annual Report, 1902*. Washington, D.C.: U.S. Government Printing Office, 1903. Pp. 177–178.

Vucinich, Alexander S., *Science in Russian Culture*, Vol. I, *A History to 1860*. Stanford: Stanford University Press, 1963.

Waksman, Selman A., *Sergei N. Winogradsky: His Life and Work: The Story of a Great Bacteriologist*. New Brunswick, N.J.: Rutgers University Press, 1953.

Zernov, Nicolas, *The Russian Religious Renaissance of the Twentieth Century*. London: Darton, Longman, & Todd, 1963; New York: Harper, 1964.

The Cultural Renaissance

Berdiaev, Nikolai A., *The End of Our Time, together with an Essay on the General Line of Soviet Philosophy*, trans. D. Atwater. New York: Sheed & Ward, 1933.

Berdiaev, Nikolai A., *The Russian Idea*, trans. R. M. French. New York: Macmillan, 1948.

Bill, Valentine T., "The Morozovs," *Russian Review* (New Haven), XIV, No. 2 (April 1955), 109–116.

Bowra, Sir Cecil M., ed. *A Book of Russian Verse*. London: Macmillan, 1943.

Coxwell, Charles F., trans. & ed., *Russian Poems*. London: Daniel, 1929.

Curtiss, John S., *Church and State in Russia; the Last Years of the Empire, 1900–1917*. New York: Columbia University Press, 1940.

Deutsch, Babette, & Abraham Yarmolinsky, *A Treasury of Russian Verse*. New York: Macmillan, 1949.

Donchin, Georgette, *The Influence of French Symbolism in Russian Poetry*. The Hague: Mouton, 1958.

Frank, Semen L., *A Solovyov Anthology*, trans. Natalie Duddington. New York: Scribners, 1950.

Gray, Camilla, *The Great Experiment: Russian Art, 1863–1922*. New York: Abrams, 1962.

Kisch, Sir Cecil, *Alexander Blok, Prophet of Revolution*. London: Weidenfeld & Nicolson; New York: Roy, 1960.

Markov, Vladimir, "The Province of Russian Futurism," *Slavic and East European Journal*, VIII, No. 4 (Winter 1964), 401–406.

ADDITIONAL READING

Markov, Vladimir, *Russian Futurism: A History.* Berkeley: University of California Press, 1968.

Maslenikov, Oleg, *The Frenzied Poets: Andrey Biely and the Russian Symbolists:* Berkeley: University of California Press, 1952.

Matlaw, Ralph E., "The Manifesto of Russian Symbolism," *Slavic and East European Journal,* XV, No. 3 (Fall 1957), 177–191.

Miliukov, Paul N., *Outlines of Russian Culture,* ed. Michael Karpovich. Philadelphia: University of Pennsylvania Press, 1942.

Mirsky, Dmitry Svyatopolk, *Contemporary Russian Literature, 1881–1925,* ed. Francis J. Whitfield. London: Routledge, 1926. Rev. ed., *A History of Russian Literature,* ed. Francis J. Whitfield. London: Routledge, 1968.

Obolensky, Dimitri, ed., *The Penguin Book of Russian Verse.* Baltimore: Penguin Books, 1962.

Pascal, Pierre, "Les grands courants de la pensée russe contemporaine," in M. F. Sciacca, ed., *Les grands courants de la pensée mondiale contemporaine* (Milan: Marzorati, 1958–), Vol. II, Pt. I (1959), pp. 5–89.

Poggioli, Renato, *The Phoenix and the Spider; a Book of Essays about Some Russian Writers and Their View of the Self.* Cambridge, Mass.: Harvard University Press, 1957.

Poggioli, Renato, *The Poets of Russia, 1890–1930.* Cambridge, Mass.: Harvard University Press, 1960.

Reeve, F. D., *Aleksandr Blok: Between Image and Idea.* New York: Columbia University Press, 1962.

Slonim, Marc, *Modern Russian Literature: From Chekhov to the Present.* New York: Oxford University Press, 1953.

Strakhovsky, Leonid I., *Craftsmen of the Word: Three Poets of Modern Russia: Gumilyov, Akhmatova, Mandelstam.* Cambridge, Mass.: Harvard University Press, 1949.

Toumanova, Princess Nina Andronikova, *Anton Chekhov, The Voice of Twilight Russia.* New York: Columbia University Press, 1960.

Yarmolinsky, Abraham, ed., *An Anthology of Russian Verse,* 1812–1960. New York: Doubleday, 1962.

Zernov, Nicolas, *The Russian Religious Renaissance of the Twentieth Century.* Darton, England: Longman & Todd, 1963; New York: Harper, 1964.

Some Imperatives of Russian Foreign Policy

Anderson, M. S., *The Eastern Question 1774–1923: A Study in International Relations.* New York: St. Martin's, 1966.

Becker, Seymour, *Russia's Protectorates in Central Asia: Bukhara and Khiva, 1865–1924.* Russian Research Center Studies, LIV. Cambridge, Mass.: Harvard University Press, 1968.

Bompard, Maurice (pseud. of Louis Maurice), *Mon ambassade en Russie, 1903–1908.* Paris: Plow, 1937.

Buchanan, Sir George W., *My Mission to Russia and other Diplomatic Memories.* Boston: Little, Brown, 1923.

Churchill, Rogers P., *The Anglo-Russian Convention of 1907.* Cedar Rapids, Ia.: Torch Press, 1939.

Crist, David S., "Russia's Far Eastern Policy in the Making," *Journal of Modern History,* XIV, No. 3 (September 1942), 317–341.

Dallin, David J., *The Rise of Russia in Asia.* New Haven, Conn.: Yale University Press, 1949.

244

ADDITIONAL READING

Dostoevsky, Fedor, *The Diary of a Writer*, trans. Boris Brasol. New York: Scribners, 1949.

Fadner, Frank, *Seventy Years of Panslavism in Russia. Karazin to Danilevsky 1800–1870.* Washington, D.C.: Georgetown University Press, 1962.

Fay, Sidney B., *The Origins of the World War.* New York: Macmillan, 1928.

Harris, David, *A Diplomatic History of the Balkan Crisis, 1875–1878: The First Year.* Stanford: Stanford University Press, 1936.

Helmreich, Ernst C., *The Diplomacy of the Balkan Wars, 1912–1913.* Cambridge, Mass.: Harvard University Press, 1938.

Hüningen, G., *Ignatiev und die russische Balkanpolitik.* Göttinger Bausteine zur Geschichtswissenschaft, X. Göttingen: Musterschmidt, in preparation.

Izvolskii, Alexander P., *Memoirs: Recollections of a Foreign Minister.* London: Hutchinson, 1920.

Jakobs, Peter, *Das Werden des französisch-russischen Zweibundes 1890–1894.* Osteuropastudien der Hochschulen des Landes Hessen. 2nd series, Vol. VIII. Wiesbaden: Harrassowitz, 1968.

Jelavich, Barbara, *A Century of Russian Foreign Policy, 1814–1914.* Philadelphia, New York: Lippincott, 1964.

Jelavich, Charles, *Tsarist Russia and Balkan Nationalism: Russian Influence in the Internal Affairs of Bulgaria and Serbia, 1879–1886.* Berkeley: University of California Press, 1958.

Kerner, Robert J., *The Urge to the Sea: The Course of Russian History.* Berkeley: University of California Press, 1942.

Kohn, Hans, *Panslavism; Its History and Ideology,* 2nd rev. ed. New York: Vintage, 1960.

Langer, William L., *The Diplomacy of Imperialism, 1890–1902.* New York: Knopf, 1950.

Langer, William L., *European Alliances and Alignments 1871–1890,* 2nd ed. New York: Knopf, 1950.

Langer, William L., *The Franco-Russian Alliance, 1890–1894.* Cambridge, Mass.: Harvard University Press, 1929.

Lederer, Ivo J., ed., *Russian Foreign Policy: Essays in Historical Perspective.* New Haven, Conn., & London: Yale University Press, 1962.

Lensen, George A., *The Russian Push toward Japan: Russo-Japanese Relations, 1697–1875.* Princeton, N.J.: Princeton University Press, 1959.

MacKenzie, David, *The Serbs and Russian Pan-Slavism 1875–1878.* Ithaca, N.Y.: Cornell University Press, 1967.

Malozemoff, Andrew, *Russian Far Eastern Policy, 1881–1904; with Special Emphasis on the Causes of the Russo-Japanese War.* Berkeley: University of California Press, 1958.

Medlicott, William N., *The Congress of Berlin and After: A Diplomatic History of the Near Eastern Settlement 1878–1900.* London: Methuen, 1938.

Paleologue, Maurice, *An Ambassador's Memoirs,* trans. F. A. Holt. London: Hutchinson, 1923–1925.

Petrovich, Michael B., *The Emergence of Russian Pan-Slavism, 1856–1870.* New York: Columbia University Press, 1956.

Pierce, Richard A., *Russian Central Asia, 1867–1917.* Berkeley: University of California Press, 1960.

Renouvin, Pierre, *Le XIXᵉ siècle de 1871 à 1914. Historie des relations internationales,* Vol. VI. Paris: Hachette, 1955.

245

ADDITIONAL READING

Romanov, Boris A., *Russia in Manchuria, 1892–1906*, trans. Susan W. Jones. Ann Arbor: University of Michigan Press, 1952.

Rosen, Roman R., *Forty Years of Diplomacy*. London: Allen & Unwin, 1922.

Sazonov, Sergei D., *Fateful Years 1909–1916; the Reminiscences of Serge Sazonov*. London: Jonathan Cape, 1928.

Schmitt, Bernadotte E., *The Annexation of Bosnia, 1908–1909*. Cambridge: Cambridge University Press, 1937.

Seaman, Lewis C. B., *From Vienna to Versailles*. London: Methuen, 1955.

Smith, Clarence Jay, *The Russian Struggle for Power, 1914–1917: A Study of Russian Foreign Policy during the First World War*. New York: Philosophical Library, 1956.

Stavrianos, Leften S., *The Balkans since 1453*. New York: Holt, 1958.

Stavrou, Theofanis G., *Russian Interests in Palestine, 1882–1914: A Study of Religious and Educational Enterprise*. Thessaloniki: Institute for Balkan Studies, 1963.

Sumner, Benedict H., *Russia and the Balkans, 1870–1880*. Oxford: Clarendon Press, 1937.

Sumner, Benedict H., *Tsardom and Imperialism in the Far East and Middle East, 1880–1914*. London: H. Milford, Oxford University Press, 1942.

Taylor, Alan J. P., *The Struggle for Mastery in Europe, 1848–1918*. Oxford: Clarendon Press, 1954.

Thaden, Edward C., *Russia and the Balkan Alliance of 1912*. University Park: Pennsylvania State University Press, 1965.

White, John Albert, *The Diplomacy of the Russo-Japanese War*. Princeton, N.J.: Princeton University Press, 1964.

Yakhontoff, Victor A., *Russia and the Soviet Union in the Far East*. London: Allen & Unwin, 1932.

Zabriskie, Edward H., *American-Russian Rivalry in the Far East: A Study in Diplomacy and Power Politics, 1895–1914*. Philadelphia: University of Pennsylvania Press, 1946.

LIST OF CONTRIBUTORS

List of Contributors

✿ ✿ ✿

ROBERT F. BYRNES is Distinguished Professor of History at Indiana University, where he has been teaching since 1956. He received his advanced degrees from Harvard University and also held a senior fellowship in the Russian Institute at Columbia University. An active promoter of Slavic Studies in the United States, he was the first director (1959–1963) of the Russian and East European Institute at Indiana University, and the founder in 1955 (and between 1960 and 1969, the director) of the Inter-University Committee on Travel Grants, which conducts scholarly exchanges between the United States and the Soviet Union and Eastern Europe. He has traveled and lectured extensively in the United States and Europe, and is the author of several publications, notably, *Anti-Semitism in Modern France*, Volume I, *The Prologue to the Dreyfus Affair* (1950), and *Pobedonostsev: His Life and Thought* (1968). He is also general editor of the seven-volume *East-Central Europe under the Communists* (1956–1957). He is now working on a study of the nineteenth-century Russian historian V. O. Kliuchevskii.

RODERICK E. MCGREW received his graduate degrees from the University of Minnesota. His dissertation was on "Nicholas I and the Genesis of Russian Officialism." He has taught at the Massachusetts Institute of Technology and the University of Missouri, where he also served as chairman of the History Department from 1962 to 1965. He is presently Professor of History at Temple University. The recipient of several research grants, Professor McGrew has contributed articles to scholarly journals and is the author of *Russia and the Cholera, 1823–1832* (1965). He is currently completing an interpretive history of Modern Europe and a series of brief studies concerning the reign of Paul I.

ARTHUR MENDEL, currently Professor of History at the University of Michigan, received his graduate training at Harvard University. Before going to Michigan in 1962, he taught at Roosevelt University, the State University of Iowa, and New York University. His principal publication is *Dilemmas of Progress in Tsarist Russia: Legal Populism and Legal Marxism* (1961). He has edited, with introductory essays and explanatory texts and notes, *The Essential Works of Marxism* (1961), *The Twentieth Century* (1965), *Paul Miliukov: Political Memoirs* (1967), and *P. V. Annenkov: The Extraordinary Decade* (1968). He is presently gathering his articles which have appeared in various journals into two collections, one on Russian Revisionism and another on studies comparing current radical thought in the West with nineteenth-century Russian radicalism. The essential theme in this latter collection is the "aristocratic rebel." Professor Mendel also has a deep interest in historiography, one which turns him ardently against the prevailing behaviorist or operationalist approach in favor of older forms of narrative history, history as art. He is attempting to put his theories into practice in a study of the reign of Nicholas II.

THOMAS RIHA is Associate Professor of Russian History at the University of Colorado in Boulder, specializing in the political and institutional history of modern Russia. He was born in Czechoslovakia and emigrated to the United States in 1947 after a year of study in England. He holds degrees from Berkeley and Harvard, and for seven years taught at the University of Chicago. He has been a visiting professor in Germany, at Marburg University, and at the University of Hawaii. He has twice visited the Soviet Union, and was a participant in the first group of graduate student exchangees at Moscow University, in 1958–1959. His publications include the three-volume *Readings in Russian Civilization* (1964); a biography of Paul Miliukov, entitled *A Russian European* (1968); and articles in *The Journal of Modern History*, *The Slavic Review*, *The Russian Review*, and *Soviet Studies*. At present he is at work on two anthologies devoted, respectively, to the revolutionary movement in Russia before 1917 and to the major cultural trends in Russia from Peter the Great to 1900.

THEOFANIS GEORGE STAVROU was born in Cyprus and came to the United States in 1952. After receiving his Ph.D. at Indiana University, he spent the 1963–1964 academic year at Leningrad

State University as a participant on the Cultural Exchange Program between the United States and the Soviet Union. Presently, he is Associate Professor of Russian and Near Eastern History at the University of Minnesota. He is the author of *Russian Interests in Palestine 1882–1914, A Study of Religious and Educational Enterprise* (1963) and of several articles on religious and intellectual history for professional journals and for the twelve-volume *Thrēskeutikē kai ēthikē egkyklopaideia (Religious and Ethical Encyclopedia)*, published in Greece. His research interests concentrate on the Orthodox Church and on Russian–Near Eastern cultural relations. He is presently completing a biography of Porfirii Uspenskii, "Precursor of Russian–Near Eastern Cultural Relations in the Nineteenth Century."

GLEB STRUVE was born in 1898 in St. Petersburg, and was educated in St. Petersburg and at Oxford University. He has lived in most European countries, engaging in journalism and literary criticism between 1922 and 1932 and serving as Lecturer and Reader in Russian Literature at the School of Slavonic and East European Studies, London University. From 1947 until he became Professor Emeritus in 1965, he was at the University of California, Berkeley, but periodically he has taught at most of the major universities in the United States and England. Best known for his *Soviet Russian Literature* (1935, 1951), Professor Struve has published numerous articles in various European languages and has edited and translated literary works from English to Russian and vice versa. He also edited or co-edited the works of Pasternak, Gumilev, Mandelstam, Akhmatova, and Zobolotskii. Though Professor Emeritus, he continues his work, and in the spring of 1969 he was visiting professor at Indiana University.

DONALD W. TREADGOLD, a Rhodes scholar, is Professor of Russian History at the University of Washington, having been on the faculty there since 1949. He is author of articles and a number of books, including *Lenin and His Rivals* (1955), *The Great Siberian Migration* (1957), and *Twentieth Century Russia* (2nd ed., 1964); editor of *The Development of the USSR* (1964) and *Soviet and Chinese Communism* (1967); contributor to several volumes, including Wayne S. Vucinich, ed., *The Peasant in Nineteenth-Century Russia* (1968). He was managing editor of *Slavic Review* from 1961 to 1965 and began a second term in that capacity on November 1, 1968. In the spring and summer of 1959 he was visiting professor at National Taiwan University; in the spring of 1965 he did research at the Institute of History of the U.S.S.R. Academy of Sciences; and

251

LIST OF CONTRIBUTORS

in the spring and summer of 1968 he did research at the Toyo Bunko, Tokyo. His work in progress, tentatively entitled "Western Thought in Russia and China," is nearing completion.

THEODORE VON LAUE was born in Germany, and began his studies at the University of Freiburg, but received his degrees from Princeton University as well as a Certificate from the Russian Institute at Columbia University. Presently, he is Professor of History at Washington University. He has taught at Princeton, the University of Pennsylvania, Swarthmore College, and the University of California, Riverside. His publication list includes *Leopold Ranke: The Formative Years* (1950), *Sergei Witte and the Industrialization of Russia* (1963), *Why Lenin? Why Stalin?* (1964), and various articles in professional journals and in volumes such as Cyril E. Black, ed., *The Transformation of Russian Society* (1960), and Ivo J. Lederer, ed., *Russian Foreign Policy* (1962).

ALEXANDER VUCINICH is Professor of Sociology at the University of Illinois, Urbana. He graduated from the University of Belgrade and received his M.A. and Ph.D. degrees from the University of California, Berkeley, and Columbia University respectively. In 1967 he spent four months in the Soviet Union on an exchange administered by the American Council of Learned Societies and the Soviet Academy of Sciences. Among his publications are *Soviet Economic Institutions: The Social Structure of Production Units* (1952); *The Soviet Academy of Sciences* (1956); *Science in Russian Culture: A History to 1860* (1963); "Science" in A. Kassof, ed., *Prospects for Soviet Society* (1968); "Science and Morality: A Soviet Dilemma," *Science,* 159 (March 15, 1968); and "Nikolai Aleksandrovich Berdyaev: His Philosophy and Social Thought," an introduction to the 1962 edition of *The Russian Idea.*

INDEX

Index

256